Resource Rebels

Native Challenges to Mining and Oil Corporations

Al Gedicks

South End Press
Cambridge, MA

Cover design by Ellen Shapiro
Cover photograph by Luke Holland
Page design and production by the South End Press collective

Printed in Canada
First edition

Library of Congress Cataloging-in-Publication Data
Gedicks, Al.
  Resource rebels : native challenges to mining and oil corporations /
Al Gedicks.-- 1st ed.
      p. cm.
Includes bibliographical references and index.
  ISBN 0-89608-641-0 -- ISBN 0-89608-640-2 (pbk.)
  1. Indigenous peoples--Land tenure. 2. Mines and mineral
resources--Environmental aspects. 3. Conservation of natural resources. 4.
Indigenous peoples--Legal status, laws, etc. 5. Social responsibility of
business. I. Title.
  GN449.3 .G43 2001
  333.8'517--dc21

                                                    2001042687

South End Press, 7 Brookline Street #1, Cambridge, MA 02139-4146
www.southendpress.org
        05 04 03 02 01   1 2 3 4 5

Contents

1. **Nigeria: Ogoni, Ijaw**
2. **Colombia: U'wa**
3. **Ecuador: Quichua, Huaorani, Shuar-Achuar, Cofan, and Siona-Secoya**
4. **Philippines: Subanen, Igorot**
5. **Mexico: Mayans**
6. **Guyana: Amerindians**
7. **West Papua: Amungme, Komoro**
8. **Manitoba (Canada): Cree**
9. **Wisconsin (USA): Chippewa, Potawatomi, Oneida, Menominee, and Mohican**
10. **Alaska (USA): Chilkat**

Map by Michael Gallagher
Midwest Educational Graphics
www.MidwestEducationalGraphics.com
Michael@MidwestEducationalGraphics.com

Foreword

Despite being the world's fifth most-capitalized industry, mining has generated remarkably few well-informed critics. Among these, Al Gedicks has been attracting deserved esteem for around 25 years. Professor Gedicks' Center for Alternative Mining Development Policy was the first of its kind and its combination of rigorous social analysis and deep respect for the views of mining's putative victims has rarely been improved upon. There is perhaps no better accolade for his work than the fact that today's key corporate players, in alliance with some of their erstwhile critics, have now started their own "alternative development initiative"—vastly ill-judged though it may be.

Professor Gedicks was among the first to make the critical connections between the emergence of a late twentieth century breed of extractive multinational, and the impending sacrifice of Indigenous Peoples' rights in mainland USA. These companies had earlier spread their wings abroad, often to have them soundly clipped, especially by post-war leftwing governments in the global South. During the eighties they reconcentrated their capital back home, trespassing on territory that had been mercifully free from encroachment. (We may forget that the United States is the first or second most important source of many of the world's minerals, as well as their most profligate consumer).

Professor Gedicks graphically mapped this process in his first book, *New Resource Wars*, in which he described the dramatic rise of native-led resistance to reconstructed extractive corporations, notably Kennecott/RTZ (Rio Tinto) and Exxon. Now he has updated—and in my view improved—this original work, bringing his incisive analysis to bear on the consequences of globalization, as it weakens much further the capacities of debt-laden governments and communities to control or benefit from the mining or upgrading of their minerals

But this is not a simplistic tale in which exploiters and exploited are easily identifiable in a medieval morality play. In their confrontations with oil and mining companies, a wide spectrum of native communities have redefined themselves as actors, rather than passive victims, and done so on the international stage (And some have also joined the mining industry). A brief fifteen years ago, only a handful of environmental or human rights organizations worldwide were prioritizing mining as a core issue. Now, every continent (except Antarctica) has several such NGO's. Just in the past 18 months, new Indigenous-led initiatives have been launched in India, Indonesia, the Philippines and western Africa.

In a back-handed acknowledgment of this upsurge in resistance, in 1995 the then-chief executive of Rio Tinto, the world's most ruthless mining company, admitted that some mining companies "are being naive about how easy it is to operate in someone else's back yard. We [at Rio Tinto] see problems virtually everywhere" These problems don't only derive from flat refusals by native peoples to countenance mining on their territory. Increasingly they are also reflected in a growing reluctance by investment institutions and insurers to bankroll projects which might never come on-stream, or end up in costly litigation (as with the Ok Tedi mine in Papua New Guinea and the Grasberg mine in West Papua) or—worst of all—hit global headlines in the shape of an unmitigated disaster. Each year since 1991, a major mine tailings containment has collapsed somewhere in the world. The latest occurred at the Baie Mare gold mine in Romania in early 2000, and was characterized by the government as the "worst environmental disaster" the country had ever faced. Within the past year, the World Bank for the first time has advised the closure of an existing mine (Ok Tedi) and Britain's state-owned Commonwealth Development Corporation has refused to finance destructive gold exploits in the Philippines.

Such reactions are raising alarms throughout an industry that has historically ridden roughshod over the opposition. Yet the corporate response is far from addressing the key issues raised in Professor Gedicks' work—notably the legacy of destruction wrought by mining for which few companies will admit responsibility (there are half a million un-rehabilitated mine sites in the United States alone); the vast amounts of compensation which must be found for existing mine-devastated communities; and the absolute right of those communities to exercise fully-informed prior consent before a single sod of their soil is turned.

Instead, the leading mining companies now boast of promoting "sustainable mining development" (an oxymoron, if there ever were one) and to recuperate their opponents as "stakeholders." This is a process clearly designed to wear down resistance to the imposition of even bigger mines in even more precarious habitats: "We are being dialogued to death" as one Indigenous Subanen opponent of mining recently put it in the Philippines. In pursuit of this agenda, the mining industry has launched a dubious new organization: Mines, Minerals and Sustainable Development (MMSD).

The companies behind this initiative, led (inevitably) by Rio Tinto, are among the most damaging in the world. Were they individuals seeking posts in public office, none of us would give them the time of day. So far, not one organization critical of mining, nor any bona fide Indigenous community, has joined up. However, with a multi-million dollar budget to pursue its program, MMSD seeks to present the beguiling face of a reformed sinner.

Reading this engrossing book will continually inform the reader about the nature of those sins, reminding her or him that they are being committed even as they read. Al Gedicks places mineral resource extraction firmly at the center—not of a technical, economic, or even purely social discourse—but an essentially moral one, which we sorely need.

—Roger Moody

INTRODUCTION

A World Out of Balance

Roberto Pérez, chief of the U'wa tribe of Colombia, paid a surprise visit to the San Francisco headquarters of the Sanford C. Bernstein investment firm in December 2000. The purpose of the visit was to deliver a letter demanding that Bernstein, a large shareholder in Occidental Petroleum, stop profiting from the destruction of U'wa lands and culture, and sell its stock in the company. Since 1992, the 5,000-members of the U'wa Nation have been organizing to prevent Occidental from drilling on sacred U'wa land. Representing the strength of the U'wa's international support, representatives from the Rainforest Action Network and Amazon Watch, two of the many environmental groups that have worked to help the U'wa, accompanied Roberto Perez to the Bernstein headquarters.

This encounter between the U'wa and the investment community signals a major shift in public perceptions of threatened native cultures in modern society. Up until recently, the tendency in the mass media has been to stereotype native people as fighting a losing battle against the onslaught of industrial civilization. But after two decades of organizing local, national, regional, and international alliances, assisted by the technology of instantaneous communication through the Internet, native voices can no longer be ignored in powerful places. A recent article in *Business Week* notes with surprising candor:

> Not long ago, the words of tribal leaders such as Pérez would not have been heard outside the forests where they were ut-

tered. Now, they echo around the world—through myriad Web sites and Western protest campaigns. The plight of indigenous groups is penetrating the boardrooms of multinationals, which are being forced to respond as never before to protect their reputations and brand names. Nowhere are the issues more contentious than in investments, such as Occidental's, that extract natural resources from developing nations. Many of these projects have long been marred by corruption, military atrocities, ecological damage, and social upheaval.[1]

While Bernstein chief executive Roger Hertog would not comment on the U'wa demand, the *New York Times* noted that after Mr. Pérez visited Boston-based Fidelity Investments in September 2000, Fidelity sold off more than $400 million of its Occidental stock.[2] What the *New York Times* failed to mention was that Mr. Pérez's visit coincided with ongoing demonstrations at Fidelity's corporate headquarters and protests around the world involving thousands of people demonstrating at over 75 Fidelity offices, creating a public relations nightmare.[3] However, a Fidelity spokesperson emphasized that the 60% divestment in Occidental was "based solely on the merits of the company, and was not connected in any way to the U'wa campaign."[4] An Occidental spokesperson reinforced the point: "The campaign of various activists, most of them centered in the U.S., has had absolutely no impact. The work is going on in Colombia."[5]

As of this writing in 2001, Occidental is still hoping to reap billions of dollars in profit through exploitation of a potential 1.5 billion barrels of crude oil on U'wa land. Occidental and its allies are willing to risk the destruction of an ancient culture (ethnocide), a pristine ecosystem (ecocide) and 5,000 lives (genocide) for what amounts to no more than three months of oil for U.S. consumers. This is a powerful argument for putting the brakes on an energy addiction that is out of control, preventing us from taking the necessary steps to a sustainable energy future based on respect for the earth and the people who inhabit it.

The last thing either Fidelity or Occidental has wanted to admit is that a well organized campaign with a focused target could disrupt the financial lifeblood of a controversial oil project. The lesson of the militant protests against corporate globalization in Seattle in November-December 1999, where the U'wa issue figured prominently, was not lost on America's corporate executives. An editorial by the dean of the Yale School of Management that appeared in the *Wall Street Journal* in the aftermath of the protests warned chief executives that many advocacy groups would

> become emboldened by the attention they received in Seattle and make global corporations an increasing focus of their activities. They will target more companies for public scrutiny about their activities abroad, from their environmental policies to their employment practices to their investments in local communities.[6]

Besides a higher level of organization and an ability to communicate their message to an international audience, there is also a greater acceptance of native traditional knowledge and prophecy in some scientific circles. Many native cultures share a belief in the idea of a delicate balance in the universe that must be maintained by reverence toward the natural world. Human actions that desecrate sacred lands or destroy entire ecosystems upset this balance. The U'wa believe that oil maintains the balance of the world and is "the blood of our mother." Not so long ago the U'wa claim that oil maintains the balance of the world would have been dismissed out of hand by the scientific community. All this has changed with our new understanding of the causes of global warming. The world's top scientists agree that the carbon dioxide (CO_2) emissions from the burning of oil, gas, and coal is a major cause of global warming or climate change. Primary responsibility for this global threat lies with the advanced industrial societies which contributed 76% of the world's total carbon emissions since 1950. The single largest contributor was the United States, with 22% of the total.[7]

The respected United Nations' Intergovernmental Panel on Climate Change (IPCC), a 2,500-member scientific body, states that no matter what we do now, the Earth's average temperature will grow one to three degrees Fahrenheit hotter because of CO_2 already in the atmosphere.[8] Due to the excessive buildup of heat-trapping "greenhouse" gases, the planet not only gets hotter, the atmospheric and oceanic systems that regulate Earth's weather become erratic. The non-governmental organization (NGO) declaration that came out of the Kyoto, Japan meeting of the Climate Convention in 1997 warned that climate change "will cause the greatest suffering to the poorest peoples and most pristine ecosystems globally."[9] The evidence for this claim is alarming.

Rising Seas, Melting Glaciers

Scientists have already documented warming oceans and melting glaciers. Rising sea levels have covered or are threatening low-lying islands in parts of the Pacific Ocean, including Samoa, Fiji, Tonga, Vanuatu, and Palau. Meanwhile, Antarctica has experienced a dramatic warming where the average temperature of the Antarctic Peninsula has increased three to four degrees Fahrenheit since the mid-1940s.[10] In 1995, a chunk of Antarctic glacier as big as the state of Rhode Island collapsed into the South Atlantic.[11] The native peoples of the Arctic environment, including the Inuit, the Yupik, the Cree, the Dogrib, and others, have been the first to notice how this warming trend has affected the ice and the availability of the foods they depend upon: the caribou, seal, bear, goose, duck, and whale.[12] "The global warming models are all consistent in one fashion in that they predict the Arctic is a very important place to feel global change," says Michael Ledbetter, director for Arctic System Science for the National Science Foundation. "Some people have likened it to the miner's canary."[13]

Infectious Diseases

We have also seen an increased incidence of floods, droughts, fires, and heat outbreaks. These changing weather patterns can produce the right environmental conditions for an outbreak of infectious disease. While the victims of extreme weather events can be found in both advanced industrial and developing countries, the consequences are more severe in the poorer developing countries. For example, Hurricane Mitch hit Central America in November 1998 killing more than 11,000 people and causing more than $5 billion damage. Moreover, the public health systems of the region were unable to deal with the aftermath of the disaster.

The intense precipitation and flooding associated with the hurricane spawned a cluster of disease outbreaks, including cholera, a waterborne disease (more than 30,000 cases), and malaria and dengue fever, transmitted by mosquitoes that flourish under these conditions (more than 30,000 cases and more than 1,000 cases respectively).[14]

Mosquito-borne diseases, such as malaria, dengue fever, yellow fever, and several kinds of encephalitis, are projected to rise in many parts of the world according to projections assuming a temperature increase of about two degrees Fahrenheit.[15]

Native Prophecy

Despite the first-hand experience of native peoples with the climatic changes produced by global warming, they were left out of the scientific discussion and debate on this issue until quite recently. In 1998, the National Aeronautics and Space Administration (NASA) sponsored a meeting in Albuquerque, New Mexico called "Circle of Wisdom: Native Peoples/Native Homelands Climate Change Workshop." During this historic meeting, tribal leaders, native scientists and spiritual elders met with a national network of scientists to exchange views on climate change and to discuss relevant native prophecies.[16] At the end of the conference the 180 native delegates from North America issued "The Albuquerque Declaration" which affirmed that "a growing body of Western scientific evidence now suggests what indigenous peoples have expressed for a long time: life as we know it is in danger. We can no longer afford to ignore the consequences of this evidence."[17]

According to the IPCC, we urgently need to reduce carbon dioxide emissions by 50-70% to stabilize the climate.[18] This means a halt to the burning of fossil fuels for energy. We cannot even afford to burn more than a quarter of the reserves contained in already known fossil fuels. Yet the oil industry currently spends $156 billion annually looking for new reserves of oil and gas.[19] This insatiable consumption of energy threatens massive deforestation, the destruction of more native cultures and the disruption of climatic stability worldwide.

Rainforests on Fire

While fossil fuel emissions from the advanced industrial societies are the primary source of CO_2 in the atmosphere, the burning of tropical forests comes in a close second. During late 1997 and early 1998 fires raged in Southeast Asia, South and Central America, Europe, Russia, China, Australia, and the United States. The World Wide Fund for Nature (WWF) reported that 1997 was simply "the year the world caught fire."[20] More tropical forests burned in 1997 than at any time in recorded history, according to WWF. "This is not just an emergency, it is a planetary disaster," said Claude Martin, Director General of WWF.[21] If all of the fires from tropical forests in 1998 were added up, it could amount to a third of the emissions from fossil fuel burning.[22]

Recent studies suggest that forests may act as carbon "sinks" which store more carbon than they give off. However, the stored carbon and other greenhouse gases are released into the atmosphere when forests are destroyed, adding to the global warming effect.[23] The Albuquerque Declaration emphasized the role of natural forests in maintaining global climate stability and that "the mining and drilling for coal, oil, and gas, as well as other mineral extractions, results in substantial local environmental consequences, including severe degradation of air, forests, rivers, oceans, and farmlands."[24]

Up to 12.4 million acres of forest and other land burned in Indonesia and Brazil. Indonesia has the third-largest area of tropical forests in the world. Those hardest hit by the fires were the native peoples who are dependent on the forest for food and shelter. In May 1998, the Indonesian press reported that some 60,000 to 80,000 people in remote parts of East Kalimantan faced starvation because of the effects of the fires on wild game and drought on agriculture.[25]

The burning of Indonesian forests in 1997 released as much carbon as all fossil fuel emissions in Europe that year.[26] The vast smoke clouds from Indonesian fires stretched over 2.5 million square miles from the Philippines in the north to Australia in the south, smothering Indonesia, Brunei, Malaysia, Singapore, and Thailand. Over 40,000 people were hospitalized for respiratory and other haze-related problems.[27]

But it was the Amazon fires that made international headlines because the greatest expanse of the world's undisturbed rainforest is in the Amazon Basin, particularly within Brazil. The Amazon region of Brazil alone had more than 44,000 fires.[28] Many news reports linked the fires to a drought caused by El Niño, a term used to describe the periodic shift in warm ocean currents. However, WWF's report placed primary responsibility on human activity, noting that over half the Amazon's fires and up to 80% of Indonesia's fires were started deliberately, often by multinational corporations trying to clear land for planting or pastures.[29] While drought conditions caused by El Niño may worsen the problem, El Niño itself does not cause fires. There is mounting evidence however, for a deadly connection between increasing greenhouse-gas emissions and El Niño events. According to WWF, "the world faces a positive feedback cycle in which climate change exacerbated by forest fires and deforestation, increases the frequency of El Niño, which in turn causes more forest burning."[30]

The 1997 fires destroyed more than 5 million acres in Brazil, including the homelands and food supplies of the Yanomami, Macuxi and Wapixhana. The poor water supplies and loss of food crops put some 22,000 native people at increased risk of malnutrition and diarrhea.[31] The number of fires in Brazil in 1997 was double that of the previous year. Even more disturbing is that scientists from the Woods Hole Oceanographic Institute in Massachusetts found that up until 1997/98, fire had been largely confined to areas used for agriculture or grazing and had not posed a major threat to intact forests. However the "drought of 1998—which built on an earlier drought in 1997—signaled the effective penetration of fire into forest ecosystems across much of the region and the possible initiation of a positive feedback loop in which rainforests are replaced by fire-prone vegetation."[32] WWF raises the possibility "of large wildfire episodes happening on such a frequent scale that the forest ecosystem will not endure."[33]

Extractive Reserves

Despite these dire projections, there is hope for the future. Native peoples throughout the Amazon Basin, which includes part of the territory of Bolivia, Brazil, Colombia, French Guiana, Ecuador, Guyana, Peru, Suriname, and Venezuela, have been building national and international alliances to win recognition of their land rights and their right to practice their sustainable development practices. In 1987, the rubber tappers and Amazonian Indians of Brazil ended a century of conflict by forming the Forest Peoples Alliance to defend the forest and the native peoples who live there.[34] The key element in this alliance was the push to create "extractive reserves," modeled on indigenous reserves, which would be set aside collectively for rubber tappers and/or indigenous peoples to manage. This proposal was intended to recognize and guarantee the rights of both groups to the lands they already occupy and use.[35] In 1988, after years of struggle, and an effective international campaign that targeted the World Bank and the Inter-American Development Bank for their role in funding destructive projects in the Amazon, the Brazilian government established the first extractive reserve. But within months of this victory, Chico Mendes, the charismatic leader of the rubber tappers, was assassinated.

"Today We Defend Ourselves with Words"

Despite the assassination of Mendes, many Brazilian grassroots environmental movements gained momentum as a result of the support they received from international environmental organizations. The late Darrell Posey's work with the Kayapo Indians of Brazil is a case in point. Posey was a North American ethnobiologist who has worked with the Kayapo from 1977 till his death in March 2001, researching Kayapo knowledge and use of medicinal plants and sustainable resource management of the rainforest ecosystem. In 1988, after speaking out against a proposed hydroelectric dam complex planned in the rainforest, Posey and Kayapo chief Paulinho Paiakan, and his cousin, Kube-i, were charged with breaking a Brazilian law against foreigners criticizing the government. Under Brazilian law, Indians are not legally citizens and can thus be prosecuted as foreigners. "In nearly 500 years of white-Indian relations in Brazil," wrote Posey, "never before had Indians been prosecuted as foreigners in their native land."[36] The dam complex, planned along the

Xingu River in central Brazil, would have flooded up to 20 million acres, and displaced 11 Indian nations, including the Kayapo.[37]

The charges stemmed from a trip to Miami in January 1988 where the three participated in an international symposium on "Wise Management of Tropical Forest" at Florida International University. The two Kayapo leaders explained how indigenous peoples preserve biological and ecological diversity while using the renewable resources to sustain themselves. They also emphasized the threats from mining, massive burning of the rainforest and mega-projects like the proposed hydroelectric dam. Representatives from the National Wildlife Federation and the Environmental Defense Fund urged the Kayapo to take their protests to the World Bank and offered to pay their expenses and organize the visit. Besides meeting with directors of the World Bank, they met with State Department representatives as well as members of Congress.

Upon their return to Brazil, police used Brazilian newspaper reports to charge that a $500 million World Bank loan for the dam had been held up as a result of their visit.[38] This was not a case where some overzealous local government official decided to prosecute a foreigner. The *New York Times* reported that the Indians' trip to Washington had attracted the attention of the Brazilian national security council and the national intelligence agency, while the order to press charges against Dr. Posey came from high officials in the Ministry of Justice in Brasilia.[39] From the perspective of the Brazilian military, which ruled the country from 1964 to 1985, any obstacle to the exploitation of Amazonian resources was a threat to the national security. In 1990, the Brazilian Superior War College released a document accusing international environmentalists and Indian organizations of colluding with the governments of developed countries to use Indian areas as entry points to control strategic parts of Amazonia.[40] This logic reduced the indigenous peoples of the Amazon to mere pawns in an international power game. The police agent that interrogated Posey told him "someone had to be behind those Indians. They would never have gone to Washington and said those things by themselves."[41]

José Carlos Castro, the president of the Brazilian Legal Society's Human Rights Commission and Posey's attorney, declared the trial to be "a politically motivated maneuver to silence the scientific community and native leaders so as not to speak out against mega-projects supported by the authoritarian government." Castro's denunciation was soon joined by the Brazilian Anthropological Association, the Brazilian Society for the Advancement of Science, the International Society of Ethnobiology, Cultural Survival, Amnesty International and hundreds of NGOs concerned with conservation, Indian rights and human rights.[42]

Despite worldwide protest, the Brazilian government continued with its case. When Kube-i was summoned to give testimony, some 400 Kayapo leaders from different parts of the forest came to the federal courthouse in Belem in warpaint. "In the old days," Paiakan told the assembled press, "my people were great warriors. We were afraid of nothing. We are still not afraid of anything. But now, instead of war clubs, we are using words. And I had to come out, to tell you that by destroying our environment, you're destroying your own."[43] The international press and television were now reporting Paiakan's original message to Washington policy makers for a worldwide audience. The Brazilian government, embarrassed at the negative publicity, finally dropped all charges against the three defendants.

If the objective of the Brazilian government's prosecution was to discourage the growing alliance between scientists, native peoples, environmentalists and Indian rights groups, the strategy failed miserably. The alliance that rallied behind the Kayapo case came together in the largest Indian gathering in Brazil's recent history. Coming together in February 1989 in the Amazon town of Altamira, the center of the proposed dam project, 600 native leaders from throughout the Americas issued "A Unified Strategy for the Preservation of the Amazon and its Peoples" to guide the alliance between native peoples and environmentalists.[44] Manuel Carneiro da Cunha, the former president of the Brazilian Association of Anthropologists, described the meeting as "a new stage in indigenous resistance—one of organized 'modern' political confrontation."[45] Shortly thereafter, the World Bank cancelled its funding of the Xingu hydroelectric project. Then, in 1991, Brazilian President Fernando Collor set aside some 19,000 square miles as reserves for the Kayapo.[46]

The Posey case illustrates the critical interplay between Brazilian domestic politics and the globalization of environmental issues. As environmentalists in the advanced industrial societies became sensitized to the issue of global warming and the terrible consequences of deforestation in the Amazon and elsewhere, they mobilized against the lending policies of major financial institutions, especially those of the World Bank. This mobilization coincided with the efforts of Amazon natives and Brazilian grassroots environmental movements to resist further destruction of the Amazon. This convergence between Brazilian and international movements resulted in substantial media coverage of the issue and effective political leverage against the policies of the Brazilian government, which wanted to avoid losing further loans from the World Bank and other international lending institutions. The result was a major shift in Brazilian policy:

> By the end of the 1980s, the direct links established between Brazilian and international lobbyists empowered local groups with resources and credibility that they never before enjoyed. These changes altered the character of the confrontations underway on the frontier, and introduced new ideas into the debate over Amazonian development policy.
>
> By the 1990s, the terms of the Amazonian debate had shifted...Indigenous cultures came to be viewed as repositories of practical knowledge, and the management systems of Indians and peasants, especially those based on forest extraction, were treated as credible alternatives in the search for new policy directions. [47]

Today the Brazilian government has recognized 20% of the Amazon, an area twice the size of California, as indigenous territory. Stephan Schwartzman, a senior scientist with the Environmental Defense Fund in Washington, DC, refers to this as "the largest expanse of tropical forest protected anywhere."[48] He also notes that Indians in Colombia, Peru and Ecuador have made substantial gains in recognition of their land rights. On a worldwide scale, indigenous peoples "occupy a substantial share of the planet's little-disturbed tropical and boreal forests, mountains, grasslands, tundra, and desert, along with large areas of its coasts and near-shore waters."[49]

It is precisely these pristine frontier eco-regions that are at greatest risk from the current drive to exploit the world's remaining energy and mineral resources.

My purpose in this book is to draw public attention to the ongoing genocidal and ethnocidal assault on native peoples worldwide. The pace of this assault has not let up in the slightest since I first identified this process in *The New Resource Wars: Native and Environmental Struggles Against Multinational Corporations*. What has changed in the interim is the extraordinary growth of the native-environmental alliance since 1993, when the United Nations (UN) declared 1993 as the International Year of Indigenous People. Later on, the UN Working Group on Indigenous Populations, the World Conference on Human Rights, and several governments, called for extending the year to a decade. The ten years 1995 to 2005 were approved, along with funding, as the International Decade of Indigenous People.[50]

As native rights movements have challenged the assault on their lands and culture, they have established an international native rights "regime" which consists of "recognized patterns of behavior or practice around which expectations converge."[51] Such expectations, or norms and rules, have had a significant influence upon the behavior of governments, international financial institutions and multinational corporations as they deal with native peoples. In the case of the Brazilian Amazon, this regime has affected the way that the World Bank evaluates their funding of development projects. While the bank does not always follow its own guidelines, there is at least a set of standards by which advocacy groups can hold this institution accountable. The case studies I present in these chapters describe how this developing international network of native, environmental and human rights NGOs have tried to strengthen these norms and make institutions accountable for their behavior toward native peoples.

If you are concerned about the mounting evidence of catastrophic climate change or the fate of the world's forests and the loss of global biodiversity, then you cannot afford to overlook the critical role of native peoples in defending their lands and culture from mining and oil corporations. Their success or failure is inextricably tied to the fate of the planet and the health and well-being of its people.

1   Raeburn, et al., 2000, p. 88.
2   Gladstone, 2000.
3   Rainforest Action Network, 2000
4   Valdmanis, 2000.
5   Ibid.
6   Garten, 1999, p. A 34.
7   Johnson, 1999, pp. 22-23.
8   International Panel on Climate Change, 1995, p. 5.
9   Rainforest Action Network and Project Underground, 1998, p. 44.
10 Berger, 2000, p. 36.
11 Flavin, 1996, p. 23.
12 Johnson, 1999. p.10.
13 Ibid., p. 12
14 Epstein, 1999, p. 64.
15 Epstein, 2000, p. 52.
16 Johnson, 1999. p. 15.
17 Albuquerque Declaration, 1998.
18 International Panel on Climate Change, 1995, p. 9.
19 Rainforest Action Network and Project Underground, 1998, p. 17.
20 Dudley, 1997.
21 Rowell and Moore, 2000, p. i.
22 Ibid., p. 14.
23 Selverston, 1999, p. 73.
24 Albuquerque Declaration..
25 cited in Rowell and Moore, 2000, p. 34.
26 Lewan, 1997.
27 Rowell and Moore, 2000, p. 35.
28 Ibid., p. 37.
29 Ibid., 2000, p. 9. In Brazil, the expansion of cattle ranching has less to
    do with feeding the world market for fast-food hamburgers and more
    to do with taking advantage of generous financial incentives. Cattle
    grazing, according to one analyst, "is quite expensive, pastures are not
    usually sustainable, and the value of the final animal product often
    does not cover investment costs." See Hecht, 1989b. However, when
    the military took power in 1964 they defined the Amazon as a
    national security zone and encouraged landless peasants to move
    there to prevent it from being overrun by foreigners. See
    Schwartzman et al., 1996, p. 37. In a Brazilian version of manifest
    destiny, the generals built roads, dams and encouraged settlers to take
    title to lands that may contain valuable gold or timber by pushing
    aside the Indians who occupied these lands.
30 Ibid., p. 12.
31 Ibid., p. 39.
32 Nepstad, et al., 1999.
33 Rowell and Moore, 2000, p. 5.
34 Hecht, 1989a, p. 38.
35 Clay, 1990a, pp. 8-9.

36   Posey, 1989, p. 16.
37   Simons, 1988.
38   Posey, 1989, pp. 14-15.
39   Simons, op. cit.
40   Wood and Schmink, 1993, p. 101.
41   Posey, 1989, p. 16.
42   Ibid., p. 16.
43   Whittemore, 1992, p. 5.
44   Posey, 1989, p. 18.
45   Da Cunha, 1989, p. 19.
46   Whittemore, 1992, p. 7.
47   Wood and Schmink, 1993, pp. 100-101.
48   Schwartzman, 1999, p. 63.
49   Durning, 1992, p. 28.
50   Brysk, 2000, p. 130.
51   Young, 1983, p. 93.

CHAPTER 1

Scouring the Globe

After strip-mining the richest minerals and and pumping the most easily accessible oil and gas deposits, multinational mining and oil corporations are scouring the globe for the remaining sources of raw materials. They are now using advanced exploration technology, including remote sensing and satellite photography, to identify resources in the most isolated and previously inaccessible parts of the world's tropical rainforests, mountains, deserts and frozen tundras. What the satellites don't reveal is the fact that native peoples occupy much of the land containing these resources.[1] The basic assumption of U.S. energy/resource policy, which is hardly ever questioned, is that other societies, mostly in the poorer countries of the Third World, should give up control of their own resources because the United States and other industrial societies refuse to control their own culture of consumption.[2]

Forty percent of the world's countries (72 of 184) contain peoples defined as native or indigenous. Worldwide, there are over 350 million indigenous people representing some 5,250 nations.[3] The invasion of these resource frontiers by multinational corporations and nation states has resulted in the systematic displacement, dispossession and, in some cases, destruction of native communities. There is no hint of this devastation in a recent advertisement for a mining exploration drilling company which features an unidentified native person with a painted face. The caption reads, "From the Brazilian rain forests to the Australian outback, JKS Boyles core drilling professionals have become familiar with dozens of unique cultures as well as drilling conditions."[4] To describe the introduction of drilling machinery onto native lands as "becoming familiar" with the native cultures is to ignore the fact that this activity usually requires a massive military presence and is frequently associated with systematic human rights abuses against native peoples, including mass killings, arbitrary executions and destruction of their food supply. It is hardly coincidental that at least half of the debts in Third World states arise from the purchase of weapons, used in part, to quash native resistance to corporate invasion of their lands.[5] At the same time that native peoples are under assault worldwide, their images are being used to sell the very products which contribute to their victimization.

Jason Clay, an anthropologist and former research director at Cultural Survival, which advocates on behalf of tribal peoples, has noted that the 20th century "considered by many to be an age of enlightenment, progress and development—has witnessed more genocides, ethnocides, and extinctions of indigenous peoples than any other in history."[6] Brazil alone lost more than 80 tribes from 1900 to 1957. During this period the native population dropped from approximately a million to less than 200,000.[7] What accounts for this extraordinary human catastrophe?

Despite endless repetition of the conventional wisdom about the inevitable disappearance of native peoples before the onslaught of "modernization," there is a specific historical process at work here that is neither abstract nor inevitable. Noted anthropologist John Bodley has put the matter bluntly:

> The disappearance of tribal cultures over much of the world in the past 150 years can be seen as the direct result of government policies designed to facilitate the exploitation of tribal resources for the health of industrial civilization.[8]

It is also called "developmental genocide" and it involves a dehumanization of those who stand in the way of the economic exploitation of valuable resources.[9] The basic element of this process involves a degradation of the victim, implying their inferiority or worthlessness. Native communities who occupy lands containing untapped resources are frequently described as "primitive," "savages" or "obstacles." From the perspective of "members of the culture of consumption," it follows that if another culture's resources appear to be underexploited, this is all the justification needed to take those resources.[10]

In response to current native land claims controversies in Canada, *The Northern Miner,* a Canadian mining industry publication, warned its readers of the serious reprecussions "if native groups are perceived as having power to put the brakes on mineral projects, for whatever reason, at any time."[11] A classic economic text put the matter quite succinctly: "Mankind has become dependent on the systematic use of the material resources of the world, and cannot afford those resources to be withheld from use through the shortcomings of communities which rule over them. This applies not only to primitive communities, but to any sovereign authorities which obstruct development."[12] This formulation easily lent itself to Cold War anti-communist crusades which tried to justify U.S. military intervention to prevent Third World societies from using their resources for their own social and economic development.[13]

According to Alfredo Vasquez Carrizosa, the president of the Colombian Permanent Committee for Human Rights, it was the Kennedy administration that "took great pains to transform our regular armies into counterinsurgency brigades, accepting the new strategy of the death squads." During the 1960s, the doctrine of "national security" gave Latin American armies free reign to

> combat the internal enemy, as set forth in the Brazilian doctrine, the Argentine doctrine, the Uruguayan doctrine, and the Colombian doctrine: it is the right to fight and to exterminate social workers, trade unionists, men and women who are not supportive of the establishment, and who are assumed to be communist extremists. And this could mean anyone, including human rights activists such as myself.[14]

During the 1970s, such counterinsurgency campaigns against native peoples affected Brazil's Surui, Paraguay's Ache, and Caqueta River groups in southern Colombia.[15] In the post-Cold War era, the rhetoric surrounding militarization has shifted from communist agitators to drug smugglers and narco-guerrillas. Noam Chomsky has

emphasized that "the current US drug programs are likely to contribute to counterinsurgency operations and destruction of popular
organizations that might challenge elite conceptions of 'democracy'."[16] Occasionally, public officials will tell the truth about the
drug war, as when U.S. congressional representatives protested
Mexico's use of U.S. antidrug equipment to suppress the native rebellion of the Zapatistas in Chiapas.[17]

The Zapatista Revolt

From the viewpoint of corporate elites, even perceptions of native empowerment can have deadly serious consequences, as illustrated by the response of Chase Manhattan Bank's "Emerging
Markets Group" to the Zapatista insurgency in Chiapas, Mexico:

> While Chiapas, in our opinion, does not pose a fundamental
> threat to Mexican political stability, it is perceived to be so by
> many in the investment community. The government will need to
> eliminate the Zapatistas to demonstrate their effective control of
> the national territory and security policy.[18]

The advocacy of state-sponsored genocide against the native
peoples of Chiapas becomes just one more part of an overall strategy of establishing a favorable climate for investors. After all, as
Zapatista Subcomandante Marcos has pointed out, these were the
"people without faces, those without voices."[19] How and why did
the faceless and the voiceless suddenly command the attention of
the international investment community?

The Indian-dominated Zapatista National Liberation Army
(EZLN) shocked the world when it seized control of four important
towns in Chiapas on New Year's Day in 1994. The uprising was
timed to coincide with the day the North American Free Trade
Agreement (NAFTA) took effect. The Zapatistas explicitly targeted
the provisions of NAFTA which would have a disproportionate effect (corporate takeover of communally-held lands, liberalization of
corn and coffee markets which displaced peasant producers, etc.) in
the poorest areas of Mexico, the areas with the greatest indigenous
population. Moreover, these are very sensitive ecological areas, such
as the Chapaneco tropical forest, which has already been devastated

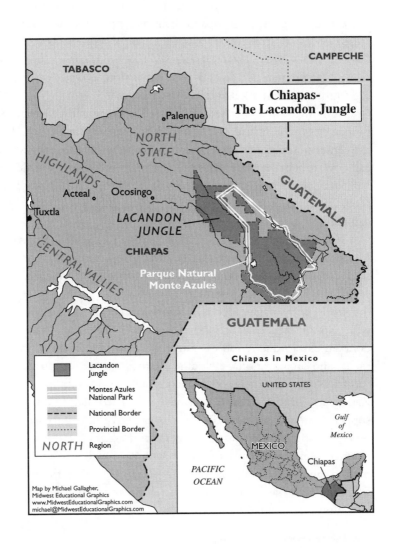

**Chiapas-
The Lacandon Jungle**

CAMPECHE

TABASCO

Palenque

NORTH
STATE

HIGHLANDS

GUATEMALA

Acteal   Ocosingo

Tuxtla

LACANDON
JUNGLE

CHIAPAS

Parque Natural
Monte Azules

GUATEMALA

CENTRAL VALLEYS

	Lacandon Jungle
	Montes Azules National Park
	National Border
	Provincial Border
NORTH	Region

Chiapas in Mexico

UNITED STATES

MEXICO

Gulf
of
Mexico

Chiapas

PACIFIC
OCEAN

Map by Michael Gallagher,
Midwest Educational Graphics
www.MidwestEducationalGraphics.com
michael@MidwestEducationalGraphics.com

by cattle-ranching, commercial forestry, hydroelectric dams, mining and oil extraction.[20] The same day the Zapatistas took control of the towns, they temporarily shut down oil exploration in the Lacandon jungle in the state of Chiapas.[21] The rebellion also inspired other protests by indigenous groups in the most important oil-producing areas of Mexico. In January 1996, for example, thousands of native Chontal Indians in the state of Tabasco blocked roads leading to 60 oil wells and demanded an end to oil expansion, as well as compensation for environmental and health damages.[22]

Both Mexican and U.S. oil interests have long known of the existence of significant oil reserves in the Lacandon jungle, which is the center of the Zapatista rebellion. Marcos has said that the Mexican government's counterinsurgency strategy in Chiapas was tied to U.S. strategic oil needs. In return for the massive U.S. bailout of the Mexican economy, the United States expects to receive future Mexican oil.[23]

The significance of the Zapatista revolt extends far beyond Mexico: "This was the first 'online' revolution, tying social revolution to the communications revolution through the Internet, providing the EZLN with instantaneous information (and the rest of the world with instantaneous information about the EZLN) and with support networks around the globe."[24] The Zapatistas have done an extraordinary job of outreach to other indigenous movements and organizations, including a representative assigned to organize North American native communities in support of the Zapatistas. Time after time, they have mobilized their international supporters to put pressure on the Mexican government to negotiate rebel demands. On at least one occasion the Zapatistas thwarted a planned Mexican military offensive with an e-mail alert and information campaign by international supporters.[25] In all of these activities, the Zapatistas have helped to establish an international regime which says that native rights are to be respected.

The Discourse of Dominance

Despite these achievements, native peoples continue to be left out of the decisions affecting their own lands throughout Latin America. For example, the former Minister of Mines in Colombia dismissed the objections of the U'wa indigenous community to the proposal to drill for oil in their traditional territory: "you can't compare the interests of 38 million Colombians with the worries of an indigenous community."[26] In fact, as we will see in Chapter 2, the government's permission to allow drilling in the traditional territory of the U'wa had little to do with the interests of 38 million Colombians and a great deal to do with the interests of the Los Angeles-based Occidental Petroleum Corporation.

The complete disregard for the prior ownership rights of native communities is evident in the case of proposed copper mining on lands of the Kuna people of Panama. Faced with the determined opposition of the Kuna, Donald McInnes, the president of the Canadian company, Western Keltic Mines, was quoted as saying, "they have explained to me that the Kunas have not permitted us to enter their territory, but I like challenges."[27]

Yet another variant of this "discourse of dominance" is the attempt to portray state and corporate efforts to take native resources under the guise of bringing economic development to the natives.[28] This justification usually involves ignoring or belittling the existing subsistence-based economies of native communities. For example, when Exxon Minerals was trying to develop a large zinc-copper mine next to the Sokaogon Chippewa reservation in northern Wisconsin (see Chapter 4) they sent their biologist to investigate why the tribe was so concerned about the proximity of the mine to their wild rice lake. But all the Exxon biologist could see was "a bunch of lake weeds."[29] As far as he was concerned, the Chippewa's wild rice-based subsistence economy was nonexistent. Or take the case of the Freeport Mining Company's displacement of the Amungme native people from their traditional gardening lands in West Papua, Indonesia (see Chapter 3). According to Freeport's chairman, James Moffett, "If we're not there, what do these people have?" In response to critics of Freeport's exploitation of Amungme lands and resources, Moffett says they "don't see what those people looked like before we got there. If they had, they wouldn't like what they saw."[30]

Beneath all the rationalizations about progress and economic development lies the insatiable consumption of minerals and energy by the world's leading industrial economies. The United States is the world's leading consumer of raw materials of all kinds with an 18-fold increase in materials consumption since 1900. While people in the industrial countries make up roughly 20% of global population, they consume far more materials and products than people in the developing nations—using, for example, 84% of the world's paper and 87% of the cars each year.[31] By 1950 the U.S. annual demand for new mineral supplies including fuels had reached two billion tons; by 1971 it had doubled to four billion tons; projections of demand put the figure at eleven billion tons in the year 2000.[32] As demand for minerals and fuels has increased exponentially in the leading industrial economies, there has been a renewed emphasis on mineral and oil investments in Third World economies. Under pressure from the International Monetary Fund (IMF) and the World Bank, half the world's states have changed their mining laws to make themselves more attractive to foreign investment.[33] The post-1991 wave of international capital investment has accelerated the pressures upon native peoples in previously unexploited regions, such as the mountains of the Philippines.

Mining Codes vs. Native Land Rights

In 1995 Philippine President Rámos signed into law a new Mining Code, drafted by multinational mining companies, which effectively gave away a quarter of the country to multinational corporations. If a similar deal had been done in the United States, an area as large as that stretching from Maine to Minnesota and south to Virginia and Kansas would be under corporate control. They can claim blocks of land of up to 200,000 acres compared to a maximum of 40,000 for Philippine companies. The mining code offers 100% foreign ownership in projects, rather than the previous 40% maximum , accelerated depreciation on fixed assets, 100% repatriation of profits and 50 year exclusive rights to exploration and development within a large concession area. The new code also lowers environmental standards by permitting increased open pit mining, for example, and gives companies the right to evict villagers from houses, farms or other "obstacles" to their operations.[34] All of these measures have been promoted as part of the Structural Adjustments

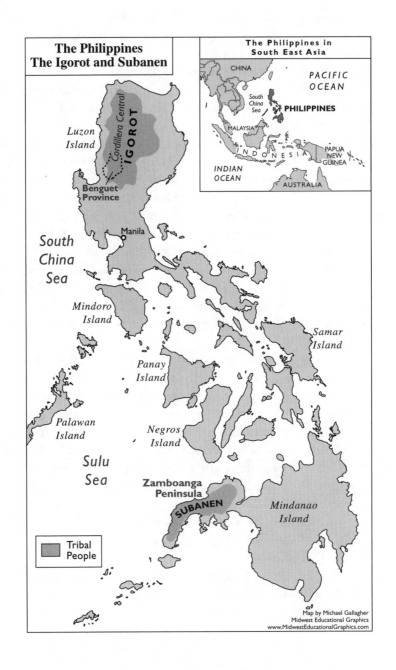

The Philippines
The Igorot and Subanen

The Philippines in
South East Asia

CHINA

PACIFIC
OCEAN

South
China
Sea

PHILIPPINES

MALAYSIA

I N D O N E S I A

PAPUA
NEW
GUINEA

INDIAN
OCEAN

AUSTRALIA

Luzon
Island

Cordillera Central

IGOROT

Benguet
Province

Manila

South
China
Sea

Mindoro
Island

Samar
Island

Panay
Island

Palawan
Island

Negros
Island

Sulu
Sea

Zamboanga
Peninsula

SUBANEN

Mindanao
Island

Tribal
People

Map by Michael Gallagher
Midwest Educational Graphics
www.MidwestEducationalGraphics.com

Program imposed by the IMF/World Bank to stabilize the Philippine economy by encouraging mineral exports and reducing the country's $39 billion debt.[35]

Since its passage, 70 mining applications have been filed covering 16.5 million acres or 23% of the country's total land area. The 1991 International Mining Annual Review reports that in terms of mineable minerals per acre the Philippines ranks second in the world for gold and third for copper.[36] Unsurprisingly, despite the fact that most of the land proposed for mining forms part of their ancestral territories, the country's 10 million tribal peoples were never consulted when the law was being drafted. Native communities were especially offended at the swift passage of the law while they have been lobbying for almost ten years for an Ancestral Domain Law that would recognize ownership and management rights to their land. The same congress that passed the Mining Act shelved the Ancestral Domain Law. The London-based international native rights organization Survival International has called the new code "the major threat to the future of tribal people in the Philippines."[37]

Among the companies that have registered mining claims is the British-owned Rio Tinto, the world's biggest mining company. This company has one of the worst records for violations of native rights around the world.[38] The company's largest single lease covers 1.5 million acres in the Philippine's Zamboanga province of Mindanao, much of it the ancestral land and sacred sites of the Subanen peoples, the most numerous of all Philippine native groups with a population of over 310,000 people.[39] At one time the Subanen had inhabited the entire Zamboanga peninsula. Today they occupy only the mountains. Settlers have taken over the best agricultural lands and loggers have already stripped most of the tropical forest cover.

While the Zamboanga peninsula is rich in gold and other minerals, the gold is found in extensive low grade deposits. Because the grade of ore is lower than those mined in the past, more ore must be mined at a faster rate, and more waste is generated for every ton of ore that is mined. The most profitable method to extract the gold is through open pit mining where large quantities of rock are blasted, bulldozed, and pulverized so that the gold can be extracted by using cyanide and other toxic chemicals to separate the minerals. Using this method, gold production can be profitable, even if it produces as little as 1 gram of gold per ton of rock.

This may be cost effective for the mining companies but devastating to the local people who find their lands and waters ruined by silt and toxic discharges from the millions of tons of tailings (mine wastes) left over from this type of mining. In Benguet province, which has been the Philippines' most important gold and copper mining region, runoff from the tailings has contaminated rice fields, killed biological life in the Itogon river and led to severe health problems among the Igorot native people.[40] When the Igorot barricaded the roads around the mine and demanded an environmental study, the government sent troops to clear the roads. The troops have remained to protect the assets of the Benguet Corporation, Asia's largest gold producer.[41]

While the government protects the large mining companies, no such concern is shown for the mining rights of the small-scale miners, which include up to 100,000 of the Igorot in Benguet province. Igorot means "people of the mountains." It is the collective term for all the native peoples of the Cordillera region, comprising seven major ethnolinguistic groups.[42] The Igorot have their own long-established mining practices which are communally controlled and do not use dangerous chemicals. Proceeds from the mining are shared in the community.[43] Under the provisions of the 1991 Small-Scale Mining Act, small-scale miners need prior approval through procedures controlled by the large mining companies.

While the mining code requires that the mining companies consult with the local community and demonstrate local consent to mining, in practice the combined power of the mining company and government agencies exert considerable pressure on communities to grant their approval. This corporate-government arrangement is spelled out in a letter from Rio Tinto's exploration manager to the government's Director of Mines:

> In opening an ancestral land for mining operations, the consent of the Subanen Cultural Community (SCC) should not be unreasonably withheld. The Government plays a major role in securing

the prior consent of the SCC before opening the ancestral land for mining operation for the State, not the SCC, is the owner of all the country's minerals, and other natural resources as enshrined in the Philippine Constitution.[44]

Despite Rio Tinto's best efforts to divide the Subanen community, thousands of Subanen signed petitions and joined protest marches against Rio's entry into their territory. Writing in support of one petition, Bishop Jímenez of Pagadian told President Fidel Rámos in 1996: "The coming of mining companies into the area is...a holocaust of nature and people, masquerading as economic development."[45] When Rio Tinto officials organized a "consultation" in the community, the Subanen challenged company officials about their record of native rights abuse in Papua New Guinea and elsewhere, thanks to information supplied by the London-based Minewatch organization. Survival International also organized a worldwide letter-writing campaign to Philippine government officials asking that no new mining concessions be granted until there is legislation guaranteeing the collective rights of tribal peoples to their ancestral lands. Meanwhile, at Rio Tinto's London headquarters, a delegation headed by the Methodist Church presented company officials with Subanen requests that the company withdraw from their territory.[46]

As native and environmental protests continued to mount against the 1995 mining code, a major mine disaster occurred on the island of Marinduque, 100 miles south of Manila, which confirmed the worst fears of the protestors. In March 1996 a concrete plug in an old drainage tunnel at the Tapian mine, burst and spilled an estimated 4 million tons of mine tailings into the Boac River.[47] The tailings, which consisted of water and fine particles including sand, mud, and traces of copper material, escaped from an open pit that was used to hold the liquid waste. The spill clogged river channels and flooded banks. Major fish kills were reported in villages where the local people relied on fish for their food and their livelihood. A social impact study after the disaster predicted that it will take 10 years for freshwater fish to return to the river.[48] The Philippine government declared the site a disaster area.

Initial blame was placed equally on the Marcopper Mining Company, which is 40% owned by Placer Dome of Canada, and on the Philippine Department of Environment for its failure to regulate and monitor the mine. The plug which burst in March had been known to be leaking several months prior to the disaster. The Philippine government, which owns a 48% share in the mine, has filed criminal charges against Marcopper executives and suspended Placer's applications for new projects. Protestors forced the government to hold public hearings on the mining code and to consider scrapping the code altogether and strengthening environmental controls on mining. This position is supported by the Cordillera Peoples Alliance, comprising more than 160 indigenous groups in the region, environmentalists, and the influential Catholic Bishops Conference and National Council of Churches.[49]

The international mining industry responded to public criticism of the mining code by openly warning the Philippine government against imposing stricter environmental standards on the industry. Twenty companies, led by Newmont of the United States and Western Mining Corporation of Australia, signed a letter to the government protesting any changes in the mining code as "inappropriate and impractical." An editorial in the London-based *Mining Journal* pointed to the favorable investment climate in Indonesia and warned the Philippine government of a possible loss of investment if it delays implementation of the mining code.[50]

The sustained protests of the Subanen led to Rio Tinto's withdrawal from their territory in 1998.[51] However, the Subanen are still waging a determined resistance against Toronto Ventures Incorporated (TVI), a Canadian mining company with claims covering 2.9 million acres at more than 20 sites in the Philippines.[52] Despite the requirement in the mining code that mining companies demonstrate local consent to mining, TVI by-passed the Subanen entirely and received permission from the local mayor who gave her permission on behalf of the Subanen. An environmental impact study which supposedly included "full consideration of the socio-economic impact" of the proposed mine never bothered to consult any representative of the Subanen.[53]

TVI's approach to community relations includes its own heavily armed security force, trained by the Philippine military, but under the direction of the company. Since 1996, TVI has maintained a checkpoint on the only road into the area. Many Subanen and the small-scale miners of the community of Canatuan, which was established 10 years ago, now find their homes within the company's compound. Armed guards prevent the movement of supplies, including food and construction materials, and restrict the free movement of the Subanen. Goods confiscated at the roadblocks can be secured only by paying extortion money to the guards.[54]

In September 1999, the Subanen set up a non-violent human barricade to prevent drilling equipment from entering their land. Armed employees of TVI broke through the barricade, beating approximately 50 Subanen with gun butts and canes. The Subanen, through their organization, the Siocon Subanen Association, had filed an ancestral land claim in 1994, well before the entry of TVI. This was fully recognized in 1997 when the legislature passed the Indigenous Peoples Rights Act. Before the Act could be implemented however, the mining industry supported a challenge to the constitutionality of the law. They argued that only the state should control mineral deposits. The Subanen are maintaing their blockade, despite violent dispersal by the police and company security guards. The company has brought injunctions against the protestors, and the military have issued a threat that any Subanen seen at the blockade with their everyday hunting knife will be shot. After international protests, the Philippine Senate has promised to investigate the situation.[55]

The pattern is the same all over the Philippines. Wherever mining companies fail to secure the consent of the native people, the area becomes militarized, the Philippine army engages in counterinsurgency operations, native people are massacred and driven from their homes to make the area secure for the mining companies. In July and August of 1995, for example, Philippine army soldiers bombed the Lumad native people of Surigao del Sur province in the hinterlands of Mindanao to make way for Australia's Climax Mining company. The Atlas Mining company , one of the country's biggest mining companies, had already laid plans for an open pit mine in the bombed areas in 1993, but had run into opposition from the native people who considered the area as their ancestral land. According to the Philippine-based Solidarity Action Group for Indigenous People, "This is what we call development aggression in its flesh and blood."[56]

Globalization and Mining/Oil Activity

What is happening in the Philippines is not exceptional. The same process can be seen in West Papua, Indonesia, Papua New Guinea, Colombia, Peru, Ecuador, Brazil, Nigeria, and elsewhere (see Chapter 2). At the root of this intensified assault against native peoples and their resources is what mining expert Roger Moody has called a "radical shift" away from financing mining projects backed by shareholders and state enterprises and toward those bankrolled by multilateral development agencies and regional banks. In 1997 the World Bank Group provided $987 million for mining projects compared to $643 million the year before.[57] The implications of this shift are both profound and disturbing:

> Only the biggest mining corporations will qualify under the stringent conditions laid down by the World Bank and the international development banks...Only huge deposits would then be exploited, although these are the very types of projects which have historically decimated or divided communities and destroyed their self-sufficiency.[58]

The inadequacy of the World Bank's lending criteria for mining projects can be seen in two of the worst cases of mine pollution on the planet: Freeport/Rio Tinto's Grasberg gold and copper mine in West Papua and the Omai gold mine in Guyana. The World Bank has no guidelines on safety requirements for tailings dams or waste rock impoundments which are used to contain toxic chemicals like cyanide and mercury. While both the United States and Canada prohibit tailings disposal in local rivers, the World Bank has no such restrictions.[59] The World Bank has provided political risk insurance for the Grasberg mine which dumps 110,000 tons of toxic mine waste into the local rivers every day and has destroyed approximately 12 square miles of lowland forest (see Chapter 3). This insurance is supposed to provide protection against losses due to war, insurrection and breach of contracts.

The Lake Wanagon Mine Waste Disaster

In May 2000, a pile of waste rock at Freeport's dump site collapsed, causing the Lake Wanagon water basin to overflow, sending a wall of water and rock into the valley below. Four workers were buried alive in the flood of mud and rocks caused by the landslide. A witness who observed the site afterwards reported that a 150-foot high wave had also destroyed pig stys, vegetable gardens and a burial ground of the Amungme tribe in Banti village, about 7 miles downstream of the basin.[60] The company blamed the collapse on heavy rainfall. Both Freeport and its British partner, Rio Tinto, tried to downplay the accident. Rio Tinto Chairman, Sir Robert Wilson, told company shareholders at their annual meeting that the accident could not have been anticipated.[61]

But environmentalists accuse Freeport of gross neglience in its handling of the wastes, citing this incident as the third spillage of the Wanagon basin in two years. Emmy Hafild, the chairwoman of one of Indonesia's largest environmental organizations (WAHLI), said that the Wanagon basin accident was caused because it could not accomodate the waste from Freeport, amounting to some 260,000 tons every day.[62] Indonesia's Minister of Environmental Affairs, Sonny Keraf, said his ministry had "warned Freeport a long time ago" about the dangers of its waste storage facility, but said that the company had not responded.[63]

Following the landslide, hundreds of local Amungme native people protested by blocking the main road to the Grasberg mine. "This incident is not the first and (local people) have been calling for years on Freeport to stop dumping rocks in their sacred lake," said the Institute for Human Rights Study and Advocacy, an Indonesian environmental group.[64] WAHLI has sued Freeport for environmental damages and has asked the court to direct the company to run a major advertising campaign correcting company misinformation saying that the accident was due to natural causes. According to WAHLI's lawyer,

an environmental report by Freeport had said that Wanagon Lake
was prone to accidents. This did not stop the defendant from
dumping huge amounts of overburden in the lake. Therefore, the
defendant knowingly and deliberately increased the risk of accidents.[65]

The report blamed the 1998 waste rock dump collapse on the rate
of dumping, not to heavy rainfall.

WAHLI's lawsuit also charges that the environmental audit report, prepared by U.S. consulting firm Montgomery Watson for
Freeport, was improperly conducted. The report praised the
Grasberg mine as "world class" and "state of the art." The siting and
design of the Wanagon basin waste pile was singled out for its
"state-of-the-practice geotechnical stability techniques."[66] The release of the report in December 1999, complete with full page newspaper advertisements, coincided with public discussions over
possible non-renewal of Freeport's mining contract in the aftermath
of the Indonesian populist uprising of May 1998 which toppled the
Suharto military dictatorship.

Further dumping at the Wanagon basin was halted until a review of the accident could be completed. That study, completed in
January 2001, was conducted by Freeport and the Institute of Technology of Bandung (Indonesia). Even if Freeport had not been involved in the study, it is doubtful whether any state-supported
research institution could be totally objective about a mining company which is the country's largest taxpayer. Unsurprisingly, it concluded that the Wanagon lake was capable of containing the
company's waste at the rate of more than 200,000 tons per day.[67]
The government, eager to have the company resume tax payments,
approved the company's resumption of normal mining operations
at Grasberg, including the placement of waste on the Wanagon
waste stockpile. WAHLI has called on the government to order
Freeport to cut down its production, close the lake and dump its
overburden at another location. WAHLI's lawsuit continues to
make its way through the courts.

The Omai Tailings Dam Disaster

The Bank also insured South America's second-largest gold mine in the heart of Guyana's tropical rainforest between Venezuela and Suriname in northeastern South America. Omai Gold Mines Ltd. is a joint venture of Montreal-based Cambior Inc. and Denver, Colorado-based, Golden Star Resources with Guayana's government holding a 5% stake. In 1995, a tailings pond gave way, spilling more than 800 million gallons of wastewater laced with cyanide and heavy metals into Guyana's biggest river over a period of four days.[68] While part of the spill was diverted into the mineworkings, most of it poured into the Essequibo River which provides fish and drinking water for the indigenous Amerindian and Creole communities along its banks.[69] The plume that travelled down the river contained a potent toxic mix of heavy metals such as arsenic, copper, cadmium and mercury, all of which were chemically bound with cyanide. Once these metals are released in the water, they become attached to micro-organisms and become part of the food chain from fish to humans. As the metals travel through the food chain they bio-accumulate, becoming more poisonous over time.[70] Even in trace amounts, they can be toxic to humans and wildlife.

President Cheddi Jaggan declared the area an environmental disaster zone and requested international assistance. A spokesman for Omai Gold Mines denied that the accident had resulted in an "environmental disaster." But a Pan American Health Association report indicated that the spill killed all aquatic life in the Omai and at the junction where the Omai and Essequibo meet. Observers reported dead hogs and fish floating down the river.[71]

A senior mining official at the World Bank defended their support of mining projects by emphasizing that mining corporations spend significant amounts to provide the best technology to safeguard the environment. "Few companies can afford to operate fast and loose," he said. "They don't want grief at their shareholders' meeting, and institutional funders don't want to see anything undertaken that puts their investment at risk."[72] This kind of narrow, economic thinking consistently ignores any concern for people and the environment. In far too many instances, the World Bank has backed mining projects that have had major destructive impacts upon both

Guyana-
The Omai Mine

Guyana in
South America

Venezuela
Suriname
French Guiana
Guyana
Brazil
Bolivia

Atlantic
Ocean

VENEZUELA

Cuyuni R.

Georgetown

GUYANA

Bartica

Mazarumi R.

Essequibo R.

Omai Mine

Berbice R.

SURINAME

BRAZIL

Map by Michael Gallagher
Midwest Educational Graphics
michael@MidwestEducationalGraphics.com
www.MidwestEducationalGraphics.com

the environment and human health. The final report of Guyana's dam review team concluded that:

> In retrospect, it is clear that the Omai tailings dam as designed and constructed was bound to fail.... [The] filter design was flawed in several respects and its construction was deficient from the very start.... We are at a loss to explain why the design and construction of these critical elements of the dam, whose importance to its safety were evidently recognized and understood, were executed so inadequately. [73]

Roger Moody, a consultant to the Amerindian Peoples Association called the accident "predictable." He visited the area in 1994 and said that the company's plan to deliberately release cyanide effluent into the Essequibo in May, 1995, prior to the dam failure, was a warning sign. "The main reason that the company was proposing this dangerous step was because it could not, for much longer, safely contain the tailings building up behind the tailings dam—especially if it accelerated the rate of milling ore," he said. "That is exactly what happened: the company did not build another tailings dam, it increased its throughput of ore, and the dam collapsed."[74]

The World Rainforest Movement, based in Great Britain, has demanded that the World Bank's Multilateral Investment Guarantee Agency (MIGA) be held accountable for not investigating the background of Cambior and Golden Star before selling them insurance.[75] Even after the disaster, MIGA continued the insurance. When asked to explain this, MIGA's senior attorney, Loren Weisberg, told Roger Moody that "this is a first rate project run by a first rate company and we had no problem in continuing the insurance."[76] An investigation would have revealed that Robert Friedland, a Canadian mining investor, was the largest single shareholder in Golden Star, and was instrumental in setting up the Omai mine.[77] Friedland's Galactic Resources Corporation was the mining firm responsible for the worst U.S. gold mine tailings disaster, at the Summitville Mine in Colorado's San Juan mountains.

Within days of its opening in 1986, the mine began leaking a cyanide solution into nearby streams and the rivers below. The constant discharge of heavy metals resulted in a 17 mile biological dead zone in the Alamosa River. Summitville suspended operations in

1991 and has become known as the "Exxon Valdez of the American mining industry."[78] Galactic declared bankruptcy and abandoned the site in 1992. The U.S. Environmental Protection Agency (EPA) has estimated that the final cost of cleaning up the cyanide and heavy metal pollution at this mine will be around $150 million. Several corporate managers of the mine were indicted by a federal grand jury and pleaded guilty to 32 counts of felony violations of the Clean Water Act as well as failure to disclose discharge of toxic waste.[79] In December 2000, Robert Friedland reached an agreement with the state of Colorado to pay $30 million over the next 10 years to help pay for the cleanup.[80]

Friedland has since moved on to invest in a new gold mine on Papua New Guinea's Lihir island which plans to dispose of toxic waste directly into the ocean. Such a practice would not be permitted in North America or Australia. The U.S. Overseas Private Investment Corporation (OPIC) had similar concerns and has refused to provide political risk insurance noting that "it could not support the project based upon initial concerns about US environmental policy regarding ocean discharge of waste."[81] Despite serious objections to the mine from groups in Papua New Guinea, the United States, Great Britain, Australia and Switzerland, the World Bank provided political risk insurance for the project.[82]

Two years after the Omai disaster, three Guyanese citizens filed suit on behalf of themselves and the 23,000 people living near the Omai river against the Canadian mining compay Cambior. The suit, filed in March, 1997 in Montreal, is asking the court to order the company to clean up the area of the spill and pay $69 million (Canadian) to compensate local people. "Multinational companies have got to realise that the days in which they could go to a Third World country, extract resources, dump toxic waste, and export the profits are over," says Shanna Langdon, former editor of *Drillbits & Tailings,* an on-line journal that reports on the environmental and human rights impact of oil and mining operations."[83]

The proliferation of lawsuits by victims of mining and oil projects which seek compensation for damages (see Chapters 2 and 3) has created an entirely new level of risk for multinational mining and oil corporations operating all over the Third World.

To continue investing under these conditions, multinational corporations need insurance; since other insurers are savvy enough to recognize the likelihood of expensive disasters, the only place they can get this insurance is from the World Bank.[84] In its role as the insurer of last resort, the World Bank provides institutional support for policies of environmental racism where ethnic and racial minorities are faced with environmental devastation and widespread human rights abuses.

This is why the mass demonstrations like the ones in Seattle in 1999, Washington, DC in 2000 and Quebec in 2001 are so significant. First, they have brought together indigenous peoples from the United States, Canada, Panama, the Philippines, Colombia, Argentina, Peru and other communities in a powerful alliance with labor, environment and human rights groups against the most powerful institutions of the global economy. Second, the protests provided a unique opportunity for sharing information about how the globalization process has affected so many lives and developing strategies to challenge those policies. Finally, the protests signalled a shift from more locally-based resistance which targets a particular corporation to more globally-based resistance which targets the entire political and economic support network for these corporations in institutions like the World Bank, the Interntional Monetary Fund, and the World Trade Organization.

One of the primary demands of the Washington, DC protests was that the World Bank stop funding the mining, oil and gas industries. "Nowhere is the incompatiblity of destruction and poverty alleviation more evident than in the World Bank Group's investments in the extractive industries," said a statement supported by over 200 non-governmental organizations from around the world.[85] Apart from investing in such projects, the Bank's International Finance Corporation and the Multilateral Investment Guarantee Agency, arrange credit and insurance for these corporations. No longer will these policies be shrouded in secrecy and made by a financial elite behind closed doors. Now these institutions will be forced to take into account the environmental and human rights impacts of mining, oil and gas projects to a much greater extent than ever before. For the first time, the public discussion and debate of these issues will involve an international advocacy community which has developed an impressive record of success on these issues.

Much of the impetus to this challenge has come out of the experiences of native and environmental rights movements in places like Ecuador, Nigeria and Colombia. In all of these places, as we will see in the next chapter, there is an inseparable connection between massive environmental degradation and widespread human rights violations.

1   Moody, 1993, p. 11.
2   Bodley, 1990, p. 7.
3   Hitchcock, 1995, p. 486.
4   *Northern Miner,* 1997, p. 18.
5   Clay, 1990b, p. 107-108.
6   Ibid., p. 106.
7   Davis, 1977, p. 5.
8   Bodley, 1977, p. 36.
9   Fein, 1984, p. 8.
10   Bodley, 1990, p. 9.
11   *Northern Miner,* 1995a, p. 4.
12   Hawtrey, 1952, p. 94.
13   Chomsky, 1970, p. 5.
14   cited in Chomsky, 1992, p. 131.
15   Brysk, 2000, p. 110.
16   Chomsky, 1992, p. 128.
17   Brysk, 2000, p. 110.
18   Silverstein and Cockburn, 1995, p. 1
19   Nash, 1995, p. 23.
20   Stea, et al., in Johnston, 1997, p. 220.
21   Ross, 1996, p. 20.
22   Chethik, 1996, p. 20; De Palma, 1996.
23   Ross, 1996, p. 20.
24   Stea, et al., in Johnston, 1997, p. 218.
25   Brysk, 2000, p. 160.
26   Project Underground, 1998, p. 10.
27   Lopez, 1996, p. 22.
28   Johnston, 1994, p. 10.
29   Gedicks, 1993, p. 61.
30   Waldman, 1998, p. A 10.
31   Gardner and Sampat, 1999, p. 46.
32   Morgan, 1973, p. 30.
33   Moody, 1996, p. 46.
34   Ibid.
35   Nettleton, 1996a, p. 4.
36   Nettleton, 1996b, p. 18.
37   Survival International, 1995a, p. 2.
38   Moody, 1991.
39   Nettleton, 1997, p. 36.
40   Survival International, 1995a, p. 2.
41   Barsh, 1999, p. 5.
42   Project Underground, 2000c, p. 16.
43   Moody, 1997a, p. 26.
44   Ibid., p. 37.
45   Ibid., p. 26.
46   Ibid., p. 27.
47   Ross, 1996, p. 12.
48   Ibid.

49 Survival International, 1999a, p. 3.
50 Nettleton, 1996b, pp. 18-19.
51 Survival International, 1998.
52 Survival International, 1999, p. 3.
53 Nettleton, 1997, p. 40.
54 Ibid., p. 41.
55 Survival International, 1999b.
56 Solidarity Action Group for Indigenous People, 1996, p. 49.
57 Project Underground, 2000a; Bosshard and Moody, 1997, p. 9.
58 Moody, 1993, p. 13
59 Whirled Bank Group, 2000.
60 *Jarkarta Post,* 2000b.
61 Burton, 2000.
62 Ibid.
63 Solomon, 2000.
64 Ibid.
65 Burton, 2000.
66 Ortman, 2000.
67 *Petromindo,* 2001.
68 Associated Press, 1995.
69 Panos, 1996, p. 13.
70 Minewatch, 1996, pp. 6-7. When heavy metals are consumed by living things, they can build up within the tissues and be passed through the food chain. This is called bioaccumulation. See Ripley, et al., 1996, p. 58.
71 *Native Americas,* 1996, p. 4.
72 Panos, 1996, 12.
73 Guyana Geology and Mines Commission, 1996.
74 Jodah, 1995, p. 10.
75 *Native Americas,* 1996, p. 4.
76 Moody, 1997b, p. 12.
77 Moody, 1994, p. 23.
78 Ibid.,
79 *Northern Miner,* 1995b.
80 Egan, 2001.
81 International Federation of Chemical, Energy, Mine, and General Workers' Unions, 1998, p. 50.
82 Whirled Bank Group, 2000.
83 Chatterjee, 1997.
84 *Native Americas,* 1996, p. 4.
85 Project Underground, 2000b.

CHAPTER 2

Big Oil, the Environment and Human Rights

As the international oil industry explores the frontier regions of the globe for new supplies, it inevitably comes into contact with the native peoples who occupy the world's remaining forests, wetlands, tundra and deserts. According to the Rainforest Action Network and Project Underground, "The high correlation between petroleum basins and indigenous communities on every continent tells a story of increasing pressure on indigenous peoples and their homelands to feed the industrialized world's growing appetite for oil and gas."[1]

The close connection between native peoples and their land has made them particularly vulnerable to changes in their ecosystems. Because of their direct dependence on the earth for subsistence, they suffer more acutely than others when toxic materials pollute their lands. In the cases of oil extraction in the Niger Delta of Nigeria, the Amazon rainforest of Ecuador and the Colombian cloud forest, there is an inseparable connection between the assault on the environment and the assault on human rights. In all of these cases, multinational oil corporations have not only degraded the environment but colluded with the governments of these countries to deny native peoples their basic political and civil rights to resist environmental damage that threatens their subsistence and their very survival.

Nigeria: Rich Land, Poor People

Nigeria, a former British colony, has been ruled primarily by military dictatorship since gaining independence in 1960. The most repressive regime was the one of General Sani Abacha (1993-1998). Nigeria is the biggest oil producer on the African continent. Oil production for export provides 80% of the government's revenue and accounts for 95% of exports. Almost one third of this oil is shipped directly to the United States.[2] Most of the oil comes from the Niger Delta, which contains the third-largest contiguous mangrove forest in the world.[3] The inhabitants of this region, which include ethnic minorities like the Ogoni and the Ijaw, have not benefited from the extraction of this oil wealth in their communities. Since oil was first discovered in Ogoniland in 1958, Shell Oil Company has extracted $30 billion worth of oil. Yet malnutrition ravages Ogoni children, and the region lacks functional hospitals and schools, paved roads, steady electricity and even running water.[4]

To understand the situation of the Ogoni one has to understand that they are one of hundreds of ethnic minorities who were subjugated and forced into the British southern protectorate that eventually became part of Nigeria. The dominant ethnic groups, located in the north, include the Yoruba, Ibo and Hausa/Fulani.[5] The unequal distribution of resources and power between the dominant ethnic groups in the north and the ethnic minorities from the southern oil-producing communities resembles a classic internal colonial situation.[6] One scholar has described the dominant groups in the military and civil bureaucracy as constituting a comprador or intermediary class serving their international masters by exploiting their compatriots:

> They proceed to forge an alliance between the MNCs [multinational corporations] and the dominant groups at the expense of minorities. This tendency is most felt in the areas of employment practices of the MNCs and their links with the local business community, both of which favor controlling local groups. Through their operations the oil MNCs also add another key element to the peripheralization process, environmental degradation, perpetrated through "ecological terrorism."[7]

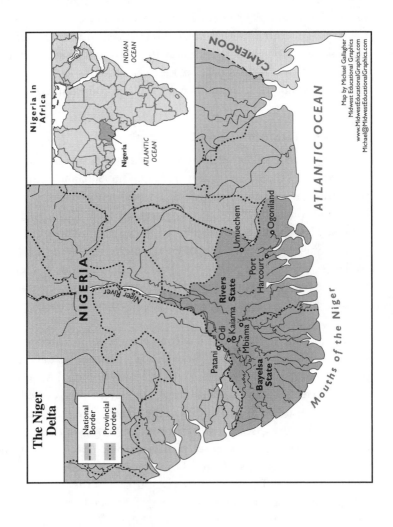

The Niger Delta

National Border
Provincial borders

Nigeria in Africa

INDIAN OCEAN

ATLANTIC OCEAN

Nigeria

NIGERIA

CAMEROON

Niger River

Patani
Odi
Kalama
Mbiama
Bayelsa State

Rivers State
Port Harcourt
Umuechem
Ogoniland

ATLANTIC OCEAN

Mouths of the Niger

Map by Michael Gallagher
Midwest Educational Graphics
www.MidwestEducationalGraphics.com
Michael@MidwestEducationalGraphics.com

All foreign oil companies in Nigeria are joint ventures with the Nigerian National Petroleum Corporation, the state oil company. As a 60% shareholder in all oil operations, the Nigerian government earns billions of dollars in royalties each year. However, successive military governments—dominated by the northern ethnic groups—have diverted the oil wealth to foreign bank accounts rather than investing in education, health and other social programs, especially where those would benefit southern Nigerian communities.[8]

"Ecological Terrorism" Against the Ogoni

The Ogoni Nation occupies 404 square miles in a coastal plain terrace of the Niger Delta, in Rivers State. The 500,000 Ogoni people in this rural setting depend upon agriculture and fishing for their livelihood. Since Shell began extracting oil from Ogoniland, the company has shown little concern for the environment or the local people. Shell has invaded Ogoni communities in search of oil and has laid oil pipelines in people's backyards and farmlands. Under the Land Use Act, passed in 1978 under the Olusegun Obasanjo military regime, land for oil operations can be appropriated for use by multinational oil corporations.[9]

Among the most serious environmental problems are the constant gas flares that burn 24 hours a day. The intense heat and gases that are released from these flares affect nearby homes, destroy food crops and render surrounding farmlands barren and wasted. Although there are no health studies of the effect of gas flares in these communities, the gaseous hydrocarbons are known hazards to life. Flaring in Nigeria contributes a measurable percentage of the world's total emissions of greenhouse gases, thus contributing to global warming.[10] The incomplete combustion of the flares also results in acid rain that deprives people of drinkable rainwater and stunts crop growth.[11] There are other options for managing the natural gas, which is a by-product of oil extraction, but this is by far the cheapest option for the company. A U.S. non-governmental delegation to the Niger Delta region met with a Shell public relations officer who denied that communities were harmed by gas flares and "even claimed that local residents benefited from these flares because they could dry their foodstuffs for free by setting them near the burning gases."[12]

Oil spillage and ruptured pipelines are another major source of environmental devastation. Major responsibility for oil spillage lies with the oil companies who fail to properly maintain, inspect and replace old and rusty pipelines. The oil blow-out in the village of Botem in 1992 lasted one week and completely destroyed the stream that provided drinking water for the village. It also destroyed aquatic life in the stream as well as extensive farmlands that have been rendered biological dead zones.[13] Villagers complain that when pipelines corrode and leak, oil workers will inspect but not repair the leak. Instead, the companies will claim sabotage, because under Nigerian law they are not obliged to clean up or compensate for the effects of spills caused by sabotage.[14] The oil spillage in the Niger Delta represents 40% of Shell's total worldwide oil spills, which is about three times as much as at Shell's operations outside Nigeria.[15]

Pipeline leaks that are allowed to go untended sometimes result in pipeline explosions. In October 1998, one such leak that flooded a large region near the village of Jesse exploded, causing the deaths of over 700 people, mostly women and children.[16] In July 2000, two separate pipeline explosions in southern Nigeria killed nearly 300 people in less than ten days. Over the past two years, thousands have been killed in similar blasts.[17] The Associated Press stories on these periodic explosions routinely place responsibility on thieves siphoning oil for personal use and ignore the role of multinational oil corporations in creating these hazards.[18] This results in the kind of victim-blaming that Shell uses when it accuses native people of taking advantage of oil spills to collect compensation. This kind of thinking can also be seen in the government's Task Force on Pipeline Vandalization. In June 2000, the task force arrested and executed three children who had gone after school to watch people scoop up the fuel from a leaking pipeline.[19]

State Terrorism Against the Ogoni

The cumulative effect of these assaults on Ogoniland, mangrove forests, air, water and health has created a crisis of survival for the Ogoni people. In 1990, the community of Umuechem staged a peaceful protest to voice its complaints about oil-related pollution. Shell requested the assistance of the Nigerian police to respond to the protest. The result was a massacre. From October 13 to November 1, 1990, the notorious Mobile Police (also known as the "kill and go") constantly bombarded the village, causing the deaths of more than 100 people. Houses were burned and looted. Most villagers were forced to leave the area.[20] Unfortunately, this repression is not exceptional. Human Rights Watch observed that "in virtually every community, there have been occasions on which the paramilitary Mobile Police, the regular police or the army have beaten, detained or even killed those involved in protests, peaceful or otherwise, or individuals who have called for compensation for oil damage, whether youths, women, children or traditional leaders."[21]

The Movement for the Survival of the Ogoni People (MOSOP), founded in 1990 by Ogoni leaders including Ken Saro-Wiwa, organized a collective response to this assault. That same year MOSOP formulated an "Ogoni Bill of Rights" and submitted it to the Nigerian government. Among the principal demands were "political control of Ogoni affairs by Ogoni people; the right to the control and use of a fair proportion of Ogoni economic resources for Ogoni development; adequate representation in all Nigerian national institutions and the right to protect the Ogoni environment and ecology from further degradation."[22] MOSOP also charged Shell with "full responsibility for the genocide of the Ogoni."[23] As a prolific author and spokesperson, Saro-Wiwa brought MOSOP's concerns to the international community when he presented the Ogoni people's case before the United Nations Commission on Human Rights in Geneva in 1992. This was widely reported by the Nigerian media and spurred on the Ogoni resistance.[24]

To call international attention to the desperate situation facing native peoples around the world, the United Nations designated 1993 as the International Year of Indigenous People. That same year, MOSOP organized the first "Ogoni Day" rally, which drew about 300,000 to the town of Bori for the largest peaceful protest against Shell's extensive oil pollution of the Ogoni homeland.

Garrick Leton, a MOSOP leader and one of the speakers at the rally, summarized the reasons for their protest:

> We have woken up to find our lands devastated by agents of death called oil companies. Our atmosphere has been totally polluted, our lands degraded, our waters contaminated, our trees poisoned, so much so that our flora and fauna have virtually disappeared. We are asking for the restoration of our environment. We are asking for the basic necessities of life—water, electricity, roads, education. We are asking, above all, for the right to self-determination so that we can be responsible for our resources and our environment. [25]

Following this demonstration, the Nigerian government established the Rivers State Internal Security Force, a military unit created specifically to deal with the Ogoni protests.[26] In 1993, Shell was forced to close its production in Ogoni following mass protests at its facilities. The Nigerian military has occupied the region ever since. The military reign of terror in Ogoni has included numerous raids resulting in the deaths of over 2,000 unarmed civilians and the destruction of 37 villages.[27] The World Council of Churches estimates that since 1993, 30,000 Ogoni have been internally displaced, and another 1,000 have fled Nigeria and endure miserable conditions in refugee camps in neighboring countries.[28] According to Ken Saro-Wiwa, the military occupation

> is meant to intimidate and terrorize the Ogoni people in order to allow Shell to recommence its operations in the area without carrying out the environmental, health and social impact studies which the Ogoni people have demanded since 1992.[29]

Besides the environmental damage, MOSOP charged that Shell had been funding the Nigerian military and providing them with arms, helicopters and boats.

In May 1994, Saro-Wiwa and eight other Ogoni leaders were arrested on fabricated charges and accused of murder by the Nigerian military. After his arrest, Saro-Wiwa was awarded the 1994 Right Livelihood Award (known as the alternative Nobel Peace Prize) for his and MOSOP's environmental campaign. Amnesty International declared Saro-Wiwa a prisoner of conscience and called his arrest "part of the continuing suppression by the Nigerian authorities of the Ogoni people's campaign against the oil companies."[30]

While Shell publicly maintained that it "ha[d] neither the right nor the competence to become involved" in the Saro-Wiwa case, it was quietly bribing witnesses to testify against Saro-Wiwa. Michael Birnbaum, who observed the trial on behalf of the Bar Human Rights Committee of England and Wales, reported that the two chief prosecution witnesses against Saro-Wiwa, and the only two to implicate Saro-Wiwa directly, had signed affidavits alleging they were bribed to give evidence against him.[31] According to Dr. Owens Wiwa, Ken's brother, Shell offered to intervene in the case if Saro-Wiwa agreed to end his protests. Saro-Wiwa responded that the campaign against Shell would stop as soon as Shell responded to the environmental concerns of the Ogonis.[32] In November 1995, a military tribunal tried Saro-Wiwa and the eight other leaders, found them guilty and hanged them. The executions provoked widespread international condemnation of both the military junta and Shell. All European Union members recalled their ambassadors for consultation. The United States withdrew its ambassador, but did not do the one thing that would have forced the Nigerian military to step down: place an embargo on Nigerian oil. The oil companies lobbied heavily against the Nigerian Democracy Act (S1419), a U.S. Senate bill that would have embargoed Nigerian oil coming into the United States. The bill died for lack of Senate sponsors.[33]

Shortly after the executions, Shell announced plans to go ahead with a liquefied natural gas plant and pipeline project in Ogoniland, funded largely through the World Bank.[34] A year later, the families of Saro-Wiwa and John Kpuinen filed suit in New York District Court against Shell for its complicity in the hanging of the two activists. Attorneys from the New York-based Center for Constitutional Rights filed suit, charging Shell with wrongful death and crimes against humanity.[35] Shell's attorneys tried to have the suit dismissed on the grounds that New York lacked jurisdiction over Shell. In 1998, Judge Kimba Wood concluded that New York had jurisdiction, but also ruled that the case should be heard in the Netherlands or England. The plaintiffs appealed this decision to the Second Circuit Court of New York and won the right to try the case in New

York. In January 2001, Shell appealed that decision to the state Supreme Court.[36]

Shell has repeatedly denied its collusion with the Nigerian military. However, a 1994 leaked memo, addressed to the governor of Rivers State and signed by Lt. Col. Paul Okuntimo, the head of the Rivers State Internal Security Task Force, stated that "Shell operations are still impossible unless ruthless military operations are undertaken for smooth economic activities to commence." Okuntimo recommends "wasting operations during MOSOP and other gatherings, making constant military presence justifiable" and "wasting targets cutting across communities and leadership cadres, especially vocal individuals in various groups." He also states that the oil companies should pay the costs of the operations.[37] Okuntimo repeated his allegations for British documentary filmmakers Glen Ellis and Kay Bishop in their powerful documentary *Delta Force*. Shell responded to the charges in *Delta Force* by categorically denying any involvement with the Nigerian military. When the filmmakers stood by their charges, Shell admitted to paying "field allowances" to the Nigerian military and providing logistical support in the form of access to Shell helicopters and boats.[38] The company has also admitted importing weapons into Nigeria to arm the police.[39] A former Shell scientist has referred to all this as the "militarization of commerce":

> Oil [is] extracted in the Niger Delta under military protection. The situation right now is that all the flow stations, that is the operational bases of the oil industry, operate under armed presence. This is a process of the militarization of commerce and the privatization of the state, and I have actually used these phrases in discussion with Shell executives.[40]

This reliance upon the military is not limited to Shell, nor to Ogoniland. The same pattern of corporate-state terrorism can be found throughout the Niger Delta.

Chevron and the Ijaw

In May 1998, about 100 members of the Concerned Ilaje Citizens peacefully occupied Chevron's Parabe offshore drilling platform to protest the company's pollution of their land and to demand compensation. They occupied the platform for three days, but did not interrupt operations. On the third day, the protestors agreed to leave after reaching an agreement with Chevron representatives that a meeting would be held at the village. Before the protestors could start leaving, however, Chevron flew in members of Nigeria's navy and notorious Mobile Police on two helicopters belonging to Chevron, and staged an attack on the unarmed protesters, killing two of them and seriously injuring another two.[41] A Chevron representative admitted to Pacifica Radio's Amy Goodman and Jeremy Scahill that the company flew in the soldiers that did the killing.[42]

Following the death of General Sani Abacha in June 1998, oil stoppages escalated, especially in Ijaw communities. The Ijaw, whose population is about 12 million, constitute the largest ethnic group in the Niger Delta. Almost two thirds of Nigerian oil flows from Ijaw territory. In October 1998, Ijaw groups took control of about 20 oil stations belonging to Shell and Chevron, at one point cutting Nigeria's oil production of 2 million barrels a day by a third.[43] The following month, nearly 500 Ijaw communities came together in the village of Kaiama and drafted the Kaiama Declaration. The declaration stated that "All land and natural resources (including mineral resources) within the Ijaw territory belong to Ijaw communities and are the basis of our survival" and demanded "the immediate withdrawal from Ijawland of all military forces of occupation and repression by the Nigerian state."[44]

Despite democratic hopes raised by the election of President Olusegun Obasanjo in early 1999, the military repression of dissent in the Niger Delta continued. In the town of Odi in Bayelsa State, Nigerian soldiers murdered at least a dozen local people.[45] Following the alleged kidnapping and killing of policemen in Bayelsa State, President Obasanjo sent over 1,500 troops to restore law and order in Odi, Mbiama, Kaiama and Patani.[46] These are all villages close to the heart of Ijaw territory where civil disobedience shut down much of Nigeria's oil production in November and December 1998, leading many in Nigeria to believe that the concern for law and order is a convenient cover for suppression of organized opposition to environmental terrorism by the oil industry. Environmental Rights Action of Nigeria, an environmental and human rights organization, claims that the reason for these attacks was spelled out by Nigeria's

Minister of Defense in an address to the Economic Community of West Africa States' ministerial committee.

> This operation, HAKURI II, was initiated with the mandate of protecting lives and property—particularly oil platforms, flow stations, operating rig terminals and pipelines, refineries and power installations in the Niger Delta.[47]

As the rebellion has spread from the 500,000 Ogoni to the 12 million Ijaw, the Niger Delta communities have become better organized and their actions more successful, inviting repression and provoking even greater protest. There can be no solution to this growing conflict that does not recognize the fundamental democratic and human rights of the peoples of the oil-producing areas. While the government of Nigeria has primary responsibility for resolving these injustices, there is no question, as Human Rights Watch has concluded, that the oil companies bear major responsibility for the conflict within and between communities that results in state-sponsored military repression.[48]

While the struggle continues in Nigeria, MOSOP activists in exile have expanded their campaign against Shell by linking up with indigenous groups in the Peruvian Amazon, where Shell is planning to invest $2.7 billion over 40 years in a gas project. The Camisea project is of particular concern, because the activity will impact the Reserve for Nomadic Kugapokori and Nahua Peoples, who have had very little contact with the Western world.[49] Similar concerns have been expressed regarding oil extraction plans within the traditional territory of the U'wa indigenous people of Colombia.

Colombia: Oil and Violence

The first native organization in Colombia emerged in the southern part of the country (Cauca department) in 1971. Since then, government security forces, drug traffickers, leftist guerrillas and paramilitary groups in the pay of landowners have killed more than 500 native leaders.[50] Why have native people suffered some of the most intense levels of violence over the past three decades of Colombia's internal war? They suffer from the same "developmental genocide" that has affected others who are considered obstacles to progress in Brazil, Mexico, the Philippines and Nigeria.

Exxon's giant El Cerrejon coal mine is located on the lands of the Guajiros, Colombia's largest group of native people, who have opposed the project. It is the largest coal mine in Latin America, and one of the richest in the world. But the mine area has become a militarized zone as Exxon has brought in troops and armored tanks to put down periodic strikes.[51] Guerrillas have also attacked the mine, causing $3 billion in damages.[52] Exxon celebrates the mine as one of Colombia's "showcases of prosperity on a barren plain," while the environmental and cultural devastation of the project has earned Exxon a place on Survival International's Top Ten list of corporate violators of native rights.[53]

Approximately a quarter of Colombian territory is legally recognized indigenous territory, and a significant part of the country's oil reserves are on indigenous land.[54] A major study of the impact of large projects on native lands singled out the oil industry as especially harmful:

> The activities of the oil industry on indigenous territories, both now and in the past, have regularly caused a significant fall in the indigenous population living in the territory concerned. This fall in population has been due to the sudden collapse in the physical, cultural and spiritual aspects of the indigenous way of life and the coercion of the affected groups in a situation in which they are unable to defend themselves against surrounding society. In certain cases, the arrival of the oil industry could have caused the extinction of indigenous groups. [55]

But the violence is not limited to native peoples. Under the Colombian doctrine of national security, the war against "subversives" justifies killing peasant and labor leaders, teachers, journalists, priests, nuns, human rights workers and unarmed citizens. The Colombian army publicly stated that 85% of the "subversives" they must attack are engaged in a "political war," not combat.[56] Human rights groups estimate that there are between 3,000 and 4,000 political killings a year, with over 70% attributed to right-wing paramilitary groups and their military allies.[57] An estimated 2 million Colombians are refugees of the violence.[58] Yet the recently approved $1.3 billion U.S. military aid package will only escalate this killing along with the numbers of refugees from the violence. Amnesty International warned that increased support for Colombian security forces would result in a "humanitarian catastrophe" in the country's conflict zones.[59]

A Drug War in Colombia?

Colombia is the third-largest recipient of U.S. military aid in the world after Israel and Egypt. According to Winifred Tate of the Washington Office on Latin America,

> The level of U.S. aid and number of advisors in Colombia on any given day are reaching levels as high as in Central America in the 1980s: For Fiscal Year 1999, the country had received 250 advisors and roughly $360 million in assistance.[60]

The total U.S. aid to Colombia's security forces has more than quadrupled from 1996 to 1999, raising serious concerns among human rights advocates because the Colombian army is the hemisphere's worst abuser of human rights.[61] In 1994, the U.S. Congress tried to cut off U.S. assistance to the notoriously abusive counterinsurgency effort and to limit military aid to units primarily involved in counternarcotics operations.[62] The distinction was meaningless. The Colombian military considered all guerrillas as "narco-guerrillas." By 1997, the oil industry had mounted a successful lobbying effort to restore and increase U.S. military aid.[63]

According to the former U.S. Drug Czar, General Barry McCaffrey, "the rapidly expanding cocaine and heroin production in Colombia constitute a threat to U.S. national security and the well-being of our citizens."[64] There are only two problems with this rationale. First, the U.S.-financed attack stays clear of the area where most narcotraffickers are located, in northern Colombia. The leader of one of northern Colombia's largest paramilitary groups, Carlos Castaño, told a national Colombian television audience that the drug trade provided 70% of his group's funding. Second, the U.S. Drug Enforcement Administration (DEA) reports that "all branches of government in Colombia are involved in "drug-related corruption."[65]

Most of the aid package will go to assist Colombia's corrupt military in its war against the guerrilla armies of the Revolutionary Armed Forces of Colombia (FARC) and the National Liberation Army (ELN). The area that will be hit the hardest, in southern Colombia, is governed by the FARC, the larger of the two guerrilla armies.[66] In addition to 18 Blackhawk and 42 Huey II attack helicopters, the Colombian armed forces will receive training and access to satellite images of areas controlled by FARC. While the FARC depends upon its control of vast areas of coca plantations in southern Colombia to finance its activity, it has also called for a development plan for the peasants that would allow them to grow alternative crops. Even the DEA admits that the FARC is not engaged in international drug trafficking.[67] However, to describe the FARC forces as "narco-guerrillas" disguises the pursuit of larger objectives, spelled out by Noam Chomsky:

> The targets of the Colombia Plan are guerrilla forces based on the peasantry and calling for internal social change, which would interfere with integration of Colombia into the global system on the terms that the U.S. demands; that is, dominated by elites linked to U.S. power interests that are accorded free access to Colombia's valuable resources, including oil.[68]

Colombia is the fourth-largest and fastest growing major exporter of oil in South America, producing 620,000 barrels per day. Even General McCaffrey has admitted his real concern is with the guerrilla threat to the region's growing oil industry:

> Colombia is the eighth largest supplier of foreign crude oil to the United States, with more than 330,000 barrels per day shipped primarily to Gulf Coast refineries in Texas and Louisiana. In 1999, oil was Colombia's largest export, accounting for approximately 31% of the country's total exports, and 24% of the central government's income. Not surprisingly, the guerrilla groups routinely attack the government-owned pipelines, 79 times in 1999 alone.... From a regional perspective, Colombia, Ecuador, and Venezuela together provide more than 20% of the US's oil imports. This statistic cannot be overlooked as we assess the importance of maintaining stability in the region.[69]

U.S. funding of the drug war includes the important Andean Amazon oil-producing countries of Peru, Bolivia, Ecuador and Venezuela. New military bases in Ecuador, Aruba, Curaçao and El Salvador, called "Forward Operating Locations,"[70] suggest an escalation of military intervention throughout the region. The new U.S. air base at Manta, Ecuador, has already been criticized as "a provocation to all of the irregular forces in Colombia," according to a leader in the Ecuadorian Congress. "Our oil has already been attacked by Colombian guerrillas, and the paramilitary groups are killing people on Ecuadorian territory, so just imagine how a military installation like this acts as an enticement."[71] The oil-producing town of Lago Agrio has been targeted as a site of arms transfers, and the local population has been identified as "vulnerable to the subversive influences of the FARC."[72] It is no accident that some of the first victims of the current escalation of the drug war are native people resisting oil drilling on their land.

Oxy Invades U'wa Lands

Shortly after President Clinton's announcement of the $1.3 billion aid grant, four U.S.-supplied helicopters carrying Colombian National Police forces attacked a group of U'wa Indians who had been peacefully blockading the road leading to the Gibraltar 1 drilling site, owned by the Los Angeles-based Occidental Petroleum Corporation (Oxy). Hundreds of police attacked the U'wa with riot batons, bulldozers and tear gas. Three U'wa children drowned when police forced them into the fast-flowing Cubujon River.[73] According to the U'wa, the governor of Northern Santander, in northeastern Colombia, where the Gibraltar site is located, said, "Those animal Indians have to be evicted violently." The military forces declared that "the oil will be extracted even over and above the U'wa people."[74]

The most intense resistance to new oil development comes from the U'wa, a native community of 5,000 members who live in the cloud forest of the Sierra Nevada de Cocuy mountains in northeastern Colombia, near the Venezuelan border. Since 1992, the U'wa have resisted attempts to explore for oil in their traditional territory, known to the oil industry as the Samore block. The U'wa believe that the project will only bring the violence that they have seen in other oil regions. The consortium pushing the project includes Oxy and Shell, each holding a 37.5% share, while Ecopetrol, the state-owned oil company, has a 25% share. The Samore oilfield is estimated to contain 1.5 billion barrels, amounting to no more than three months' worth of oil for U.S. consumers.[75]

The U'wa have threatened to commit mass suicide if Oxy and Shell go ahead with their exploration plans, preferring to die "with dignity, as opposed to slowly."[76] The U'wa have a long history of resisting colonial domination. When the Spanish Conquistadors were enslaving native peoples to dig for gold, the U'wa retreated into the mountains. Rather than endure subjugation, a portion of the tribe plunged to their deaths over a 1,400-foot cliff.[77] Today, the U'wa see their very existence threatened by Oxy and the Colombian government who "are insisting on ignoring our territorial rights over land we have occupied for thousands of years. We are the owners of the territory on which they aim to exploit petroleum, without recognizing the constitutional rights of community lands for our ethnic group which are inalienable, non-negotiable, and irremovable, protected by public laws over collective property."[78]

The U'wa reserve, which is a small fraction of their ancestral territory, lies at the headwaters of the critical Orinoco River basin. Inside the U'wa territory are multiple lakes and underground reservoirs that feed national parks and tributaries to surrounding inhabited regions.[79] The U'wa believe that "oil is the blood of Mother Earth" and that to take the oil is "worse than killing your own mother."[80] The U'wa have already seen the consequences of oil extraction just north of their reserve, where guerrilla attacks on oil pipelines have spilled over 1.7 million barrels of crude oil into the soil and rivers (the Exxon Valdez spill involved only 36,000 barrels).[81] In 1997, environmental, peasant and human rights groups and the Arauca Oil Workers Union issued a report citing Oxy's Cano Limón facility as "the best example that petroleum exploitation should not be permitted in Samore at any price."[82]

Previous oil projects led to the extermination of the Yariguie and the decimation of the Motilon tribe in the department of North Santander. In the southern department of Putumayo, Texaco and

Colombia
The U'wa Territory

Northern Santander

Barrancabermeja

Girbraltar I Drill site

Venezuela

Unified U'wa Reservation

Original U'wa Territory

Santander

Arauca

Sierra de Cocuy National Park

Samoré Block

Caribbean Sea

Casanare River

Casanare

Kajka Ika
Ancestral U'wa Territory

Boyacá

PANAMA

VENEZUELA

Barrancabermeja

Cauca R.

Medellín

Meta R.

Orinoco R.

Pacific Ocean

Bogotá

COLOMBIA

Cali

Guaviare R.

Putumayo Province

BRAZIL

Caqueta R.

ECUADOR

Putumayo R.

PERU

National Border

Provincial borders

Map by Michael Gallagher,
Midwest Educational Graphics
www.MidwestEducationalGraphics.com
michael@MidwestEducationalGraphics.com

Colombia in South America

Panama

Venezuela

Colombia

Ecuador

Brazil

Peru

Ecopetrol contaminated fresh water supplies and forced the relocation of Inga, Siona and Cofan Indians.[83] And in Ecuador in 1996,
Oxy brought in the military to force the Siona and Secoya peoples of
the Amazon to give up their land.[84]

The U'wa have turned to both national and international law to
preserve their land from oil exploitation. The Colombian Constitution of 1991, in which indigenous leaders played a critical role, for
the first time provided for the rights of indigenous peoples and communities in regard to territory, politics, economic development, administration and social and cultural rights.[85] When the U'wa filed
suit in Constitutional Court to stop oil exploration on their land, the
court cited these rights in ruling that the U'wa must be fully consulted before the government could approve the project. One
month later, this decision was overruled by the Council of State,
which asserted state ownership of mineral rights above all other
considerations. The U'wa then took their case to the Organization
of American States (OAS). The National Indigenous Organization
of Colombia, along with the Earthjustice Legal Defense Fund and
the Coalition for Amazonian Peoples and their Environment, presented the U'wa case in Washington, DC, in 1997. The OAS issued a
report recommending an immediate and unconditional suspension
of all oil activities in the Samore block and legal recognition of the
entire territory of the U'wa.[86]

Militarized Commerce, Privatized State

Since the first major oil field at Cano Limón was discovered in
1984 by Oxy, there have been over 500 pipeline bombings by the
ELN, which is committed to disrupting foreign oil companies and
which favors nationalization of the industry.[87] The growth of the oil
industry and of the guerrilla armies has gone hand in hand. Colombia's National Planning Department estimated that rebel hits during
1990-94 cost the industry $12 billion at the very least.[88] The Colom-
bian government has responded "by militarizing these areas and ter-
rorizing the local population, whom they presume to be guerrilla
supporters."[89] The policy of murdering trade unionists, human
rights observers and anyone supporting the guerrillas is called

"draining the sea to kill the fish" and is a U.S.-designed counterinsurgency plan for guerrilla warfare.[90]

Since 1991 the Colombian military has worked with a U.S. Defense Department and Central Intelligence Agency (CIA) team to create "killer networks that identified and killed civilians suspected of supporting guerrillas."[91] Human Rights Watch has documented that several leaders of the powerful Workers' Trade Union (USO) were assassinated by the Colombian navy around the city of Barrancabermeja in the department of Santander in 1992 and 1993.[92] The USO represents workers employed by Ecopetrol. The workers have consistently opposed the government's attempts to privatize the state's oil industry and turn it over to foreign oil companies like Oxy, Shell and British Petroleum (BP).[93]

Human rights abuses have risen dramatically in the areas with the most intense oil activity. Illegal detentions are a serious problem in the department of Arauca, where BP's large Cusiana oil deposit is located, while forced disappearances have risen in the department of North Santander, site of the Cano Limón-Covenas pipeline.[94] Native communities in these oil-producing areas have been caught in the crossfire among Colombian armed forces, leftist guerrillas and right-wing paramilitary groups. Both Colombian and U.S. government officials deny that they have any connection to or responsibility for the activities of the paramilitaries. Human Rights Watch has assembled overwhelming evidence to the contrary:

> It is time to clear the smokescreen of official denial and identify this lethal partnership for what it is: a sophisticated mechanism, in part supported by years of advice, training, weaponry and official silence by the United States, that allows the Colombian military to fight a dirty war and Colombian officialdom to deny it. The price: thousands of dead, disappeared, maimed and terrorized Colombians. [95]

Part of the government's militarization of the oil production and pipeline zones involved a "war tax" of $1 per barrel on foreign oil companies to pay indirectly for the protection of the armed forces. However, beginning with the exploitation of the large Cusiana oil reserve in 1995, BP and Oxy began negotiating protection agreements directly with the military and private security firms.

According to the *Oil and Gas Journal*, multinational oil companies spend 8% of their investment on security in Colombia, as compared to 1% in the rest of Latin America.[96]

In 1996, the army assigned 3,000 troops to the area surrounding BP's Cusiana installations.[97] Meanwhile, Oxy contracted for the maintenance of two new counter-guerrilla army units to deter ongoing guerrilla attacks on the Cano Limón pipeline.[98] Oxy also accused Roberto Cobaría, chief of the U'wa, of opposing exploration on tribal lands because of pressure from the ELN.[99] In the context of the government's war against the guerrillas and the wave of paramilitary violence, the suggestion that the U'wa were guerrilla sympathizers was the equivalent to a death threat. Afterwards, the U'wa chief was pulled from his bed in the middle of the night by a group of hooded men with assault rifles. The assailants held him to the ground and demanded that he sign an agreement to let Oxy explore or lose his life. When he refused, the gunmen beat him. Cobaría continues to speak out, but under the threat of death.[100]

An unpublished government report has accused BP of collaborating with soldiers involved in kidnappings, torture and murder.[101] The report, prepared by a high-level team, including the Colombian Attorney General and the presidential advisor on human rights, alleges that BP gave photos and videotapes of local people protesting oil activities to the Colombian military, which proceeded to arrest and kidnap activists for being "subversives." Despite urging by the European Parliament, former Colombian President Ernesto Samper refused to publish the report.

The Murder of North American Activists

International attention was focused on the U'wa people's struggle when three international indigenous rights activists—Terence Freitas of Los Angeles; Ingrid Washinawatok, a Menominee Indian from Wisconsin; and Lahe'ane'e Gay of Hawaii—were murdered in Colombia in March 1999. They were kidnapped by FARC gunmen and were found slain along the Arauca River in Venezuela. Terry Freitas was one of the founders of the U'wa Defense Working Group (UDWG) and had devoted the last two years of his life to supporting the U'wa in their campaign to stop Occidental's oil project. Ingrid Washinawatok and Lahe'ane'e Gay were assisting the U'wa in setting up an educational program to maintain and promote their traditional culture. The news of the murders was especially painful for me because I had known Ingrid, first as a student of mine and more recently in her capacity as executive director of the Fund for the Four Directions in New York, which had helped to fund a project through which I worked with Wisconsin tribes in opposing mining projects next to their lands. Ingrid was a proud member of the American Indian Movement and a co-chair of the Indigenous Women's Network.

In response to the news of the murders, Apesanahkwat, the tribal chairman of the Menominee, charged that the U.S. government bore some responsibility for the killings. He said that the U.S. government had sent money for arms to the Colombian government four or five days after the kidnapping, knowing that these arms would be used against the FARC rebels who held the kidnap victims.[102] According to an in-depth investigative report by Jeff Wollock, a frequent reporter on native issues, the CIA and U.S. military intelligence had been intercepting FARC communications prior to the kidnapping, as part of a Colombian military offensive called "Operation Total Eclipse." The objective was to protect Occidental's oil pipeline.[103] The intercept was still in progress when Terry, Lahe and Ingrid were kidnapped, and continued throughout their entire ordeal. The intercepted tapes were later played on Colombian radio. They leave no doubt that from the very beginning, FARC intended to kill them. While FARC pays lip service to the U'wa struggle against Occidental, they have not respected the territory or the culture of the U'wa. In response to FARC's apology for the murders, the vice-president of the National Organization of Indigenous Peoples of Colombia said: "The act is an atrocity that cannot be forgiven. They killed our brother and sisters from North America, and now they are apologizing? That is unacceptable."[104]

And what about U.S. and Colombian intelligence? They knew from the very beginning of the kidnapping what was going to happen to Terry, Lahe and Ingrid, but did nothing to save their lives. An editorial in the Colombian newspaper *El Espectador* in March 1999 raised the question of complicity in the murders:

If Army intelligence has been intercepting the 45th Front [of FARC] for over a month now, why did they allow the situation to deteriorate and not do anything to save the lives of those three Americans?… As far as is known, military intelligence serves to prevent and to alert the country to new challenges and possible acts that can affect the life of its citizens. But an intelligence that is only capable of operating ex post facto fails to remove certain suspicions as to its real reach and projection.[105]

The Occidental Campaign

The UDWG, a coalition of non-governmental organizations, was formed in the United States in 1997. Its mission is to secure the rights of the U'wa people and the protection of their environment. Members include Action for Communities and Ecology in the Rainforests of Central America (ACERCA), Amazon Watch, Center for Justice and International Law, Colombian Human Rights Commission (DC), Earthjustice Legal Defense Fund, Earth Trust Foundation, Native Forest Network, Project Underground, Rainforest Action Network and Sol Communications. In April 1999, the UDWG organized the "International Week of Action for the U'wa," which included protests at Oxy headquarters, press events and the appearance of U'wa leaders at Oxy's annual shareholders' meeting. The *Wall Street Journal* commented upon the effectiveness of the coalition in putting Oxy in a difficult position: "By personalizing the global fight over natural-resource extraction with the brooding faces of the U'wa…environmentalists are tugging at heartstrings like never before."[106]

With the help of the Sinsinawa Dominican Sisters, who own Oxy shares, the U'wa were able to speak to the directors and shareholders about their determination to resist drilling on their lands. The nuns' proposal to hire an outside firm to analyze the potential impact of the U'wa suicide threat on the company's stock price won approval from an unprecedented 13% of shareholders. Social justice resolutions rarely receive more than 2 to 3% of the vote. Shell had already announced its intent to sell off its share of the Samore project the previous year. While the company cited financial reasons,

Colombian government officials suggested that Shell did not want to risk another "Nigeria."[107]

Following the U'wa blockade of Oxy's Gibraltar 1 drill site in November 1999, the *Oil and Gas Journal* commented that "the continuing standoff with the U'wa has escalated to a critical mass, to the point where the next step by either side could put the white-hot spotlight of the world on a single well." The editorial put the conflict in the context of worldwide flashpoints on indigenous rights and oil operations in places like Nigeria and Indonesia:

> It is not too much of a stretch to imagine events cascading into the kind of situation that attracts an intense spotlight for well beyond the duration of those events. If the U'wa were to carry out their grim threats, the result would certainly garner the kind of worldwide shock and approbation that the Exxon Valdez oil spill did in 1989—with comparable repercussions lingering for years.[108]

From the perspective of the global oil industry, the outcome of the U'wa-Oxy conflict could affect the ability of the industry "to explore for and develop oil and gas resources in the sociopolitically high-stakes arena that is Latin America's rainforest."[109] The U'wa conflict has already raised the stakes for Occidental in neighboring Ecuador, where the powerful indigenous confederation CONAIE has demanded that Oxy leave Ecuador and Colombia because of its "inhuman and aggressive attitude" toward native peoples. In June 2000, a delegation of 50 indigenous rights and environmental activists delivered a letter to Oxy's Quito office, promising nonviolent direct actions against the company's facilities in Ecuador if Oxy did not abandon its proposal to drill on U'wa land.[110]

Meanwhile, the Rainforest Action Network, Amazon Watch and other environmental groups have targeted Fidelity Investments and the Sanford C. Bernstein investment firm to divest their shares of Oxy stock. After a ten-month campaign, Fidelity sold more than 60% of its holdings in Occidental. Since the beginning of the campaign, Bernstein has increased its holdings by 10 million shares to become Oxy's largest investor.[111]

The international campaign also raised the U'wa issue during the 2000 U.S. presidential campaign by exposing candidate Al

Gore's financial ties to Occidental. The Gore family owns at least half a million dollars' worth of Occidental stock. Gore's father, a former U.S. senator, also served on Oxy's board of directors for 28 years.[112] U'wa campaigners from the Native Forest Network, Action for Community and Ecology and the Rainforest Action Network were arrested in January 2000 outside of Gore's New Hampshire presidential campaign headquarters during a sit-in. They were demanding that Gore use his deep family and financial ties to Occidental Petroleum to block the company's plan to drill on U'wa territory.[113] U'wa supporters continued to confront Gore along the campaign trail, including an ad in the *New York Times* asking "Who is Al Gore? Environmental Champion or Petroleum Politician? The U'wa people need to know."[114] Many of the protestors have read Gore's bestselling book, *Earth in the Balance,* in which he praised the indigenous peoples who were on "the front lines of the war against nature now raging throughout the world" and expressed hope that "the relentless and insatiable drive to exploit and plunder the earth will soon awaken the conscience of others who are only now beginning to interpret the alarms and muffled cries for help."[115]

Ray Irani, CEO of Oxy, was not one of those whose conscience was awakened. In January 2000, he filed a restraining order against five human rights and environmental groups who have been pressuring Oxy to pull out of U'wa territory. The targets of the order were the Action Resource Center, Amazon Watch, Project Underground, Rainforest Action Network and Student Action for the Environment.[116]

In February 2000, Oxy vice-president Lawrence Meriage testified before the U.S. Congress in a subcommittee hearing on the military aid package to Colombia. He said that the only two groups that were intent on blocking their project were "extremists" in Colombia and "several fringe nongovernmental organizations in the US." While Meriage did not name the organizations, he said they were "de facto allies of the subversive forces that are attacking oil installations, electric power stations and other legitimate business enterprises."[117] Meriage further suggested that both U.S. environmentalists and Colombian guerrillas were using the U'wa. The suggestion that the U'wa are "dupes" is an important aspect of the discourse of dominance that justifies taking native lands. In the culture of the colonizer, there is no room for the idea that native peoples are capable of managing their own natural resources or responding to attempts to separate them from their lands and culture.

Meriage's comments also try to do away with the critical distinction between nonviolent social protest and guerrilla warfare. This is an essential component of the military's counterinsurgency strategy. Social protest, said General Luís Carlos Camacho Leyva, a former Colombian defense minister, was simply "the unarmed branch of subversion."[118] The U'wa demanded that Occidental withdraw the charges of being guerrilla sympathizers because it puts U'wa leaders and supporters in grave danger of arrest, torture and murder in an already militarized region around the Samore block.

An investigation conducted by *The Nation* has revealed that besides the unprecedented level of military assistance for Colombia, the Clinton administration provided strong support for Oxy's drilling plans through Energy Secretary Bill Richardson. He met with Colombian government officials on the company's behalf and even hired a former Oxy lobbyist to work in a key international policy position at the Energy Department.[119] Moreover, former Vice-President Gore oversaw an item in the Defense Authorization Act that resulted in the sale of the Elk Hills Naval Petroleum Reserve to Oxy. The unprecedented closed bidding process was the largest privatization of federal property in U.S. history and tripled Oxy's U.S. oil reserves overnight.[120]

The U'wa won a temporary victory in March 2000, when a Colombian court ordered Oxy to halt all construction work on the Gibraltar 1 drill site because it is on the sacred ancestral land of the tribe. The judge ruled that drilling on the site would violate the "fundamental rights" of the U'wa, including their right to life, as defined by the Colombian Constitution. Oxy responded by filing an appeal to the injunction. Ecopetrol said the government would also appeal the ruling. In May 2000, a Colombian high court revoked the injunction that had suspended Oxy's drilling, once again setting aside its own precedent-setting indigenous protection laws to protect multinational oil interests.

U'wa Denied Travel Visas

Over 1,000 people marched in Los Angeles during the Democratic Party convention in August 2000 and called on Al Gore to take action for the U'wa. Members of the U'wa had intended to travel to Los Angeles to confront Gore, but were denied visas by the U.S. embassy in Bogota. This was the first time U'wa leaders had been denied entry into the United States. According to Atossa Soltani of Amazon Watch, an official in the U.S. embassy in Colombia said that the U'wa were denied travel visas because "We don't consider the U'wa to be working in the best interest of the U.S. government." Congresswoman Cynthia McKinney (D-GA), a member of the International Relations Committee and ranking member of the International Operations and Human Rights Subcommittee said, "The current administration [Clinton] just doesn't get it. That's why the young people are taking to the streets—to redefine U.S. interests to respect human rights over corporate greed."[121]

In October 2000, the Colombian Agrarian Reform Institute declared the 500-meter area surrounding the company's drill site a "petroleum reserve zone," and military personnel have placed land mines around the Gibraltar 1 drilling site to keep the U'wa and other protesters from blockading drilling rigs.[122] U'wa leaders are currently trying to halt the drilling by challenging the company's license. They have just presented the Colombian government with legal documents showing that the King of Spain granted them legal title to the surface and sub-surface mineral rights on the land they claim as their territory. In 1873, the Colombian government claimed all sub-surface mineral rights except those previously ceded by royal land deeds.[123]

Oxy began test drilling on November 3, 2000. It has said it will take about seven months to complete the well. The international campaign filed another shareholder resolution with Oxy around the same time, calling on the company to assess the risks and liabilities of its controversial Colombian operations. The U'wa campaign continues on many fronts within Colombia and internationally.

Ecuador: Oil and Ethnocide

The Amazon is the world's largest rainforest. The Amazon region of northeast Ecuador, known as the "Oriente," consists of over 32 million acres of tropical rainforest lying at the headwaters of the Amazon river network. The region contains some of the most biologically diverse rainforests on earth as well as a considerable number of endangered species. Within one square kilometer of rainforest are 400 tree species.[124] According to tropical ecologist Norman Myers, the area "is surely the richest biotic zone on Earth" and "deserves to rank as a kind of global epicenter of biodiversity."[125]

The area is also the homeland of eight groups of native people, representing from 25 to 50% of the Oriente's population. Estimates of the native population range from 90,000 to 250,000 and include the Shuar, Achuara, Quichua, Cofan, Siona, Huaorani and Secoya.[126] All of these native peoples exhibit a high degree of dependence upon the rainforest environment. They rely on hunting, fishing and gathering to complement small-scale, shifting cultivation of cash and subsistence crops. They also depend on streams, rivers and lakes for fishing, gathering, drinking, cooking, bathing and transportation.[127] The areas now inhabited by native peoples are "refuge zones" where the native peoples fled to escape enslavement by the rubber barons during the Amazonian rubber boom from the late 1800s through the 1920s.[128]

But native retreat from the onslaught of Western "progress" was only temporary. Shell Oil Corporation began exploration around 1920.[129] With exploration came roads into the jungle, and with the roads came the missionaries and a flood of land-hungry immigrants from the coastal and highland regions. In 1942, Ecuador lost nearly a third of its national territory when one half of the Oriente was annexed by Peru, with the encouragement of Occidental Petroleum.[130] In 1950, after years of unsuccessful exploration, Shell left the Oriente.

The modern era of oil activity began in 1967, when Texaco-Gulf first struck oil at Lago Agrio, just north of the territory of the Huaorani. By 1972, the 310 miles of the Trans-Ecuadorian pipeline connected the Lago Agrio across the Andes to the Pacific port of Esmeraldas. In that same year, Ecuador had become the second-largest oil producer in South America.

Twenty-eight international oil corporations joined the oil rush and constructed a grid of more than a dozen 500,000-acre geometric drilling "blocks" over the Amazon.[131] Since that time, the Oriente has become a major center of oil activity with over 300 oil wells, roads, pipelines and pumping stations encompassing over 2.5 million acres of forest.[132] Since the annexation of part of the Oriente by Peru, the area has also been a national security area. With the expansion of oil company infrastructure and roads, the Ecuadorian military has played a major role in defending oil company sites from native peoples protesting the invasion of their homelands.[133] In some cases the Ecuadorian military has forcibly removed native peoples from their lands.[134] At one point the U.S. Agency for International Development (AID) fabricated reports of Cubans in Huaorani territory to justify increased military "pacification" campaigns.[135]

Through Petroecuador, the state's oil corporation, Ecuador became the majority financial partner in the Texaco consortium. While the oil boom produced increased revenues for Ecuador, the economic benefits were concentrated in the hands of a small elite and the military. The numbers of people in poverty rose during the oil boom, from under 50% in 1975 to 65% in 1992.[136] At the same time, the national debt rose from $200 million in 1970 to over $12 billion today. Contrary to the claims of the industry, oil revenues have not provided either a stable or a sustainable basis for the Ecuadorian economy. In 1982, the crash in oil prices led to a further reduction in the standard of living for the majority of the population. In order to receive loans desperately needed to meet payments on this debt, the IMF and World Bank required Ecuador to make "structural adjustments" that have cut back social spending, increased oil production for export and devalued the local currency, making manufactured goods more expensive as the price of agrarian products fell or stagnated.[137] Oil production now accounts for 70% of Ecuador's exports, and oil revenues finance the nation's massive $12.4 billion foreign debt obligations.[138]

**Ecuador-
The Oriente Region**

COLOMBIA

Esmeraldas

*Pacific
Ocean*

Rio Esmeraldas

Lago Agrio

COFAN

Shushufindi

SIONA

COFAN SECOYA

Quito

ECUADOR

LOWLAND
QUICHUA

Rio Napo

HIGHLAND QUICHUA

Oriente Region

HUAORANI

LOWLAND
QUICHUA

Rio Curaray

Rio Daule

Pastaza
Province

Rio Tigre

Rio Babahoyo

Rio Morona

Rio Pastaza

Guayaquil

SHUAR-ACHUAR

**Ecuador in
South America**

Rio Zamora

Colombia

Ecuador

Peru

Brazil

PERU

	Oriente Region
	Pastaza Province
....	Provincial borders
COFAN	Indigenous territories

*ATLANTIC
OCEAN*

Map by Michael Gallagher,
Midwest Educational Graphics
www.MidwestEducationalGraphics.com
michael@MidwestEducationalGraphics.com

Neither the Ecuadorian government nor the oil companies recognize the rights of native peoples who have lived in the rainforest
for thousands of years. Under Ecuadorian law, vast amounts of native territory are treated as "unoccupied lands." The peoples who
occupy the rainforest are viewed as "undeveloped," "backward" or
"uncivilized."[139] Since Ecuador's independence in 1830, the government has pursued a policy of assimilation and "civilization" of the
Indian people, who comprise 40 to 50% of Ecuador's 12 million
people.[140] This strategy has led to their political disempowerment
and economic exploitation. The government "views the Amazon as
a frontier to be conquered—a source of wealth for the debt-bur-
dened state and an escape valve for demographic and land distribution pressures."[141] The unequal distribution of resources and power
between the dominant ethnic groups in Quito and the natives of
Oriente is a classic internal colonialism situation.[142] "In some cases,"
reports Survival International, "oil wells have been placed actually
within lands that have been already properly titled to Indian communities—making conflict inevitable."[143]

Oil development has had a particularly devastating impact upon
the Cofan Indians. After Texaco-Gulf established its base camp at
Santa Cecilia in 1970, the lands of the Cofan were reduced by oil
wells, roads and a 315-mile pipeline "cutting the Cofan territory into
ribbons of nationalized infrastructure."[144] Ecuador encouraged
waves of colonists into Cofan territory who proceeded to take over
the native gardens so that the Cofan can no longer make a sustainable living in their homeland. Estimates of the number of settlers in
the Oriente range from at least 250,000 to 300,000.[145] With the in-
flux of non-native peoples into traditional native territory, natives
were exposed to previously unknown diseases and epidemics to
which they had no resistance:

> With the coming of the petroleum companies came the epidem-
> ics. We didn't know anything about the flu, the measles; almost all
> the region was hit. Many fled. Those that stayed were finished....
> [We]couldn't keep living the old way. It was all contaminated.[146]

This process has also resulted in a deforestation rate of almost a
million acres a year in Oriente, one of the highest rates in Latin

America.[147] Before Texaco drilled its first well in their homeland, the Cofan were a small but thriving nation of some 15,000. Today, after 30 years of oil development, they number approximately 650.[148] The Siona, Secoya, Quichua and Huaorani all experienced some displacement from their homelands.

These activities also forced the last native Tetetes from their lands near Lago Agrio, the boom town near Texaco's first commercial oilfield. This displacement is widely believed to have hastened their extinction as a people.[149] Oil development activities have also been linked, directly and indirectly, with problems in food supply and malnutrition. A 1997 human rights report by the OAS notes that "the sectors of Orellana, Shushufindi and Sacha, which are centers of petroleum development activity, register the highest indicators of malnutrition in Ecuador."[150] Shushufindi, where Texaco built its main Amazon refinery, was a Cofan village.[151] A 1987 study by the Ecuadorian government warned that oil development led by Texaco had placed the local native groups "at the edge of extinction as a distinct people."[152]

An Environmental Free-Fire Zone

Since 1972, oil companies have extracted almost 2 billion barrels of crude oil from the Oriente with devastating environmental consequences. In 1991, Judith Kimerling, a former environmental attorney in the New York State Attorney General's office who helped prosecute the Love Canal case, brought the issue of oil company complicity in the destruction of the rainforest to public view with the publication of *Amazon Crude*, a book which has become the *Silent Spring* of Ecuador's growing environmental movement.

In 1989, Kimerling went to Ecuador and was shocked and surprised to find toxic waste pits in the rainforest. Up to this time, says Kimerling, the literature in the environmental community basically said there was no harm from the oil industry.[153] However, she documented that over 200 oil wells, designed and built by Texaco, generated more than 3.2 million gallons of toxic waste each day. These wastes contain hydrocarbons, heavy metals and toxic levels of salts. "Virtually all of these wastes," she noted, "are discharged into the environment without treatment or monitoring, contaminating countless rivers and streams that supply water and fish to surround-ing communities."[154]

Accidental oil spills from the Trans-Ecuadorian Pipeline alone have discharged an estimated 16.8 million gallons of crude into the headwaters of the Amazon River, 1.5 times the amount spilled by the Exxon Valdez disaster. Texaco neither developed a spill contin-gency plan nor cleaned up the spills.[155] And, as we've seen in the case of the Niger Delta, most of the gas that is extracted with the oil is burned as a waste, contaminating the air with greenhouse gases and the elements of acid rain (nitrogen oxides and sulfur dioxide). The chemical pollution from nearby oil facilities has caused much native territory to be uninhabitable and has severely degraded native peo-ples' remaining lands and strained their subsistence lifestyle.[156] This separation from their lands has broken down traditional cultures; forced many natives into seeking work away from their communi-ties; and brought prostitution, alcoholism, violence, poverty, malnu-trition and disease to these communities.

The unwillingness of the government of Ecuador to exercise any kind of regulatory control or oversight regarding oil activity has resulted in what Kimerling calls "an environmental free-fire zone."[157] In June 1992, Texaco withdrew from Ecuador and turned over its operation to Petroecuador. While Texaco's Ecuadorian rev-enues ended, its legacy had just begun.

The environmental crisis that has resulted from substandard in-dustry practices is inseparable from the ongoing public health crisis. In 1993, the Center for Economic and Social Rights (CESR), a New York-based health and human rights group, sent a team of doctors, scientists and lawyers from Harvard University to the Oriente. They found that sections of the rainforest are now so contaminated that Indians and colonists living there are exposed to high risks of cancer and neurological and reproductive problems. Water studies found that "drinking, bathing and fishing water samples contained levels of PAHs [polycyclic aromatic hydrocarbons] 10 to 1,000 times greater than [the] U.S. Environmental Protection Agency's safety guide-lines."[158] Furthermore, these water contaminant patterns can be traced to waste water sources at nearby oil facilities.

The report charged that the government of Ecuador's failure to prevent the contamination of the Oriente constitutes a violation of its citizens' human rights to health and a healthy environment. This was one of the first occasions where human rights advocacy focused on the rights to health and a clean environment. It provided an important stimulus to the growing alliance between native and environmental movements in Ecuador. In 1980, the Confederation of Indigenous Nationalities of the Ecuadorian Amazon (CONFENIAE) emerged and brought these issues to the national political agenda. One of the most important allies of the native peoples of the Amazon has been the environmental movement.[159] In 1990, Acción Ecológica, a Quito-based national environmental group, launched its "Amazon for Life" campaign to call national attention to the environmentally and socially disastrous effects of oil development in the northern Oriente. The campaign, building on an already established North/South NGO network, also opposed a proposed World Bank loan for increased oil exploration. Since 1990, the campaign has grown into an international alliance of hundreds of environmental and human rights organizations.[160]

Indigenous Mobilization

While the Ecuadorian government and the oil companies would like the Indians to believe that oil exploitation is the only possible path to development, this view is emphatically rejected by CONFENIAE: "we the indigenous peoples say that development which destroys our rivers, our land and our lives is not real development."[161] In 1992, 1,500 natives from Ecuador's Amazon rainforest walked 140 miles to Quito, the country's capital. International NGOs, such as Oxfam America and the Rainforest Action Network, helped cover the marchers' expenses.[162] In Quito, they negotiated with the government for titles to about 13,000 square miles of ancestral lands. "The urgency we have is that the Amazon Indian Peoples [in Ecuador] have already lost almost the majority of our traditional territory," said Leonardo Viteri, coordinator of the Organization of Indigenous Peoples of Pastaza.[163] The Indians received title to their lands, which protected them from further colonization, but did not prevent the state from giving oil companies exploration rights on these lands. The Indians gained surface rights, but the state reserved sub-soil rights. Moreover, even these surface rights could be terminated if the communities "impede or obstruct" oil or mining activity.[164] "The Indians must understand that Ecuador lives off oil," said Diego Bonifaz, who was President Rodrigo Borja's chief negotiator with the Indians.[165]

While the march did not slow down the oil rush, it did garner unprecedented popular support throughout Ecuador and marked a growing political sophistication in the native rights movement. During this time, Acción Ecológica and indigenous groups coordinated efforts with U.S. and European environmental and human rights groups to publicize multinational oil corporations' assault on the environment and the people. "Texaco is viewed as the chief human rights violator," says Paulina Garzon of Acción Ecológica. "Texaco has invaded the forests, killed the rivers and animals, created a health disaster and destroyed indigenous groups like the former Tagiere."[166]

National and international attention became focused on this issue when, in November 1993, five native groups from the Oriente filed a $1.5 billion lawsuit against Texaco to "remedy the negligent, reckless, intentional and outrageous acts and omissions of defendant Texaco, Inc., in connection with its oil exploration and drilling operations."[167] It is a class-action lawsuit brought under the Alien Tort Victims Act, which allows foreign citizens to sue U.S.-based defendants for violations of international law.[168] As a result of the lawsuit, the victims of Texaco's contamination have formed an organization, Front for the Defense of Amazon Life, which has united the previously divided communities of Indians and colonists in the Lago Agrio area. While the initial focus of the organization was to press their legal claims in the Texaco case, "by 1996, the new organization had extended its work to monitoring oil and timber activities, working closely with local and international environmental groups."[169]

If the case is allowed to proceed, it will fundamentally alter the present power imbalance between multinational oil and mining corporations and the Third World communities where many of their operations are located. "If they're successful in suing Texaco, it'll have repercussions around the world," said Jeff Kerr, a correspondent for *Petroleum Intelligence Weekly*.[170]

David Dickson, a Texaco spokesperson from the company's White Plains, New York, office, called the allegations in the complaint "outrageous and categorically untrue." He said that the company "consistently operated under sound industry practices and complied with all Ecuadorian laws."[171] Except that Ecuador didn't have any environmental laws that could effectively regulate the industry. And so the industry routinely cut corners on the proper disposal of its wastes. Cristóbal Bonifaz, a lead attorney for the native groups, charges that rather than pump unmarketable crude oil back into the wells, as is customary in the United States, Texaco dumped millions of gallons of crude oil into human-made lagoons in the region, causing massive contamination. "In an effort to gain greater profits, Texaco deliberately implemented drilling practices that had as their built-in waste disposal mechanism the constant dumping of crude oil into the environment," Bonifaz said.[172] Texaco has since agreed to a $40 million cleanup program that has been widely criticized as inadequate by both environmental groups as well as the Ecuadorian Ministry of Energy and Mines Environmental Protection department. Ecuador suspended part of Texaco's cleanup in 1996 on the grounds that results were not proving sufficient to undo the damage.[173]

The Rainforest Action Network (RAN) and Acción Ecológica launched a consumer boycott, and are encouraging people to cut up their Texaco credit cards and send them to the oil giant's corporate headquarters in Westchester County, New York. In April 1994, RAN organized a three-day protest of Texaco's plunder and pillage in Ecuador and Burma. Demonstrators, including Ecuadorian and Burmese natives, marched from Wall Street to White Plains and then to the company's Harrison, New York, headquarters. More than two dozen police were called in from surrounding towns, and nine demonstrators were arrested as they chanted, "Texaco Must Go."[174]

Less than a week later, in an unprecedented decision, Federal District Judge Vincent Broderick ruled that the native groups had a right to argue their case against Texaco in a U.S. court. In his ruling,

Judge Broderick cited the UN's 1992 Rio Declaration, which declares a fundamental and inalienable human right to a clean and healthy environment. He also ordered Texaco to release some 75,000 pages' worth of documents relating to the parent company's responsibility for damages caused by the company's Ecuadorian operations.

However, one year later, Judge Broderick died of cancer, and the case was passed along to Judge Jed Rakoff. In November 1996, Judge Rakoff dismissed the case, saying that the U.S. courts were not the appropriate forum for arguing this case. The plaintiffs have claimed that they cannot receive justice in Ecuador because the judiciary is biased and there is a prohibition on class-action lawsuits. Moreover, an Indian leader stated in an affidavit submitted to the court that "there is a history in Ecuador of the armed forces and police repressing the indigenous peoples who challenge the Texaco company and other oil companies.... This repression includes detention without charge, torture and killings."[175] Aside from the problems in Ecuador, the primary motive for hearing the case in New York is that the decisions that led to the devastation in Ecuador were made at Texaco's corporate headquarters in White Plains. Just when it seemed that the case would be sent back to Ecuador, the U.S. Court of Appeals for the Second Circuit reversed Judge Rakoff's ruling in a unanimous decision, saying that the lawsuit could not be dismissed until it was clear that an adequate "alternative forum" existed.[176]

While the case has yet to come to trial, it has resulted in widespread publicity, including a two-part story on ABC's *Nightline* in October 1998. It has also inflicted heavy costs on Texaco, "both financially and in terms of management time," according to a political risk consultant report.[177] What is most troubling about the lawsuit, from the perspective of the oil industry, is that it upsets all the old assumptions about the benefits of having repressive Third World governments do the bidding of the multinational oil companies in securing the flow of oil and profits without interference from democratic social movements. In their review of the Ecuadorian class-action lawsuit, the *New York Times* observed that "pliable governments, which may once have been a possible advantage for foreign investors, could actually prove a liability, as citizens take on the companies directly."[178] Grassroots native movements have led to numerous confrontations with oil corporations not just about past abuses, but their future plans as well.

ARCO Meets Native Resistance in Pastaza Province

Pastaza Province extends from the central Andes eastward to the Peruvian border, covering 11,500 square miles. The Organization of Indigenous Peoples of Pastaza (OPIP) formed in 1978 as state pressure to colonize and develop the area encroached upon native lands.[179] In 1988, the California-based Atlantic Richfield Company (ARCO) began oil exploration on Quichua land without consulting local communities. Quichua actions at the site halted exploration for a year. The willingness of the government and the companies to use force against those who resist oil activity has convinced many native communities that they need to negotiate with companies to reduce the worst social and environmental impacts of oil development. However, when ARCO resumed operations in 1990, they had found pro-oil communities in the interim and refused to recognize OPIP as the legitimate representative body of the native people of the region. The pro-oil native group, located near the oil well sites, had only been established in 1993, after ARCO had announced its discovery.

OPIP put forward a very different concept of land rights than ARCO. The native people who assembled in Villano, near the well sites, spoke of "territory" or "lands" that referred to ancestral space, not private property.[180] "The people near the oil wells do not own this land," explained Leonardo Viteri, the director of OPIP's research institute. "Nor does petroleum simply affect one community. ARCO's concession is 200,000 hectares; we all manage this land and will all be affected by oil."[181]

When ARCO refused to meet with OPIP representatives, OPIP joined forces with CONAIE, CONFENIAE and Acción Ecológia and occupied the Quito offices of the Minister of Energy and Mines in January 1994. Outside the office, about 150 protestors formed a human chain around the building, effectively halting all activity at the ministry. Luís Macas, the president of CONAIE, explained that the occupation was in protest against the state's oil policy, which "is contemptuous of indigenous peoples and provokes social, cultural and environmental conflicts."[182] The minister met with the protestors and the following morning arranged a meeting between ARCO and OPIP, emphasizing that dialogue between oil companies and native groups is part of doing business in the Ecuadorian Amazon.

As ARCO has expanded into neighboring areas, it has met increasing opposition. In 1998, ARCO was granted a 500,000-acre oil concession, known as Block 24, on Shuar and Achuar territory. Once again, ARCO engaged in divide-and-rule tactics, offering individual communities roughly $2,500, plane rides and food contributions for an agreement to permit oil exploration. ARCO-Ecuador spokesperson Herb Vickers explained that the company "has concentrated on working more on the local level, because, in its opinion, the large indigenous organizations no longer represent the people."[183]

In September 1999, almost 400 Shuar and Achuar peoples gathered in the town of Macas in Pastaza province to demonstrate their opposition to ARCO's operations on their ancestral lands. Carrying signs and chanting, "No more Texacos," they marched to a court office to present a legal injunction meant to prevent ARCO from entering tribal territory or approaching communities without the consent of the general tribal assembly.

The Indigenous Movement Takes Center Stage: The 1994 Uprising

Ecuador's indigenous movement took a giant step forward with the founding of CONAIE in 1986. The new organization brought together three powerful regional organizations representing the highland indigenous groups, the coastal groups and the Amazonian Indians. All 12 indigenous groups were now united in one organization. Their ability to organize massive protests was dramatically demonstrated in June 1994 when indigenous organizations shut down the country for two full weeks.

The protests were directed against the Agrarian Development Law, which would have broken up communal lands in favor of privatization. The law would also have privatized water resources and put grazing lands and forest lands used by native people up for sale. Indigenous leaders criticized the government's rural development legislation as the brainchild of a U.S. AID-funded think tank.[184] They also criticized the Ecuadorian government for allowing the World Bank to help write a hydrocarbon law designed to open up the oil sector to foreign companies.[185] This kind of meddling in Ecuador's legislative affairs is inevitable when 85% of new loans in the country come from these Multilateral Development Banks (MDBs).[186]

The massive civil disobedience in Ecuador was rooted in the same resentment against neoliberal economic reforms and IMF-imposed structural adjustments as the Zapatista revolt in Mexico. Peasants, small farmers, trade unions and popular organizations demonstrated against the new law, blocking roads and cutting off food supplies to the cities. Indigenous communities also took over oil wells in the Amazon to protest the privatization of the state oil company and to place a moratorium on further oil exploration in the Oriente.[187]

Similar to the Zapatista revolt, an international network assisted Ecuadorian grassroots organizers by supplying them with critical information and opportunities to exert political pressure on key players:

> Building on networks created in previous campaigns against Texaco and the World Bank, CONAIE turned to the emerging Ecuador Network, which had formed an economics task force (including BIC [Bank Information Center], Development Gap, and Oxfam America) to help NGOs with information about MDB loans.[188]

This international network played a critical role as the government of President Sixto Duran-Ballen declared a state of siege. Several radio stations run by native people were taken over by the military, and news of the uprising was suppressed.[189] When native leaders meeting in Quito learned that they were going to be arrested, they sought and received sanctuary in the National Bishops' Headquarters.[190] As violence escalated in the streets of Ecuador, CONAIE had direct discussions with the World Bank and the Inter-American Development Bank (IADB). The Ecuador Network also brought in the OAS Human Rights Commission and Nobel Peace Prize winner Rigoberta Menchú to put pressure on the government to negotiate.[191] The president of the IADB was visiting Ecuador when the uprising began and met with Duran-Ballen's cabinet, telling them he "wanted the I[A]DB to be part of the solution, not part of the problem."[192]

The mobilization ended when the government agreed to church-sponsored national-level negotiations with CONAIE. The government conceded the major demand of the movement: the withdrawal of plans to break up communal lands. "This was the first time in Ecuadorian history," said Nina Pacari, a lawyer and a leader in CONAIE, "that an indigenous movement forced the government to enter into a serious dialogue about national policies."[193]

When the mobilization ended, indigenous leaders went back to their communities and took up the urgent demand that the government recognize the different nationalities that exist in Ecuador, whose collective rights are ignored in national decision-making. They also demanded the right of indigenous people to be "consulted about plans for exploration of non-renewable resources on their territories."[194] Both demands were incorporated into the language of the first article of the new Constitution in 1998. This was a major achievement of the indigenous movement, because now government policy had to acknowledge that Ecuador is a "pluricultural" and "multi-ethnic" state. The ability of the indigenous movement to link indigenous and non-indigenous popular movements was again demonstrated in the uprising of January 21, 2000.

"The People Are Now in Power"

In response to a worsening economic crisis and the widespread popular perception that President Jamil Mahuad was biased toward powerful banking interests, a coalition of Indians, peasants and urban workers, supported by junior military officers, occupied Parliament and the Judiciary and surrounded the presidential palace, forcing Mahuad's resignation in 1999. Indigenous representation in the government was recognized as essential by the three-member Junta of National Salvation, which attempted to succeed Mahuad. The junta included an army colonel, a former supreme court judge and Antonio Vargas, the president of CONAIE. Addressing the Ecuadorian nation, Vargas, an Amazonian Quichua, declared, "The people are now in power and we are going to triumph!"[195]

President Clinton responded immediately, threatening an economic boycott of Ecuador and ordering the U.S. embassy in Quito to pressure conservative generals to act.[196] Within 24 hours, senior military officers imposed Mahuad's vice-president, Gustavo Noboa, as the new president. Noboa pledged to continue the disastrous economic policies of his discredited predecessor and authorized mass arrests of peasants and trade union activists. Despite this setback, "the right of Indians to protest and, yes, even to govern has been established," says Pacari. "Something very fundamental has emerged for us from this experience: a sense of possibility."[197]

Is Ecuador a Unique Case?

While there are some special conditions that facilitated the movement in Ecuador—its small size and a common indigenous language (Quichua) in both highlands and lowlands[198]—there are many conditions that Ecuador shares with Brazil, Mexico, Colombia and other countries. Among the most important conditions facilitating the emergence of a native rights movement is the extent of a country's international connections through flows of private investment, economic aid and military aid. States that are more dependent on international resource flows are more vulnerable to pressure for human rights reform than those not receiving such resources.[199] We saw this clearly in the transnational network of native, environmental and human rights NGOs that developed to oppose Occidental in Colombia, Shell in Nigeria, multilateral bank loans for dams in the Brazilian Amazon and Texaco in the Ecuadorian Amazon.

Second, ethnic identity and conflict are heightened by the corporate drive to penetrate the world's remaining resource frontiers. Indigenous political organizations began to form throughout the Amazon during the 1970s to defend their lands and culture from colonization. Once they recognized the magnitude of the threat they faced, local organizations united in regional federations.[200] In Ecuador's Pastaza Province, we have seen how ARCO's oil exploration rallied the Quicha native community behind OPIP's defense of native lands and culture.

Third, in many parts of Latin America, the Catholic Church has played a key organizing role in the native rights movement. It was the World Council of Churches that sponsored the 1971 Barbados Conference that "launched the international indigenous rights movement."[201] As early as 1972, the church sponsored the regional meeting of local native organizations that resulted in the formation of ECUARUNAR, a regional organization similar to CONFENIAE. Leaders of both these organizations established the statewide organization CONAIE. [202]The same pattern of church sponsorship of regional assemblies can be seen in Brazil.[203]

Fourth, many of the transnational networks promoting native rights have achieved some response and recognition from multilateral banks, private corporations and international bodies like the United Nations. While these efforts have not necessarily changed the behavior of governments, they have nonetheless succeeded in creating political space for the native groups to organize their communities.[204] In many cases international linkages have protected the physical safety of native leaders. This was clearly shown during Ecuador's 1994 indigenous uprising, when the government ordered the arrest of CONAIE's native leaders. The Catholic Church provided sanctuary to the leaders, and the Ecuador Network pressured the government to negotiate an end to the uprising. Similar network pressures helped to clear Darrell Posey and the Kayapo leaders of subversion charges in Brazil. The ability of a transnational native and environmental network to influence multilateral bank loans in Brazil and Ecuador not only affected governmental decisions regarding resource extraction, but also provided an opportunity for native organizations to have their concerns addressed by changes in state constitutions. These constitutional changes have included land rights (Colombia), the creation of extractive reserves (Brazil) and recognition of native cultures in a multi-ethnic state (Ecuador). All of these have had a positive effect upon native organizations, strengthening local movements and expanding the scope of native participation in democratic politics.

Finally, the communication of information through transnational networks provides important political leverage for native groups in countries where their voices are all too often ignored. "At the core of network activity, " write network analysts Keck and Sikkink:

> is the production, exchange and strategic use of information. This ability may seem inconsequential in the face of the economic, political or military might of other global actors. But by overcoming the deliberate suppression of information that sustains many abuses of power, networks can help reframe international and domestic debates, changing their terms, their sites and the configuration of participants. [205]

Paulinho Paiakan, the Kayapo chief, put the matter succinctly when he said, "instead of war clubs, we are using words." When those words are broadcast over radio, television and the Internet, they can have a powerful effect in faraway places. We have already seen how information about the ecological consequences of deforestation and global warming has affected the terms of the debate about Amazonian development. We have also seen how the Zapatistas' strategic use of the Internet to alert their international supporters thwarted a planned Mexican military offensive.

What about worst case scenarios like the Ogoni in Nigeria? The Nigerian military government ignored international protest over the arrest of Ken Saro-Wiwa and proceeded to execute him, along with eight other Ogoni leaders. But why would the Nigerian military risk international condemnation by killing them? A group of pastors in Port Harcourt told the World Council of Churches that "the government could not forgive Ken for making the Ogoni issue public. They got angry because he took the case to the world, and the world listened. They were determined to silence him."[206] In other words, the generals were afraid of world public opinion and the possible cutoff of economic and military aid. This was a crass, power-driven calculation, but it nonetheless acknowledged that they faced a major problem in their international relations because of their treatment of the Ogonis. This is evidence that a process of socialization or social learning is already going on.[207] General Sani Abacha's first move after killing Saro-Wiwa and the other Ogoni leaders was to hire a number of lobbyists and public relations firms to improve Nigeria's image in Washington and prevent any cutbacks in U.S. aid to his regime.[208] Meanwhile, the Ogoni have prevented Shell from operating in their territory since 1993, when mass protests shut down Shell's operations. The international campaign against Shell has mounted a boycott of Shell gas stations, filed shareholder resolutions demanding corporate accountability and generally shamed the corporation around the globe. Shell has spent millions of dollars on public relations since 1993 to counter its "image problem."[209]

While these efforts to rehabilitate Shell's image are an insult to the Ogoni people, they are nonetheless testimony to the power of international networks to focus world attention on gross human rights violators. In the following chapter we will examine a worst case scenario for human rights in Indonesia and show how information about systematic human rights abuse has enabled native groups to exert pressure on a powerful mining corporation doing serious damage to native lands and people.

1   Rainforest Action Network and Project Underground, 1998, pp. 3-4.
2   Human Rights Watch, 1999a, p. 6, 26.
3   Quarto, 2000, p. 7.
4   Esparza and Wilson, 1999, p. 23.
5   Nwiado, 1996, p. 41.
6   Adeola, 2000, p. 693; Hechter, 1975, p. 30; Gedicks, 1985.
7   Naanen, 1995, p. 50.
8   Human Rights Watch, 1999a, pp. 2-3.
9   Esparza and Wilson, 1999, p. 5.
10 Human Rights Watch, 1999a, p. 72.
11 Nwiado, 1996, p. 42.
12 Esparza and Wilson, 1999, p. 5.
13 Nwiado, 1996, p. 42.
14 Esparza and Wilson, 1999, p. 6.
15 Idemyor, 1999, p. 58.
16 Ibid.
17 Onishi, 2000.
18 Aigbogun, 1998.
19 Environmental Rights Action, 2000.
20 Esparza and Wilson, 1999, p. 18.
21 Human Rights Watch, 1999a, p. 11.
22 Naanen, 1995, p. 68.
23 Saro-Wiwa, 1992, p. 81.
24 Naanen, 1995, p. 69.
25 Kretzman, 1995, p. 11.
26 Human Rights Watch, 1999a, p. 125.
27 Idemyor, 1999, p. 56
28 Robinson, 1996, pp. 60, 81.
29 Kretzman, 1995, p. 8.
30 Ibid.
31 Birnbaum, 1995.
32 Wiwa, 1996, p. 28.
33 Silverstein, 1998, p. 36.
34 Cohen, 1996, p. 38.
35 Kretzman, 1997, p. 19.
36 Green, 2001
37 Human Rights Watch, 1999a, p. 169.
38 Ibid., p. 20.
39 Duodo, 1996.
40 Ake, 1996.
41 Esparza and Wilson, 1999, p. 18.
42 Goodman and Scahill, 1998.
43 Onishi, 1998, p. 1.
44 Human Rights Watch, 1999a, p. 130.
45 Project Underground, 1999a.
46 Esparza and Wilson, 1999, p. 20.
47 Project Underground, 1999a.
48 Human Rights Watch, 1999a, p. 18.

49 Kretzman, 1997, p. 19.
50 Wollock, 1999, p. 31.
51 Weissman, 1990, p. 8.
52 *North American Mining*, 1997b, p. 23.
53 Wilson, 1996, p. 11; Survival International, 1992.
54 Organizacion Nacional Indigena de Colombia, 1996, p. 298
55 Ibid., p. 295.
56 Human Rights Watch, 1998, p. 44.
57 Youngers, 1998, p. 34.
58 Krauss, 2000.
59 Marquis, 2000.
60 Tate, 2000, p. 19.
61 Isacson, 2000, p. 1, p. 8.
62 Human Rights Watch, 1996, p. 4.
63 Wright and Kretzman, 1999.
64 McCaffrey, 2000, p. 2.
65 Chomsky, 2000, p. 30.
66 Wolf, 1999, p. 6.
67 Youngers, 1998, p. 35.
68 Chomsky, 2000, p. 30.
69 McCaffrey, 2000, p. 4.
70 Tate, 2000, p. 17.
71 Rohter, 2000, p. 8.
72 Simon, 2000, p. 55.
73 *Earth Island Journal,* 2000, p. 23
74 U'wa, 2000.
75 Project Underground, 1998, p. 1.
76 Dudley and Murillo, 1998, p. 45.
77 Project Underground, 1998, p. 4.
78 U'wa, 2000.
79 Project Underground, 1998, p. 5
80 Murillo, 1999, p. 46.
81 Ibid., p. 11.
82 Project Underground,1998, p. 13.
83 Dudley and Murillo, 1998, p. 45.
84 Project Underground 1997a, p. 1.
85 Avirama and Marquez, in Van Cott, 1995, p. 85.
86 Project Underground, 1998, p. 24.
87 Zackrison and Bradley, 1997, p. 1.
88 Barrett, 1997, p. 44.
89 Dudley and Murillo, 1998, p. 44.
90 Wolf, 1999, p. 6.
91 Human Rights Watch, 1996, p. 3.
92 Ibid.
93 Dudley and Murillo, 1998, p. 42.
94 Ibid.
95 Human Rights Watch, 1996, p. 96.
96 Barrett, 1997, p. 44.

97   Dudley and Murillo, 1998, p. 46.
98   Project Underground, 1998, p. 12.
99   *Los Angeles Times,* 1997.
100 Project Underground, 1997a, p. 3
101 *Earth Island Journal,* 1996-97, p. 15.
102 Knol, 1999.
103 Wollock, 1999, p. 21.
104 cited in Wollock, p. 30.
105 Ibid.
106 Waldman, 1999.
107 Project Underground, 1998, p. 25.
108 *Oil and Gas Journal,* 1999, p. 18.
109 Ibid., p. 21.
110 Project Underground, 2000g.
111 *Oil and Gas Journal,* 2000.
112 Silverstein, 2000, p. 12.
113 Project Underground, 2000d.
114 *New York Times,* 2000a.
115 Gore, 1993, p. 285.
116 Project Underground, 2000d.
117 Silverstein, 2000, p. 15.
118 Human Rights Watch, 1996, p. 16.
119 Silverstein, 2000, p. 12.
120 Cockburn, 2000, p. 3.
121 McKinney, 2000.
122 Rainforest Action Network, 2000b.
123 *Oil and Gas Journal,* 2000.
124 Rainforest Action Network and Project Underground, 1998, p. 21.
125 Myers, 1988.
126 Kimerling, 1991, p. 34.
127 Ibid., p. 37.
128 Whitten, 1978, p. 49.
129 Ibid.
130 Kimerling, 1991, pp. 34, 37.
131 Cooper, 1992, p. 41.
132 Ibid., p. 43.
133 Rainforest Action Network, 1991, p. 4.
134 Simon, 2000, p. 53.
135 Brysk, 2000, p. 110.
136 Center for Economic and Social Rights, 1994, p. 8.
137 Pacari, 1996, p. 26.
138 Parlow, 1991, p. 36.
139 Whitten, 1978, p. 59.
140 Veilleux, 1992, p. 36.
141 Kimerling, 1996, p. 61.
142 Whitten, 1976.
143 Survival International, 1987.
144 Whitten, 1978, p. 39.

145 Organization of American States, 1997, p. 109.
146 Ibid., p. 110.
147 Smith, 1989.
148 Kimerling, 1994, p. 206.
149 Ibid.
150 Organization of American States, 1997, p. 91.
151 Switkes, 1994, p. 8.
152 Jochnick, 1995, p. 13.
153 Rowell, 1996, p. 219.
154 Kimerling, 1994, p. 205.
155 Kimerling, 1996, p. 65.
156 Kimerling, 1994, p. 206.
157 Kimerling, 1991, p. 48.
158 Center for Economic and Social Rights, 1994, p. xii.
159 Van Cott, 1995, p. 137.
160 Treakle, 1998, pp. 225-226.
161 Pandam in Center for Economic and Social Rights, 1994, p. x.
162 Brysk, 2000, p. 155.
163 Steller, 1992.
164 Kimerling, 1996, p. 69.
165 Associated Press, 1992.
166 Jochnick, 1995, p. 13.
167 Arthaud, 1994, p. 218.
168 Press, 1999, p. 12.
169 Brysk, 2000, p. 169.
170 Schemo, 1998a.
171 Maull, 1993.
172 Mokhiber, 1993, p. 15.
173 González, 1996.
174 Lipka, 1994.
175 Inter Press Service, 1994.
176 Press, 1999, p. 15.
177 Bray, 1997, p. 42.
178 Schemo, 1998a.
179 Sawyer, 1996, p. 28.
180 Ibid., p. 29.
181 Ibid.
182 Ibid.
183 Project Underground, 1999b.
184 Treakle, 1998, p. 243.
185 Ibid., p. 229.
186 Ibid., p. 224.
187 Pacari, 1996, p. 23.
188 Treakle, 1998, p. 246.
189 Ibid., p. 245.
190 Brysk, 2000, p. 214
191 Ibid., p. 157
192 Treakle, 1998, p. 247.

193 Ibid., p. 24.
194 Project Underground, 1999b.
195 Collins, 2000, p. 41.
196 Petras, 2000, p. 7.
197 Collins, 2000, p. 46.
198 Brysk, 2000, p. 25.
199 Risse, 1999, p. 24.
200 Selverston, in Van Cott, 1995, p. 136.
201 Brysk, 2000, p. 86.
202 Selverston, in Van Cott, 1995, p. 139.
203 Brysk, 2000, p. 78.
204 Risse, 1999, p. 25.
205 Keck and Sikkink, 1998, p. x.
206 Robinson, 1996, p. 53.
207 Risse, 1999, p. 23.
208 Silverstein, 1998, p. 36.
209 Robinson, 1996, p. 46.

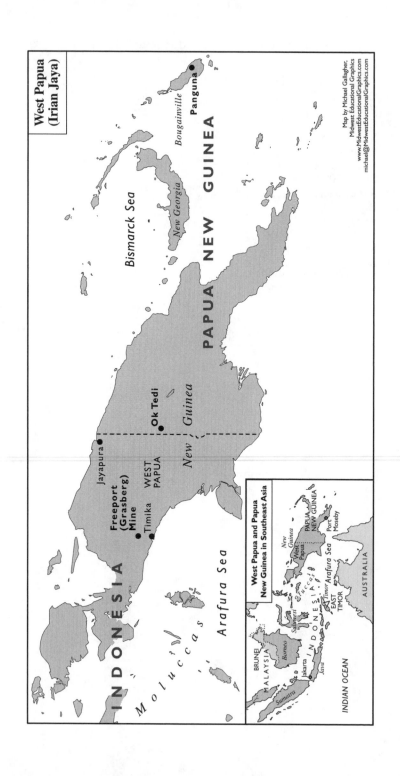

West Papua
(Irian Jaya)

Map by Michael Gallagher,
Midwest Educational Graphics
www.MidwestEducationalGraphics.com
michael@MidwestEducationalGraphics.com

Panguna

Bougainville

Bismarck Sea

New Georgia

PAPUA NEW GUINEA

Ok Tedi

New Guinea

Jayapura

Freeport
(Grasberg)
Mine

WEST
PAPUA

Timika

INDONESIA

Moluccas

Arafura Sea

West Papua and Papua
New Guinea in Southeast Asia

New
Guinea

PAPUA
NEW GUINEA

West
Papua

Port
Moresby

Arafura Sea

Timor

EAST
TIMOR

AUSTRALIA

M

Sulawesi

I N D O N E S I A

BRUNEI

MALAYSIA

Borneo

Jakarta

Java

Sumatra

INDIAN OCEAN

CHAPTER 3

West Papua

The Freeport/Rio Campaign

Some of the most controversial mining projects on the planet are the gold and copper mines started on the island of New Guinea in the 1960s. New Guinea is the world's second-largest island. In 1975, the eastern half of the island achieved independence from Australia and became Papua New Guinea; that nation now includes several eastern-lying islands as well. The western half of the island, known as West Papua, had been earlier invaded and annexed by Indonesia. Separated by 2,300 miles of ocean waters from the rest of the Indonesian archipelago, the new easternmost province under Jakarta's rule was renamed Irian Jaya.

But the incorporation into the Indonesian fold has been far from copacetic. "The people of West Papua," according to one geographer, "are different in all respects from their rulers in Java [Indonesia's central island]: language, religions, identity, histories, systems of land ownership and resource use, cultures and allegiance."[1] Papuan people are Melanesian, not Indonesian. Melanesians also live in Papua New Guinea, the Solomon Islands, Vanuatu, Kanaky, Fiji and the Torres Straits Islands, which lie between New Guinea and Australia. Along with the other "outer" island provinces of Sumatra, Kalimantan and Sulawesi, West Papua has been forcibly incorporated into the Indonesian colonial empire primarily because of the former Dutch colony's substantial resources:

Copper, gas, oil, nickel, gold and silver and especially space in which to settle its huge surplus population are some of the attractions which led Indonesia to colonize West Papua. Mineral extraction, industrial fishing, logging and a plantation economy are all undertaken by international companies with the support and backing of Indonesian businesses.[2]

Anthropologist David Hyndman has summarized the experience of many of the Melanesian native peoples with these projects: "As Fourth World Melanesians in the vicinity of the projects experienced ecocide; incorporation into larger regional, national and international socioeconomic networks; and conversion of their natural resources into national and transnational resources, they responded with social protest."[3] This chapter—a case study of the Freeport mining project in West Papua—illustrates both the dynamics of the West Papuan social protest movement and its linkage with international environmental and human rights advocacy groups.

New Orleans-based Freeport McMoRan, together with the world's biggest mining company, Rio Tinto (formerly Rio Tinto Zinc), runs the world's largest gold mine and the third-largest copper mine, Grasberg, situated in West Papua.[4] The open pit mine has been carved out of a snow-capped mountain, considered sacred by the native peoples, more than 13,500 feet above sea-level in the central highlands of the island. Freeport was the first foreign company to invest in Indonesia after General Suharto came to power in 1965 by overthrowing the Sukarno government and launching a blood-bath that led to the slaughter of at least 500,000 people.[5] Freeport's CEO, James Robert ("Jim Bob") Moffett calls Suharto a "compassionate man."[6]

Evidence uncovered after the 1965 massacre showed that the United States not only condoned the massacre but actively participated in it. Investigative reporter Kathy Kadane wrote that in 1965, high-ranking U.S. diplomats and CIA officials provided lists of Indonesian Communist Party (PKI) members to the Indonesian army. Robert Martens, a former political officer at the U.S. embassy in Jakarta, told Kadane: "[The lists were] a big help to the army. They probably killed a lot of people, and I probably have a lot of blood on my hands, but that's not all bad. There's a time when you have to strike hard at a decisive moment."[7] Noam Chomsky reflected on the absence of remorse from government officials when Kadane's revelations were published in the *Washington Post* in 1990:

> The general satisfaction over the Indonesian slaughter and its aftermath helps us understand the criteria by which terror should be evaluated.... We do not regard murder, torture, slaughter, and mutilation as pleasurable in themselves. To be acceptable, they must meet the condition of salutary efficacy.... The only mass-based political force in Indonesia stood in the way of the goals of privileged sectors of the West. Therefore, its destruction was hailed as a great achievement, in no way inconsistent with the fabled yearning for democracy that guides our every thought, in fact, a necessary step towards achieving the blessings of democracy.[8]

In 1967, not long after the military overthrow of the Sukarno government, Indonesia granted Freeport the right to exploit West Papua's mineral resources—two years before the so-called "Act of Free Choice" (or "Act of No Choice," as many Papuans dubbed it) ceded West Papua to Indonesia.[9] Apparently Freeport assumed that the 1969 referendum by which the West Papuans were to determine their relationship to Indonesia was a foregone conclusion.[10] At the official opening ceremony of the mine in 1973, President Suharto renamed the territory Irian Jaya—an acronym for "Follow Indonesia Against Holland." Henceforth the Papuan, or Melanesian, population, who numbered about a million would be renamed Irianese and use of the geographical name West Papua was forbidden.[11]

Both Freeport/Rio Tinto and Indonesia have benefited from this colonial takeover at the expense of the native Papuans. The value of the Grasberg mine exceeds $60 billion. In 1997, Freeport removed $1.5 billion of copper, gold and silver ore from Grasberg,[12] delivering a $208 million profit that year.[13] While 1998 falls in copper and gold prices dented profits appreciably, the mine has since expanded dramatically, reaching a daily throughput of up to 240,000 tons of ore by mid-1999.[14] The company's intention is to increase this rate to 300,000 tons a day "when metal prices improve"[15]—which will make it probably the largest creator of mineral wastes of any mine on the planet.

But while the mine has been very profitable for Freeport and Rio Tinto, it has been an unmitigated disaster for the Amungme, the 13,000 native people who live around the mine; the Komoro, who live downstream from it; and others who live in the company's vast exploration lease, some of which borders on the famed Lorentz National Park.

Anti-Colonial Resistance

Indonesia invaded West Papua in 1962 as the Dutch were preparing to hand over power to the local Melanesian people.[16] The attack failed, but President Kennedy pressured the Dutch into surrendering West Papua to the United Nations on the grounds that Indonesian President Sukarno might otherwise join the communist world. Sukarno had just concluded an important arms deal with Moscow and was threatening another invasion of West Papua.[17] Washington's special UN ambassador, Ellsworth Bunker, negotiated a highly controversial New York Agreement, which provided for UN control of the territory for seven months before handing it over to Indonesia. The Papuans were never consulted during this entire process. Their right to self-determination was sacrificed on the altar of Cold War politics.

From the time West Papua was forcibly incorporated into Indonesia in 1963, the native population has resisted Indonesian authority just as they resisted their former Dutch colonizers.[18] Indonesia has responded to Papuan resistance with military force and programs of forced assimilation. One of the most important parts of forced assimilation is the transmigration program, which involves moving Javanese settlers and military units from the overcrowded island of Java to West Papua in what one geographer has called "the world's largest invasion" financed by the World Bank, the European Economic Community, Asian Development Bank, the United States and the United Nations Development Program, among others.[19]

Under Indonesian law, native peoples must give up "their customary rights over land and resources to so-called national development projects, which include mines."[20] Because Indonesia has declared transmigration a national priority, the traditional land rights of native people are also not allowed to stand in the way of transmigration settlements.[21] Hyndman has described the collusion between Indonesia and Freeport to mine gold and copper on native land as "nothing short of economic development by invasion."[22] Bechtel Construction paid several hundred Amungme ten cents (U.S.) per hour for unskilled construction work, but once the mine was operating, only 40 continued to be employed.[23] Of the 18,000 jobs connected with the mine, only 1,500 are filled by West Papuans, and only 400 are filled by local people.[24]

Freeport's disregard for the rights of the Amungme sparked a protest in 1977 in which villagers, with the assistance of independence fighters from the Free Papua Movement (OPM), blew up a Freeport ore pipeline. The Indonesian military responded by sending U.S.-supplied OV 10 Bronco attack jets to strafe and bomb villagers. The retaliation was code-named Operation *Tumpas* ("annihilation"). Papuans claim that thousands of men, women and children were killed in this action; the government admits to 900.[25] Reports of the use of these counterinsurgency aircraft did not appear in the world press until a year later. These same Broncos were also being widely used in East Timor to defeat the guerrilla resistance to Indonesian occupation.[26] While the U.S.-backed Indonesian massacre in East Timor received some limited coverage internationally, the comparable massacre in West Papua received hardly any notice.[27]

After the uprising, the government forcibly resettled entire communities away from the mine to the makeshift township of Timika, near the coast.[28] In 1991, when a second contract was signed between Freeport and the Indonesian regime, the government was empowered to "assist the Company in arrangements" to remove even more communities from their traditional land.[29] This cozy relationship between Freeport and the Indonesian government has made this one of the most controversial, and one of the most militarized, mining operations on the planet.

By this time, Freeport was finally acknowledging its responsibility in dumping over 110,000 tons of untreated mine waste (tailings) into the rivers of West Papua every day.[30] This practice is illegal in the United States. The company claims that the tailings are non-toxic, but it has refused requests from the Indonesian Forum on the Environment for independent testing and monitoring. The extent of the company's concern for secrecy was dramatically illustrated when Danny Kennedy of the Berkeley, California-based mining watchdog group Project Underground was deported in February 1997 for attempting to ship samples of the river's water to the United States for analysis.[31]

Moffett once described his company's operations as "thrusting a spear of economic development into the heartland of Irian Jaya."[32] Those who are most directly affected by Freeport's operations have a far different view of the situation, but must be careful about what they say and to whom. When *Tifa Irian*, a local newspaper, began reporting on the environmental destruction and negative social impacts of the mine, Irian Jaya's General Director of Conservation warned that "anyone who does anything against Freeport is also against the government."[33] In 1998, Amungme spokesperson and matriarch Yosefa Alomang wanted to address Rio Tinto shareholders at the company's annual meeting in London, on the plight of her people. Her personal experience with human rights abuse has transformed her into a leading critic of Freeport/Rio's impact upon her people. She was taken from her home by solidiers one night in October 1994 and locked in a police station closet for three weeks.[34] Prior to her trip to London she was visited several times by Indonesian security forces who tried to intimidate her, and when she arrived at the airport, she was prohibited from leaving the country.[35]

Under these circumstances, local NGOs must find ways to circumvent their own government and seek assistance from the international human rights and environmental community to put pressure on their government from the outside. Organizations like Amnesty International and Survival International have been doing this kind of advocacy for human rights and native rights for a long time. What is innovative is the way in which traditional human rights issues have been coupled with environmental issues in a new generation of international organizations.

Transnational Advocacy Networks

The renewed assault on resource-rich native lands has been met by a rapid increase in the number of native organizations. Native rights advocate Julian Burger has emphasized that these organizations "are now a distinct new force in world politics, and their struggles can no longer be considered marginal to the main concerns of governments and, more generally, mankind."[36] In the last several years, we have seen a variety of transnational enviromental and native rights advocacy networks coming together to assist native communities under siege by the international oil and mining industries. Some of the major actors in these advocacy networks include the following: international and domestic non-governmental research and advocacy organizations, local social movements, foundations, the media, churches and trade unions.[37]

The major impetus to the emergence of these networks is the understanding that the land rights of native communities in the Third World and even in some situations in advanced capitalist countries like the United States, Australia and Canada are routinely ignored, and major mining and oil projects are undertaken on native lands without the consent of those communities. In these situations, where governments are unresponsive or hostile toward the assertion of native land rights, "the boomerang pattern of influence characteristic of transnational networks may occur: domestic NGOs bypass their state and directly search out international allies to try to bring pressure on their states from outside."[38]

Organizations such as Project Underground in the United States bring together native rights, human rights and environmental issues in a network bound together by shared values, a common understanding of the problem and by ongoing exchanges of information and other forms of assistance. The role of information, easily and rapidly communicated by e-mail and fax, is a critical element in the success of these networks. The strategic use of information can "generate attention to new issues and help set agendas when they provoke media attention, debates, hearings and meetings on issues that previously had not been a matter of public debate."[39] Equally important is that the demands of native peoples are "framed in terms of existing international norms by internationally famous and

charismatic leaders."[40] Recent examples of such leaders would include Chico Mendes and Paulinho Paiakan of Brazil, Ken
Saro-Wiwa of Nigeria and Rigoberta Menchú of Guatemala.

Environmental and native rights activists have been compiling
a database of multinational mining corporations and their worldwide operations for years. Publications like Roger Moody's *The Gulliver File: Mines, People and Land: A Global Battleground* provide local
communities with the track records of hundreds of mining companies so that they can "intervene against mine plans or insist on better
ones."[41] Also important to the success of these networks is the dramatic testimony of the people directly affected by environmental
and human rights abuses that makes the case for action "more real
for ordinary citizens."[42] Shareholders in corporations may find it
easy to ignore the effects of corporate policies on native peoples if
those native peoples are halfway around the globe. Bring the people
suffering from corporate-sponsored human rights abuses into the
annual shareholders' meeting, and it is much more difficult to ignore
their concerns. Finally, the international contacts provided by these
networks "can amplify the demands of domestic groups, pry open
space for new issues and then echo back these demands into the domestic arena."[43]

Project Underground sees itself on the frontlines of a worldwide battlefield, "exposing the environmental and human rights
abuses by the corporations involved and building capacity amongst
communities facing mineral and energy development to achieve
economic and environmental justice."[44] The Project's Freeport
Campaign has acted as a catalyst for about 20 international and Indonesian NGOs, from England's Minewatch to the U.S.-based Sierra Club, Australia's Mineral Policy Institute and the Indonesian
Forum on the Environment, which is itself a coalition of 335 organizations from all over Indonesia. The broad aim of the campaign is to
target a range of interests, from industry insurers and private investors to the public, in order to pressure Freeport and Rio Tinto to act
in a socially responsible fashion toward the people and environment
around their operations in West Papua/Irian Jaya.

This is no small task, given the absence of U.S. media coverage
of the issue and Freeport's ability to restrict media access to its re-

mote Grasberg mining operations. When Bill Elder, a news anchor for New Orleans Channel 4, asked Jim Bob Moffett for permission to visit the mine, he was told he could do so only if he was accompanied by Freeport escorts and only if he agreed to use equipment provided by the company. Elder turned down Moffett's offer and went on his own. In Sydney, Australia, the Indonesian consulate denied his entry into West Papua and told him he had to get permission from Freeport.[45] A professor at Tulane Law School in New Orleans put it bluntly: "Nobody visits Freeport's operations in Indonesia without, at the very least, Freeport's permission."[46] In those cases where journalists report unfavorably about Freeport, the company threatens legal action and/or spends millions on print and TV ads trying to create a favorable public image.[47]

In the case of Garland Robinette, a co-anchor at the New Orleans CBS affiliate, who did several stories critical of Freeport's environmental practices, the company offered him a job as Freeport's vice-president of communications. Robinette accepted the offer in 1990 and developed the Planit Communications division to sell Freeport as environmentally responsible in the eyes of the public. The company sponsors "Focus Earth" infomercials for local TV and sends speakers to the local schools to talk about recycling and environmentally responsible corporations.[48] In 1993, Planit became an independent company, but retained Freeport as its biggest customer. Ironically, it was precisely this obsession with secrecy, security and its corporate image that provided an opening for the Freeport Campaign network.

Framing the Issue

The first and most important challenge for the Freeport Campaign was how to present the issues to the public in a way that would mobilize key constituencies to take concerted action. In their survey of issues around which transnational advocacy networks have organized most effectively, Keck and Sikkink note that one of the issue characteristics that appear most frequently is that "involving bodily harm to vulnerable individuals, especially when there is a short and clear causal chain (or story) assigning responsibility."[49] While the native people of West Papua have suffered repression at the hands of

the Indonesian army since the first big mine (at Erstberg) began operating in 1972, Freeport was able to maintain some distance from
this activity, at least in its public image.

All this changed in April 1995, when the Australian Council for
Overseas Aid (ACFOA), the largest NGO in Australia concerned
with development and human rights, released a report documenting
the killing or disappearance of dozens of native people in and
around Freeport's 5.75 million-acre concession at the hands of the
Indonesian army between June 1994 and February 1995.[50] In
reponse to the ACFOA report, the Catholic Church of Jayapura (the
capital of West Papua) issued its own report based on first-hand in-
terviews with Amungme eyewitnesses.[51] The report documents that
from 1994 to mid-1995, summary executions, arbitrary detentions
and torture occurred on numerous occasions in Freeport's concession area. The church report also charged that three civilians died
while being tortured by Indonesian soldiers at a Freeport workshop.
Freeport denies the workshop exists and adamantly denies that its
security forces were involved in any killings. "We have an excellent
relationship with the chiefs of the tribes," said Freeport senior
vice-president Thomas J. Egan. Any reports of civil unrest are "certainly not the case," he told a *Business Week* reporter.[52]

However, critics like Danny Kennedy of Project Underground
argue that Freeport is directly involved in these ongoing atrocities
and point to Freeport's close relationship with the Suharto regime.
"The Indonesian government owns a 9% share in the mine and supplies soldiers, who are fed and sheltered by Freeport, to guard the
mining areas."[53] Moreover, a 1995 U.S. State Department report on
Indonesia confirmed that

> where indigenous people clash with development projects,
> the developers almost always win. Tensions with indige-
> nous people in Irian Jaya, including the vicinity of the
> Freeport McMoRan mining concession near Timika, led to
> a crackdown by government security forces, resulting in the
> deaths of civilians and other violent human rights abuses.[54]

The publicity following the reports of human rights abuses provided a further opening for the Amungme to draw attention to the

environmental devastation they were suffering from current and planned mining expansion. By the company's own estimates, the Grasberg mine dumped more than 40 million tons of tailings into the Ajkwa River in 1996.[55] Environmental groups say that the enormous amounts of mine waste, which contain dissolved arsenic, lead, mercury and other potentially dangerous metals, have destroyed roughly 26 square miles of rainforest, ruining palm trees that are the source of sago, a traditional staple in the native people's diets.[56] Residents along the Ajkwa River have been warned against drinking the polluted water by the provincial environmental authorities.[57] Freeport's expansion plans call for dumping 300,000 tons of tailings per day into the Ajkwa River. Even before these plans were confirmed—and the projected disposal rate was 190,000 tons a day—Freeport's own consultant admitted that over the 40-year life of the mine 3.2 billion tons of waste rock will be dumped into the local river system. Much of this rock is acid-generating and has already polluted a nearby lake.[58]

Most of the capital for Freeport's plant and exploration expansion (which has now reached $1 billion) came from Rio Tinto, which, as of May 1999, owned 14.5% of Freeport McMoRan Copper and Gold, the parent company of PT (Limited Company) Freeport Indonesia.[59] The British company's investment came, in early 1995, at a time when Freeport's cash-flow was running perilously low.[60] Not only was Rio Tinto's 40% contribution to the expenses of expansion critical to Freeport's fortunes; its share of the copper from Grasberg (136,000 tons in 1998) was the main factor in boosting Rio Tinto's copper output by 17% in 1998—helping make it one of the world's major producers of the metal.[61]

Freeport's expansion plans could involve the relocation of an estimated 2,000 people.[62] Shortly after Rio Tinto announced its involvement with Freeport, the London-based Partizans (People Against Rio Tinto Zinc and its Subsidaries) called on the company not to sign the agreement until shareholders had an opportunity to discuss the implications. The involvement of Partizans added yet another transnational advocacy network to the Freeport Campaign. Formed in 1978, at the request of aboriginal communities in North Queensland, Australia, Partizans brought the concerns of native peoples to the attention of Rio Tinto directors by buying shares of Rio Tinto stock. From 1980 to the present, this has enabled nearly 60 native people to attend the company's annual meetings and question its board. At the 1982 annual meeting, Partizans protesters took over the platform, and, for the first time at a British company's public meeting, the police were called in to eject an aboriginal delegate and 30 supporters. The event was headline news around the world the next day. When Partizans joined the Freeport Campaign, it brought more than 15 years of experience in networking with other campaigns around the issues of multinational mining, native peoples' land rights, and the effects of Rio Tinto and other mining companies on the environment and people's health.[63]

However, the company refused to delay signing the agreement. Rio Tinto closed the deal just before the annual shareholders' meeting that year, a move designed, according to Partizans, to preempt any attempt to block the agreement.[64] As Partizans noted when the deal was finalized, Rio Tinto's experience in neighboring Papua New Guinea did not bode well for the Amungme and other native groups. The company had operated the Panguna copper/gold mine on Bougainville island until 1989, when it was shut down as a result of a guerrilla insurgency in response to Rio Tinto's disregard for native land rights and irresponsible mine waste disposal practices.[65]

By 1995, the Freeport Campaign was able to frame the issue as the inseparable connection between protecting one of the world's most pristine ecosystems and protecting the vulnerable people who live in it. By joining the issues of human rights abuse and environmental degradation, the Freeport Campaign enabled the Amungme to go beyond the relatively weaker human rights advocacy network and tap into the stronger international advocacy network of environmental groups.[66] The first targets of the campaign included a U.S. government insurance agency and the World Bank.

Targeting Responsible Parties

Jim Bob Moffett once dismissed the pollution from his company's West Papua mining operation as "the equivalent of me pissing in the Arafua Sea"[67] (the body of water into which the Ajkwa River flows). This arrogant disregard for the devastating impact of the mine was still apparent when the Overseas Private Investment Corporation (OPIC), a U.S. federal agency that provides support for U.S. companies overseas, cancelled Freeport's $100 million political-risk insurance policy in October 1995. The insurance—carrying an annual premium of $1 million—provided Freeport with protection against damage to its assets from war, insurrection and unilateral breach of contract by the Indonesian government.[68] But, as a federal agency, OPIC is also enjoined to take into consideration any adverse environmental or social consequences of projects it endorses. Following OPIC's public announcement, Moffett went on live television in New Orleans saying, "There's been no claim by OPIC that we have an environmental problem."[69] However, when OPIC's letter to Freeport was leaked from within the agency (supporting materials later became available under the Freedom of Information Act), there was no question that there was an environmental problem. OPIC said that "massive deposition of tailings and the sheetflow of tailings" from Freeport's mine into the Ajkwa River "has degraded a large area of lowland rainforest," posing "unreasonable or major environmental, health, or safety hazards with respect to the rivers...the surrounding terrestial ecosystem, and the local inhabitants."[70]

The cancellation of Freeport's insurance was the first and only time OPIC has ever cancelled a client's insurance for environmental reasons. Moreover, the cancellation was confirmed despite a major lobbying effort by former Secretary of State Henry Kissinger, who was a member of Freeport's board of directors and also a lobbyist who was paid about $400,000 per year for his services for Freeport. President Suharto also made a personal appeal to President Bill Clinton during a meeting at the White House.[71]

Freeport immediately launched a multimillion-dollar media strategy to respond to the OPIC decision and the unfavorable news coverage that followed. In addition to buying ads in *Newsweek* and *U.S. News & World Report,* the company took out two full-page ads in the December 5, 1995, *New York Times* that blamed unnamed "foreign special-interest groups" for promoting "misleading accusations about our environmental record" which the ads claimed was "a model of development." The ads also attacked the U.S. Agency for

International Development (AID) for giving funds to Freeport's detractors.[72] This was a reference to the Indonesian Forum for the Environment (WAHLI). Prior to OPIC's announcement, the Jakarta-based WAHLI, along with the International NGO Forum on Indonesian Development (INFID), had been asking Freeport to neutralize its tailings before dumping them into the river and to allow independent testing of the river's water quality. WAHLI also filed a lawsuit in Jakarta against the Indonesian government for failing to follow national environmental laws when it issued mining permits to Freeport.

The company responded to the WALHI lawsuit by sending a letter to AID asking that it cut off all funding to the "newly radicalized" WALHI for "openly affiliating with radical international NGOs such as Earth First!, Friends of the Earth, Global Response and Greenpeace." It was a ploy that dismally failed. WALHI was also accused of "organizing protests" and using "access to the media to manipulate public discourse," a charge that of course would never be made against Freeport for its full-page ads in the *Times*.[73] OPIC's decision to cancel Freeport's insurance was not just bad publicity for the company, but a vindication of the claims that had been made by a transnational advocacy network for years.

The Freeport media counter-offensive continued with an article on "environmental imperialism" in *Forbes* magazine, which featured a picture of Jim Bob Moffett standing at his desk with the caption, "Forced to his knees by environmental control freaks." The article made the case that U.S. AID "has become a virtual partner of the environmental extremist organizations" in imposing "environmental fascism" on U.S. companies operating aborad. The article accused Lori Udall, the Washington director of the Berkeley, California-based International Rivers Network, of being part of an international conspiracy to "hold the financial institutions that are involved in Freeport's activities in Irian Jaya accountable" and of arranging for Indonesian activists to come to Washington, DC, to meet with OPIC officials about Freeport's environmental violations and complicity in human rights abuses.[74]

In this bizarre reinterpretation of history, the imperialists are not the multinational corporations acting in concert with Suharto and the Indonesian military, but environmental and human rights activists. In other words, what upset Freeport the most about the OPIC insurance cancellation was the ability of the Freeport Campaign network to dramatically reinforce the attack on the company's environmental and human rights abuses. In this way, it became clear to a government agency whose primary objective was to facilitate U.S. foreign investment that this company had gone so far beyond the limits of acceptable capitalist profit-maximizing behavior as to threaten the political stability of an already highly militarized police state system in West Papua.

Freeport Campaigners then set their sights on a World Bank affiliate that also insured the Grasberg operation.[75] The Multilateral Investment Guarantee Agency (MIGA) offers insurance against political risks to companies in developing countries. MIGA had sold a $50-million policy to Freeport in 1990—the first contract the fledgling agency had ever made. "OPIC has done the right thing," said Danny Kennedy, who was then an activist with the Australia-based Action for Solidarity, Equality, Environment and Development (A SEED). "We are calling on the World Bank, which also guaranteed Freeport's mine, to follow their example immediately."[76]

But before pressure on MIGA could become effective, Freeport's own browbeating and blustering had apparently succeeded. Following an environmental assessment by the Australian consulting firm, Dames & Moore, which identified many problems with the mine but concluded the company was striving to remedy them, OPIC reversed its earlier decision. It would renew Freeport's political risk insurance from April 1996 until the end of that year, at which point it would reassess the situation in the light of improvements effected by the company.[77] This decision regrettably had more to do with pro-Freeport political maneuvering (in particular by Kissinger Associates) than logic or consistencies within OPIC. The one essential measure Dames & Moore did not recommend was the cessation of tailings disposal in the Ajkwa River system, even though this was clearly the only way that OPIC's original objections to the Grasberg operations could be addressed.

MIGA had planned to send a three-member team to West Papua in late 1996 as part of its own investigation of Freeport, when the company announced that it no longer required political risk insurance—whether from MIGA or OPIC. The timing of Freeport's announcement was seen by many critics as an attempt to preempt a full-scale investigation of the charges against Freeport and the possible disclosure of more damaging information.

On the other hand, the cancellations occurred just months after the most serious indigenous demonstrations at West Papuan mining towns since the beginning of the mining operations. Surely this was precisely the time that insurance against political risks was most required. The revolt started following an incident when a tribal man was hit by a car driven by a Freeport employee. Survival International estimated that 6,000 tribal people attacked Freeport's offices and facilities (but not people) in three towns connected with the mine.[78] On March 12, 1996, they marched to the airport to meet the incoming plane of Jim Bob Moffett. Said an Amungme tribal leader:

> Because Jim Bob Moffett and Freeport are deaf to our complaints and demands, because the Government continues to ignore the problems of the Amungme and Komoro people and all the other native inhabitants of Irian Jaya, we have been forced to use this kind of language to tell them what we want.[79]

When Moffett met with the Amungme Tribal Council, LEMASA, the executive director of the organization said that local tribes were in agreement that "Freeport operations should be shut down."

Following this meeting, LEMASA was warned by Brigadier-General Prabowo, Suharto's son-in-law and commander of the notoriously brutal special forces army unit, KOPASSUS, that this was tantamount to a declaration of war.[80] Clearly Freeport and its partner Rio Tinto felt they could rely on brute force to protect their interests better than a U.S. government agency and a World Bank affiliate that were coming under public pressure.

After the revolt, the Indonesian army announced that a rapid deployment force battalion from the army's strategic command had been sent to the area to protect mining company property. Freeport also invested $35 million for barracks and other facilities for this military task force.[81] In December 1996, the Indonesian armed forces (ABRI) had created a special unit of no less than 6,000 troops (more than one soldier for each adult Amungme) to "safeguard" the mining complex. It was, declared the Indonesian human rights organization TAPOL, "the only task force of its kind to exist anywhere in Indonesia."[82] According to Kennedy of Project Underground, "the mining concession is now the most militarized district in all of Indonesia. The military presence surpasses even that of occupied East Timor, where invading Indonesian forces have been fighting a popular resistance for more than 21 years."[83]

But there was still a token velvet glove barely covering the iron fist. Freeport also said that it would allocate at least 1% of its gross revenues for the next ten years, an estimated $15 million per year, in support of "a comprehensive social development plan based upon the input of indigenous leaders during a year-long series of meetings."[84] However, none of the "indigenous leaders" that Freeport consulted included members of LEMASA, the representative organization for the native people living in the mining area. Instead, Freeport set up seven local foundations to be the recipients of the revenues. LEMASA rejected the 1% Trust Fund as any kind of solution to the grievances that led to the March revolt. They also noted that 96% of the revenues went to government and military projects.[85]

The response of the Indonesian army to the revolt against Freeport left little doubt that the grievances of the native people would not be taken seriously in Jakarta. If the Amungme and other native groups wanted to press their claims against Freeport, they would have to find a more hospitable forum than their own government. With the help of the Freeport Campaign network the Amungme shifted the conflict from the West Papuan rainforest to the corporate headquarters of Freeport in New Orleans, Louisana.

Tom Beanal and Yosefa Alomang v. Freeport McMoRan

In April 1996, Tom Beanal, a leader of the Amungme Tribal Council, filed a $6-billion class-action lawsuit in New Orleans district court charging Freeport with human rights abuses, the robbery of Amungme ancestral lands, violations of international environmental law "tantamount to acts of eco-terrorism" and the "planned demise of a culture of indigenous people whose rights were never

considered" during the course of the company's mining operations.[86] Freeport spokesperson Garland Robinette strongly denied
the allegations contained in the lawsuit, claiming, "There is no basis
in law or in fact for the claims." Richard C. Adkerson, vice-chairman
of Freeport, called the suit "frivolous and opportunistic."[87]

With the help of Friends of the Earth and Project Underground,
Beanal came to New Orleans to meet with Martin Regan, the attorney handling the lawsuit, and to provide testimony in response to
Freeport's attempt to have the case dismissed. The night before his
testimony, he spoke at Loyola University through an interpreter:

> [G]old and copper have been taken by Freeport for the past 30
> years, but what have we gotten in return? Only insults, torture, ar-
> rests, killings, forced evictions from our land, impoverishment
> and alienation from our own culture.... Even the sacred moun-
> tains we think of as our mother have been arbitrarily torn up by
> them, and they have not felt the least bit guilty.... During the last
> 30 years, we tried to find justice, but we never found it. And now
> comes Mr. Martin [Regan], and I can see justice. I come here to
> ask for justice.[88]

Beanal found the students at Loyola University especially recep-
tive to his message. Freeport had already been targeted by a local environmental group, the Delta Greens, for dumping radioactive
gypsum waste into the Mississippi River from the company's phos-
phate processing plants in New Orleans.[89] According to U.S. Environmental Protection Agency records, during the 1990s, Freeport
was the worst polluting company in the United States, based on the
quantity of toxic materials released into the air, water and soil.[90] To
reverse the company's anti-environmental image, Moffett donated
$600,000 to Loyola to endow a chair in environmental communica-
tions. The chair was part of Freeport's Environmental Research
Consortium of Louisana, which includes the University of New Orleans (UNO), Louisana State University, Tulane University and Xa-
vier University.[91]

Instead of improving the company's image, the controversy
that erupted at Loyola only served to focus public attention on
Freeport's abysmal record. "By using an endowed environmental
chair at Loyola in his efforts to disguise Freeport's role in ecological

destruction and environmental injustice," wrote Loyola University philosophy professor John Clark, "Moffett presented the university with an inescapable responsibility to confront the issue."[92]

In April 1995, Assistant Law Professor William P. Quigley sponsored a resolution that the $600,000 be returned to Freeport, citing "crimes against humanity in places like Indonesia as well as Freeport's lack of commitment to preserving the environment throughout the world."[93] While administrators at this Jesuit-run university sought to delay any campus-wide discussion of the endowment controversy, news of the OPIC decision prompted Professor Clark to organize a protest march. Protesters, including Loyola faculty and students, marched outside Moffett's house carrying signs that read, "Jim Bob kills for profit." Similar protests occurred at the University of Texas at Austin, which has also received large financial endowments from the company. After the New Orleans protest, Moffett asked the university to return the $600,000 gift. A journalist for the local New Orleans paper, the *Times-Picayune*, concluded that "Moffett asked for his money back to show his displeasure at Loyola University's failure to stifle dissent."[94]

If Moffett's objective was to buy off university dissent the same way he had bought off media dissent, by hiring his critics, he was partially successful. After the OPIC news broke, the *Times-Picayune* received letters supporting Freeport's record from the president of Loyola University and UNO's chancellor and its dean of the College of Business. Tulane University paid for a full-page ad in the *Times-Picayune* applauding Freeport's environmental record.[95]

A year after filing the lawsuit, a federal district court judge dismissed the case, but left the door open for Beanal to amend his case with more specific allegations and refile it. More importantly, Judge Stanwood Duval ruled that Beanal and other tribal people had standing to bring damage claims against Freeport in a U.S. court. At that point, Yosefa Alomang became the chief plaintiff and Freeport lost all attempts to prevent a hearing taking place.[96] Both the federal court case and Louisiana state court case were ultimately unsuccessful.[97] Despite the loss, the case was an important rallying point for thousands of Papuans seeking to hold Freeport's corporate executives accountable for their behavior in West Papua. Fortunately, they did not put all their energies exclusively into the lawsuits.

Exerting Leverage over Freeport

Echoes of the human rights allegations in the Beanal/Alomang lawsuit also figured prominently in a shareholder resolution filed by the Seattle Mennonite Church prior to Freeport's 1997 annual meeting. By working with religious denominations who own minority shares in a variety of multinational corporations, transnational advocacy networks can bring controversial issues directly before shareholders and ask them to vote for actions to be taken by the board of directors to address these concerns. Even if activists are unsuccessful in getting enough votes to compel action by the company, a large number of votes, usually anything over 3%, has enormous symbolic value. It represents a public criticism of the company's corporate management and forces a company to state its position on issues in a public fashion. Resolutions that garner at least 3% are automatically carried over to the following year's meeting.

Taken in conjunction with the lawsuit, the shareholder resolution represented a further challenge to Freeport's ability to control public discussion and debate about its Grasberg mine.[98] The church asked Freeport's board of directors to end the company's relationship with the Indonesian military and postpone expansion of mining operations until the company can resolve ongoing disputes with tribal people. The church also asked Freeport to release all of its environmental audits and to allow independent environmental monitoring.

CEO Moffett began the meeting by noting that the Beanal lawsuit had been recently re-filed and called it an effort to "intimidate and shake down" the shareholders.[99] When it came time for the Mennonite proposal, Moffett advised Bob Pauw, a Seattle immigration attorney, that he had two minutes to speak to the resolution. Before he could finish his statement, Moffett cut him off. After Pauw's presentation, Moffett told Project Underground's Danny Kennedy that he had one minute to address the Mennonite proposal. Kennedy told Freeport board members that they should support the shareholder resolution because it made good business sense. He also pointed out that the revised Beanal lawsuit was very similar to one now pending in Los Angeles federal court against Unocal, which has been sued for human rights violations that occurred in relation to its natural gas pipeline project in Burma. In that case, a federal judge found Unocal potentially liable if it could be shown to be "accepting benefits of and approving" human rights abuses by the military.[100]

The Mennonite proposal garnered 2.5% of the shares that were voted. While this was not enough for the proposal to be carried over to the next year's meeting, it was an impressive showing, especially in the context of the unprecedented security that Freeport had employed to preempt any protest at the meeting. Meanwhile, in London, Freeport's partner, Rio Tinto, was also being challenged for its complicity in human rights abuses at the Grasberg mine. The main challenger was the World Development Movement (WDM), one of Britain's most influential development campaign organizations, which in 1996 focused on Rio Tinto and the West Papua mine as a key instance of unacceptable multinational exploitation.[101] The WDM presented Rio Tinto's board of directors with a petition calling on the company to withdraw its 12% shareholding in Freeport unless the company addressed the claims of the Amungme and Komoro peoples.[102] Rio Tinto defended its involvement in the Grasberg mine and avoided any response to the specific claims of the Amungme and Komoro. The inability of the Freeport Campaigners to engage the board of directors of either Freeport or Rio Tinto in a dialgoue at their annual meeting prompted a change of tactics the following year.

Activists in advocacy networks are constantly evaluating how to exert leverage over more powerful actors. The two most common forms of leverage are material and moral ones.[103] With the publication of alternative annual corporate reports, the Freeport Campaign network was able to identify both material (financial liability) and moral (public shaming) sources of leverage.

Prior to the 1998 Freeport annual shareholders' meeting, Project Underground produced an independent annual report on Freeport's Indonesian operations and distributed it to the company's top 100 institutional investors, financial reporters and mem-

bers of the company's board of directors. The report, "Risky
Business: The Grasberg Gold Mine," attempted to persuade investors that they were not being told the entire story about the company's pattern of human rights violations around the Grasberg
mine, and that this exposed the company to future risks and liabilities, including the ongoing litigation against the parent company.[104]
Project Underground arranged for a shareholder briefing on the report the day before Freeport's annual meeting. In addition to several
shareholders and reporters, Freeport senior vice-presidents Thomas
Egan and Paul Murphy showed up. They were quite upset with Project Underground for charging Freeport security and police with responsibility for the beating death of a Dani tribal person in "Risky
Business." The company had explained the death as due to malaria
and dehydration in an internal company memo obtained by Project
Underground and reproduced in the report. Egan and Murphy
threatened to sue Project Underground for libel. When Danny Kennedy produced a Polaroid photo of the beaten man, obtained from
the man's family, there was no further discussion of the issue. However, during the annual meeting the next day, Moffett took Kennedy
aside and told him "I'm gonna take you down."[105]

In Europe and Australia, the Freeport Campaign network had
meanwhile secured the commitment of the world's largest miners'
union, the Brussels-based ICEM (International Federation of
Chemical, Energy, Mine and General Workers' Union) to publish its
own alternative annual corporate report. Entitled "Rio Tinto:
Tainted Titan: The Stakeholders Report," it covered several of the
company's more unacceptable operations, focusing particularly on
the Grasberg mine. Copies of the report were distributed to shareholders and the public at the 1998 shareholders' meeting. Rio Tinto
had early access to the report through the ICEM's own website.

The report identified "stakeholders" such as native groups,
trade unions, environmental groups, churches, human rights groups
and aid agencies who "have raised significant concerns over the
company's systematic failure to address human and workers' rights
and environmental protection at many of its operations around the
world."[106] The report emphasized that the cost of ignoring these
concerns will affect the company's bottom line. "With respect to

occupational health and safety and indigenous peoples there is an increasing risk that the company will be involved in expensive litigation over compensation."[107] Rio Tinto's directors did not have to look very far to be reminded of this fact. In 1996, Broken Hill Proprietary (BHP), Australia's largest company, settled a class-action lawsuit brought by native leaders surrounding its Ok Tedi mine in Papua New Guinea that will cost the company about $400 million. The settlement requires the company to come up with a plan to stop mine tailings from entering the local river.[108]

When confronted with questions about the report during the meeting, Rio Tinto's chairman, Robert Wilson, announced that he hadn't seen it until just minutes prior to the meeting. Nonetheless, shareholders were given a detailed rebuttal to the report immediately after the meeting—a rebuttal that could only have been prepared in advance.[109]

One indication of the effectiveness of the Freeport Campaign's shareholder actions is the fact that Freeport moved the shareholders' meeting from its traditional location in New Orleans to Wilmington, Delaware the following year. Critics claimed that the company moved the meeting to avoid negative publicity. Lending credibility to this interpretation was the fact that neither the company's board of directors nor CEO Moffett attended the meeting. This did not stop Freeport Campaign activists and shareholders representing religous groups from attending and raising concerns about the company's Grasberg mine. The network also brought John Rumbiak, a human rights worker from West Papua. Rumbiak told shareholders, "My people are fighting against you so that you can recognize our dignity as human beings."[110] It was Freeport's failure to respond to Amungme grievances that prompted the lawsuit against the company, said Rumbiak. At the same time that campaign activists were talking to shareholders, Yosefa Alomang was protesting outside Jim Bob Moffett's mansion in New Orleans.

Just in case anyone had any doubt about the international networking capability of the Freeport Campaign, on the same day as the protests in New Orleans and Wilmington, yet another Amungme representative, Paulus Kanongopme, attended the annual shareholders' meeting of ABN Amro, a Dutch bank that is financing

Freeport. He told the bankers that Freeport has adversely affected an area the size of Belgium either through mining or from the in-migration that the company has attracted to the region. "My people have been killed by ABN Amro's investments," said Kanongopme. A top executive of ABN Amro expressed shock at the situation of the mine and assured Kanongopme that ABN Amro would maintain pressure on Freeport to conduct an independent environmental audit.[111]

Assessing the Freeport Campaign

Has the Freeport Campaign's transnational advocacy network been successful in presenting the issues in a way that could mobilize others to take action? If one looks at the public discussion and debate that has been generated in the media, financial institutions, government agencies, U.S. courts and shareholder meetings on two continents, it is clear that Freeport McMoRan is facing demands for corporate accountability that Jim Bob Moffett would have considered inconceivable prior to 1995.

Despite a well-funded public relations effort to counter the negative publicity about human rights abuse and environmental devastation, Freeport was unable to prevent an unprecedented finding of environmental recklessness by a government insurance agency, repeated, well-documented charges of human rights abuses by respected NGOs and church agencies, well-organized protests at shareholder meetings in New Orleans and London or a multibillion dollar lawsuit filed on behalf of thousands of native people pushed off their land to make way for Freeport's Grasberg mine.

The Freeport Campaign network was able to provide both technical information about the environmental impacts of the Grasberg mine and dramatic first-person accounts of human rights abuses to international constituencies as part of a strategy to assist local communities in West Papua in achieving some measure of economic and environmental justice. While conditions in the communities immediately around the mine have not improved and are even more oppressive, the organizational capability of native organizations such as LEMASA has increased and extended its reach into the very center of Freeport's corporate headquarters in New Orleans.

By 1997, a report by one of the largest corporate consultants on political risk noted that international NGOs have raised human rights and environmental issues pertaining to Freeport/Rio Tinto's West Papuan/Irian Jayan operations so successfully that they are now "as much a part of the mine's political risk profile as Arungme [sic] tribespeople."[112]

Following the Indonesian populist uprising of May 1998 and the removal of Suharto from office, there have been increasing calls for a public accounting of Freeport's cozy ties to the former dictator and a reconsideration of Freeport's mining contract for the Grasberg mine. The company has been forced to agree to pay increased royalties and to agree to a further government stake in Freeport McMoRan Copper and Gold.[113] Before the Indonesian general elections in June 1999, the government also suspended the company's exploration permit in outlying areas for "political and security reasons"—a euphemism for the antagonism of local communities.[114] For a period, between mid-1998 and early 1999, the Indonesian press and parliament rung with accusations of complicity between ex-President Suharto and his cronies—including a former mining minister, the timber tycoon Bob Hassan, an investor group led by Aburizal Bakrie and Freeport, in particular Jim Bob Moffett. Bakrie and Freeport were accused of corruption in dealing in Freeport shares, contributing to the fiction that the U.S. company was divesting to Indonesians when it was actually consolidating control.

A checklist of these accusations appeared in the *Wall Street Journal*, which also summarized the history of environmental problems and human rights abuses at the Grasberg mine.[115] Although Freeport vehemently denied these claims, it did not prevent the Indonesian House of Representatives from calling Moffett to defend the company's reputation in Jakarta.[116] More important—though given less attention—was the fact that a parliamentary commission had reported the month before that Grasberg "has not proved to be of sufficient benefit to the local people."[117]

"Freeport got away with murder," allegedly declared Mohammad Sadli, Indonesia's foreign investment czar at the time Freeport signed its first mining contract in 1973.[118] What is certain is that the company and its essential helpmate, Rio Tinto, continue to get away with practices that would not get past an initial social and environmental assessment in much of the rest of the world—in particular, the countries where the two companies are registered, and to which they return their fattest profits.

While the Freeport Campaign cannot take credit for the popular uprising against Suharto, it can certainly take some credit for the intense scrutiny of Freeport's Grasberg mine in a post-Suharto Indonesia. The international connections provided by the Campaign network did indeed overcome the media blackout on West Papua, provide new venues where environmental and human rights issues could be addressed, empower native communities to challenge Freeport's policies and mobilize key constituencies to put pressure on Freeport to act in a socially responsible fashion. The Freeport Campaign network—inside and outside the country—has so far not stopped the environmental degradation and human rights abuses, but it did make it significantly more costly and politically risky for the company to continue doing business as usual. This was dramatically illustrated in the political response to the latest Freeport environmental assault.

Freeport McMoRan in the National Spotlight

Following the May 2000 landslide from Freeport's Lake Wanagon waste site (see Chapter 1), WAHLI launched a national campaign for an environmental audit of the Grasberg mine and a renegotiation of the terms of environmental management and income distribution. The announcement of this campaign had been preceded by the visit of a government commission to the Grasberg mine. The commission's report had asserted that the mine resulted in socioeconomic injustice, rampant human rights abuse and political tension.[119] On May 8 and again on May 18, protests against Freeport in Jakarta shut down the company's offices and prevented a thousand employees from this and several other firms from going to work.[120] The protesters attacked Freeport's environmental record at Grasberg and demanded that the company return a larger share of the profits to the communities in West Papua.

The Indonesian government of President Abdurraham Wahid has already ordered Freeport to cut its output from the Grasberg mine while the government investigated the May 4th landslide. The company agreed to cut its output by around 30,000 tons from its current level of 230,000 tons per day (tpd).[121] Given the company's recent investment to boost production to 300,000 tpd, it will lose money on its capital investment no matter what level of production is permitted. The company has also been ordered to clean up the pollution that has been caused by the toxic materials dumped by the landslide and to compensate the losses suffered by local villagers. The Indonesian government has also asked a new human rights commission to investigate possible abuses by Freeport at Grasberg.[122]

The Freeport situation is not exceptional. After sponsoring a national meeting to discuss the problems caused by gold mining, the Mining Advocacy Network (JATAM), an Indonesian non-governmental organization, called for the immediate cessation of all mining activties in Indonesia. According to JATAM, "Indonesia is standing at the verge of a massively serious ecological disaster, created largely by the mining industry."[123] U.S. AID responded immediately by cutting funding for JATAM. The group had received $75,000 to protect the rights of communities to manage their natural resources and also to assist in monitoring the impact of mining operations. Newmont Mining, a Denver-based U.S. mining company, had complained to the U.S. embassy that taxpayer funds were being used to fund a campaign against a U.S. company. The issue came to a head after the director of JATAM attended Newmont's annual meeting and told shareholders about the company's dumping of toxic mine tailings directly into the rivers and coastal waters in North Sulawesi, yet another of Indonesia's outer islands.[124] WAHLI's funding may also be cut because of its criticism of Freeport McMoRan's Grasberg mine.

Indonesia's Minister of Environment Sonny Keraf assured reporters for the *Wall Street Journal* that President Wahid had no intention of shutting down Freeport's mining operations, though he wouldn't rule out a renegotiation of its contract. The chances that President Wahid would take any drastic measures against Freeport are very slim. After taking office, President Wahid invited Henry

Kissinger, former U.S. Secretary of State and Director Emeritus of Freeport's board, to be an unpaid adviser to the Indonesian government. Kissinger's trip to Jakarta coincided with the increasing demands for renegotiating Freeport's mining contract. His first piece of advice to the president was to honor the Freeport contract negotiated under the Suharto dictatorship. "Investors also expect an assurance of law enforcement," Kissinger told a legislative defense commission.[125] The reference to "law enforcement" was a reminder that Freeport McMoRan expected the same level of military assistance for its operations as the Suharto dictatorship had provided.

However, the political upheavals in Indonesia made investors nervous. In April 1999, Standard & Poor lowered its rating on $3.3 billion worth of Freeport debt and preferred stock, citing the firm's ties to Suharto and the possibility that it could face "retribution and reprisals."[126] After the May 2000 landslide, investors' concern over the future of the company's Indonesian mining operations caused Freeport's stock price on the New York Stock Exchange to fall more than 50% from above $21 at the start of 2000 to $10.38 in May.[127]

From Revolt to Secession

The May 2000 environmental disaster at Freeport's mine also spurred the demands of the Papuan peoples for complete independence from Indonesia. Former governor of West Papua, Freddy Numberi, noted that the conflict between the local people and Freeport was the primary factor that had triggered the demand for independence.[128] Following the historic June 2000 Papuan People's Congress, Tom Beanal, deputy chairman of the Papuan People's Presidium Council, said that there is now unanimity and determination to separate from the Indonesian Republic and to become a fully sovereign state.[129] Over 6,000 West Papuans gathered in the provincial capital of Port Numbay, formerly known as Jayapura, for the largest pro-independence gathering in over 30 years.

While rejecting the demand for independence, Indonesian President Wahid has warned the military against resorting to violence in West Papua. Referring to recent military massacres in East Timor

following the August 1999 independence vote and to the more recent massacres of independence supporters in Aceh, another exploited outer island, Wahid said the military must not act like they
did on those occasions. At the same time that the president urges
calm, he warns that security forces will act to maintain order. In December 1999, Indonesian soldiers arrested Yosefa Alomang, the
class-action plaintiff, as part of a general political crackdown.[130] Indonesian troops increased from 8,000 to more than 12,000 just before the June 2000 Papuan People's Congress.[131] Indonesia's armed
forces are reported to be training and funding East Timor-style
anti-independence militias, which have already attacked and tortured dozens of villagers in the province. Since November 2000, the
Indonesian government has "systematically closed down the political freedoms that had emerged in Papua since the fall of Suharto."[132]
This has included the arrest of pro-independence leaders on
charges of subversion, the military occupation of Jayapura in December 2000, on the eve of an independence rally, and the systematic repression of peaceful flag-raising ceremonies by
independence supporters.

The Papuan people have asked for negotiations to settle the
question of West Papua's political status through just and democratic means. They have also called upon the international community to provide protection to the Papuan Nation while this issue is
being negotiated. Based upon Indonesia's response to similar independence movements in East Timor and Aceh, and the military occupation of West Papua today, there is every reason to fear a
blood-bath.

The response of the U.S. government will be critical for the
Papuan Nation. The U.S. embassy in Jakarta said that Washington
doesn't support "independence for Papua or any other part of Indonesia."[133] As in the recent past, the U.S. government can be counted
upon to defend the interests of U.S. mining companies in Indonesia.
The *Engineering and Mining Journal* recently reminded its readers that
"Indonesian mining operations have achieved higher rates of return
compared to mining operations elsewhere in the world" and that the
country has the potential to become a "truly world-class mining center over the long term."[134]

Project Underground's Freeport Campaign can be expected to play a vital role in opposing further U.S. support for a military response to the West Papuan struggle for self-determination.

A Code of Conduct for Mining and Oil Corporations?

In response to the escalating violence by Indonesian military and police in West Papua and Aceh, Rep. Cynthia McKinney (D-GA) and eight other congressional representatives wrote to former Secretary of State Madeline Albright that "it is imperative that the U.S. refrain from all re-engagement with the Indonesian military at this time."[133] Despite repeated warnings from the international human rights community about the possibility of another East Timor-style blood-bath, U.S. military assistance and training of the Indonesian military continues as before.[134] Similar demands to stop the flow of British military assistance to the Indonesian military have been ignored.

While U.S. Secretary of State Albright and British Foreign Secretary Robin Cook were not willing to admit complicity in the Indonesian violence, they were enthusiastic about the joint U.S. State Department and U.K. Foreign Office initiative announced in December 2000, aimed at curbing human rights abuses at mining and oil facilities in places like West Papua, Colombia and Nigeria. Seven leading U.S. and U.K. oil and mining companies announced their support for a set of voluntary principles to ensure that companies act to stop abuses by public or private security forces protecting company operations. The seven include five oil companies—Chevron, Texaco, Conoco, BP Amoco and Shell—and two mining corporations, Rio Tinto and Freeport McMoRan. Noticeably absent from the list were Exxon-Mobil, Unocal, Occidental, and many others with a history of human rights abuses. "The initiative," according to the London *Financial Times*, "arises out of numerous incidents in the past decade in which large oil and mining companies have come under sharp criticism from human rights groups for killings carried out by security forces in states such as Nigeria and Colombia."[135] Among the principles they've agreed to are the following: instructing security personnel they hire to use only the minimum force necessary to protect company property, pushing for investigation of alleged abuses by security people or local government forces, noninterference with peaceful demonstrations and tolerance of collective bargaining efforts by workers.[136]

Robin Cook said the pact should "greatly reduce the scope for human rights abuses associated with the way companies protect themselves and their employees overseas."[137] These principles are completely voluntary and there is no commitment to monitor compliance. Nonetheless, they do provide a standard against which independent human rights groups can measure corporate compliance and apply the pressure of international public opinion.

However, these standards do not address the systematic relationship between the activities of multinational mining and oil corporations in Third World countries and the flow of U.S. and U.K. military aid, equipment and training of repressive military forces in places like Colombia, Indonesia and Nigeria. Companies like Freeport McMoRan not only employ private security forces to protect their mines (as in West Papua); they also lobby Congress and the president for increased U.S. military aid to Indonesia.[138]

Between 1975 and 2000, the U.S. arms industry sold an estimated $1.1 billion worth of weaponry to Indonesia's military. Following Indonesia's invasion of East Timor in December 1975, U.S. military aid more than doubled, from $17 million to $40 million, and U.S. arms sales jumped from $12 million to $65 million.[139] U.S. Secretary of State Henry Kissinger, who personally approved the sales, had earlier given the green light to Suharto's invasion while attending a state dinner in Jakarta with the dictator.[140] Now Kissinger uses his government connections to lobby on behalf of Freeport McMoRan in Washington and Jakarta. However, if one is to believe the editors of the *New York Times*, companies like Freeport just happen to find themselves in "violent places" with no particular responsibility for the preexisting violence:

> Oil and mining companies do not have the luxury of relocation. They often find themselves working in poor and violent places where protecting a mine or pipeline is a challenge. Occasionally the security forces hired by American or European corporations have gone too far. In the Indonesian province of Irian Jaya [West Papua] in the mid 1990s, military men hired as guards at Freeport

McMoRan's Grasberg gold and copper mine were accused of killing civilians. The security forces contracted by British Petroleum in Colombia, and Shell and Chevron in Nigeria, among other companies, have been accused of similar abuses. [143]

What the *New York Times* cannot admit is that these places *became* violent as a direct result of the extractive activities of these corporations. Culturally insensitive, environmentally hazardous and economically unjust resource exploitation provoked local resistance that was then repressed with massive military force made possible by imperial powers like the U.S. and the U.K. No amount of voluntary compliance with ethical guidelines will address the systemic violence of U.S. military aid to repressive regimes in resource-rich countries in the Third World.

1   Nietschmann, 1986, p. 5.
2   Whittaker, 1990, p. 5.
3   Hyndman, 1988, p. 281.
4   *Engineering and Mining Journal*, 1999, p. 16ww.
5   Udin, 1996, p. 21.
6   Press, 1996, p. 32.
7   *In These Times,* 1990, p. 5.
8   Chomsky, 1990, p. 21.
9   Under threat of execution, 1,025 representatives preselected by the Indonesian government were allowed to "choose" Indonesian rule on behalf of 800,000 people. See Budiardjo and Liong, 1988, p. 33.
10 Minewatch, 1990, p. 1.
11 Nietschmann, 1986, p. 6.
12 Waldman, 1998.
13 *Mining Journal,* 1999.
14 *Indonesian Observer,* 1999.
15 *Jakarta Post,* 1999.
16 Monbiot, 2000.
17 Budiardjo and Liong, 1988, p. 9
18 Ibid., p. 4.
19 Nietschmann, 1986, p. 7.
20 Marr, 1993, p. 4.
21 Nietschmann, 1986.
22 Hyndman, 1988, p. 285.
23 Ibid.
24 Runyan, 1998, p. 18.
25 Osborne, 1985, p. 5.
26 Jardine, 1995.
27 Budiardjo and Liong, 1988, p. 69.
28 Marr, 1993, p. 74.
29 Contract of Work, 1991, Article 18, clause 3.
30 P. T. Freeport Indonesia.
31 Minewatch, 1993, p. 2.
32 *Far Eastern Economic Review,* 1991.
33 Survival International, 1998b.
34 Knight, 1998.
35 Survival International, 1998b.
36 Burger, 1987, p. 44.
37 Keck and Sikkink, 1998, p. 9.
38 Ibid., p. 12.
39 Ibid., p. 25.
40 Van Cott, 1995, p. 30.
41 Moody, 1992, p. 13.
42 Keck and Sikkink, 1998, p. 21
43 Ibid., p. 13.
44 Project Underground, 1996.
45 Bryce, 1996, p. 67.
46 Houck, 1996, p. B7.

47 Both Robert Bryce and Daryl Slusher of *The Austin Chronicle* have received threatening letters from Freeport. See *Austin American-Statesman,* 1995, p. B1.

48 Press, 1995, p. 130.

49 Keck and Sikkink, 1998, p. 27.

50 Australian Council for Overseas Aid, 1995.

51 Catholic Church of Jayapura, 1995.

52 Shari, 1995, p. 66.

53 Kennedy, 1997b, p. 24.

54 U.S. Department of State, 1995.

55 Bryce, 1996, p. 66.

56 Press, 1996, p. 34.

57 *Jakarta Post,* 1997.

58 Dames and Moore, 1996, p. 36.

59 Brookes, 1996.

60 Partizans, 1995.

61 Rio Tinto, 1999.

62 Survival International, 1995b, p. 3.

63 Partizans, 1990.

64 Moody, 1999.

65 Moody, 1991, pp. 70-71.

66 Van Cott, 1995, p. 35.

67 Australian Financial Review, cited in Bryce, 1995.

68 *South East Asia Mining Letter,* 1995.

69 Cited in Bryce, 1996, p. 67.

70 Press, 1996, p. 34.

71 Bryce, 1995.

72 Berry, 1996.

73 Press, 1996, p. 34.

74 McMenamin, 1996.

75 Freeport conducted a massive lobbying effort in Washington, DC, to get OPIC to reinstate the company's insurance. In April of 1996, the agency reinstated the company's insurance through the end of 1996. In exchange for the reinstatement, Freeport agreed to create a $100 million trust fund to be used for remediation of the site after the mine closes. See Bryce and Brackett, 1996, p. 12.

76 Chatterjee, 1995.

77 Project Underground, 1996.

78 Survival International, 1996. p. 2.

79 Indonesia Human Rights Campaign, 1996, p. 1.

80 Ibid., p. 3.

81 McBeth, 1997.

82 Indonesia Human Rights Campaign, 1997.

83 Kennedy, 1997b, p. 24.

84 Murphy, 1998, p. 3.

85 Lembaga Masyarakat Amungme (LEMASA), 1997.

86 Beanal, 1996.

87 *Texas Observer,* 1996.

88 Clark, 1997.
89 Chatterjee, 1996, p. 13.
90 Press, 1995.
91 Fox, 1997, p. 268.
92 Clark, 1997.
93 Bonura, 1995, p. 1.
94 Gill, 1995.
95 Houck, 1996.
96 Freeport McMoRan, 1998.
97 Abrash, 2001, p. 41.
98 Freeport tried to persuade the Securities and Exchange Commission (SEC) that the Mennonite resolution should be dismissed because the request to end company cooperation with the military would violate its contract of work with the Indonesian government. The Mennonites argued otherwise, and the SEC allowed the resolution to go before the shareholders.
99 Bryce, 1997.
100 Project Underground, 1997b.
101 World Development Movement, 1996.
102 Kennedy, 1997a.
103 Keck and Sikkink, 1998, p. 23.
104 Kennedy, et al., 1998.
105 Personal interview with Danny Kennedy, June 22, 1999.
106 International Federation of Chemical, Energy, Mine and General Workers' Unions, 1998, p. 1.
107 Ibid., p. 18.
108 *Multinational Monitor* 1996, p. 5. Also see Imhof, 1996, pp. 15-18.
109 Moody, 1999.
110 Project Underground, 1999c.
111 Ibid.
112 Bray, 1997, p. 45.
113 *Indonesian Observer*, 1999.
114 Agence France Press, 1999.
115 Waldman, 1998.
116 Agence France Press, 1998.
117 *Indonesian Observer*, 1998.
118 Waldman, 1998.
119 *Jakarta Post,* 2000a.
120 Project Underground, 2000c.
121 Marshall, 2000.
122 Tarabay, 2000.
123 Project Underground, 2000c.
124 Knight, 2000.
125 Allen, 2000, p. 12.
126 Zagorin, 1999, p. 62.
127 Madani and Solomon, 2000.
128 Kompas, 2000.
129 Suara Pembaruan, 2000.

130 Ondawame, 2000, p. 35.

131 Kilvert, 2000.

132 Chauvel, 2000

133 Dow Jones Newswires, 2000.

134 *Engineering and Mining Journal,* 2000, p. ww8.

135 McKinney et. al., 2000.

136 In May 2001, the U.S. Congress approved the Foreign Relations Authorization Act which calls on the U.S. government to press for the withdrawal of Indonesian troops from West Papua and Aceh. It also urges the U.S. State Department to press the Government of Indonesia to allow independent human rights and environmental monitors access to Freeport's facilities in West Papua and Exxon Mobil's facilities in Aceh. See Indonesia Human Rights Network, 2001.

137 Alden and Buchan, 2000.

138 *Christian Science Monitor,* 2000.

139 Ibid.

140 Press, 1997.

141 Washburn, 1997, p. 26.

142 Jardine, 1995, p. 10.

143 *New York Times,* 2000b.

CHAPTER 4

A Multiracial Anti-Mining Movement

One of the critical differences between the situation of native peoples in post-colonial nation-states like Indonesia and advanced capitalist countries like the United States, Canada and Australia is the existence of legal structures that can and have been used by native peoples to assert tribal sovereignty over land and natural resources and to oppose destructive mining projects. For the past 25 years, one of the smallest and poorest Native nations in the United States has successfully prevented some of the most powerful multinational mining corporations in the world from constructing a large mine next to its tiny, 1,800-acre reservation at the headwaters of the Wolf River in northeastern Wisconsin. The determination of the Sokaogon Chippewa, one of the six bands of the Lake Superior Chippewa Nation, to resist unwanted mining has developed into a multiracial anti-mining movement that "can provide a model not only to environmental alliances, but to grassroots education and organizing campaigns that operate without large staffs and funding proposals," showing how "imagination and community support can outfox the world's largest multinational corporations."[1]

Mole Lake: Where the Food Grows on the Water

On March 29, 1995, the U.S. Army Corps of Engineers held a public hearing on the Mole Lake Sokaogon Chippewa Reservation to take comments on Exxon/Rio Algom's proposed underground zinc-copper sulfide mine next to the reservation near Crandon, Wisconsin. Tribal members testified about the historical origins of their present reservation and the significance of the wild rice that they harvest from Rice Lake on the reservation.

Fred Ackley, a tribal judge, recalled the history of the creation of the reservation at the hearing:

> The government asked our chief why he wanted this reservation in this spot. Our chief walked over and gave him a handful of wild rice, and he said, "This is the food of Indian people. This is why I want my reservation here on this lake. There are six or seven other lakes in this area where my people have been harvesting food for a long time." So he wanted his reservation right here on this lake for the wild rice.
>
> Through the hard times that we've had to live as Indian people here in Mole Lake, we realized that money and everything else that the white people had didn't count. Because what the Great Spirit gave us was the food for our people—subsistence to go on another year, to have another offspring, to bury another elder. Also, he taught us how to pray for that every year. We've been doing that every year here in Mole Lake. We still pray for everything we get. We do it our way.

Charles Ackley, the son of Chief Willard Ackley, still harvests and sells wild rice. He testified about the threat to wild rice from the proposed mine:

> East of us here, where this mine is supposed to take place, is all spring-fed. And if they start fooling around underground, there are going to be a lot of lakes going dry east of us here. And suppose that Exxon taps into our underground water spring? What is going to happen to our water situation in our community? And do we all want to risk that to have a mining company come into our area and do that?

Rose Van Zile, a grandmother and veteran wild rice harvester, also spoke against the proposed mine:

> Right now I'm saying I don't want this mine here. I don't want it to be part of my everyday life. When I grow old, I'd like to have my grandchildren here to comfort them, the way my grandpar-

ents comforted me and gave me the enjoyment of going to school, coming home, having my dinner and relaxing and knowing that I have a safe place to come home to every night. And when I rest, I don't have to worry about the water or the wild rice.

I went out there for 23 years of my life, and I picked rice. I still do today. And yes, I'm mad. I'm damned mad at this mining. To me, no mining in Mole Lake. That's what I say. That's what my grandson is going to say. That's what my children are going to say. No mining in Mole Lake. Thank you very much.

From Spearfishing Conflict to Mining Conflict

Indian tribes in the northern portions of Wisconsin, Minnesota and Michigan are seriously threatened by sulfide mining operations in ways that are difficult for non-Indians to perceive. For Indian people, natural resource harvest is more than a means to provide food. It is a cultural activity that renews both the Indian person and the resource that is harvested.[2]

Recent court rulings have upheld the reserved rights of the Lake Superior Chippewa Nation to hunt, fish and gather on public lands ceded to the U.S. government in 19th-century treaties.[3] For the past decade, Chippewa spearfishers have had to defend those treaty rights against northern Wisconsin residents who have accused the Chippewa of depleting the fish populations. After disproving the racially motivated charges and peacefully resisting mob violence, the Chippewa now face the prospect of toxic contamination of their fish, deer and wild rice resources as a result of large-scale mining projects in the Chippewa's ceded treaty lands. The focal point of recent Chippewa resistance to environmental degradation to their traditions is Exxon's attempt to construct a large underground mine next to the Mole Lake reservation.

In 1975, Texas-based Exxon Minerals discovered one of the ten largest zinc-copper sulfide deposits in North America adjacent to the reservation near Crandon, Wisconsin. Situated at the headwaters of the Wolf River in Forest County, the proposed mine is the largest of a series of metallic sulfide deposits planned for development in northern Wisconsin. The Crandon/Mole Lake mine

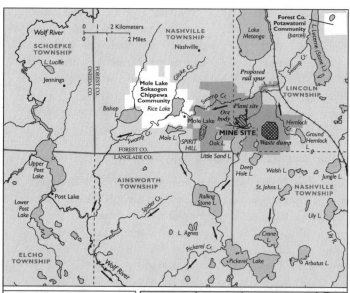

The Proposed
Crandon Mine
in Wisconsin

☐ Reservation and other tribally owned lands

▨ Company-owned mine site property

⚒ Proposed plant site complex

◉ Proposed Tailings Management Area

➤ Ore body

→ Direction of water flow from mine site

— County boundary

--- Township boundary

⊢⊣ Railroad

⊢⊣ Proposed rail spur

©Map by Zoltán Grossman, mtn@igc.org
Mine area GIS linework supplied by John Coleman, Great Lakes Indian Fish & Wildlife Commission (GLIFWC). Proposed mine (fee, purchase option, lease, easement, or buffer zone) from 1994 *Notice of Intent* fig 2-3, and CMC *Land Ownership Map*, May 1995. Mole Lake lands from 1995 plat. More information: www.treatyland.com

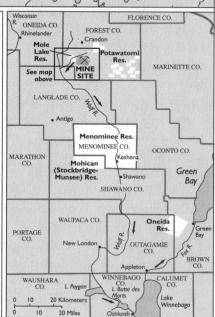

would extract approximately 55 million tons of sulfide ore during the 28-year life of the project.

In 1993, after prolonged opposition by enviromental and Native American groups, Kennecott Copper, a subsidiary of Rio Tinto, began an open pit copper sulfide mine on the Flambeau River outside Ladysmith, Wisconsin. The Flambeau mine is tiny in comparison to the Exxon project. But it represents the "foot in the door" the mining industry has been after since 1968, when Kennecott first discovered the orebody at Ladysmith. "Discovery of the Flambeau deposit," Kennecott geologist Ed May wrote, "has opened the way to the development of a new domestic mining district."[4] In 1982, Exxon Minerals' chief lobbyist James Klauser told the Wisconsin Manufacturers and Commerce Association that the state could host up to ten major metal mines by the year 2000.[5] In 1987, Governor Tommy Thompson appointed Klauser to head up the Wisconsin Department of Administration, a state agency that oversees the mine permitting process.

Exxon's proposed underground shaft mine at Mole Lake would disrupt far more than its surface area of 550 acres. Over its lifetime, the mine would generate an estimated 44 million tons of waste. Half of the projected mine waste is rocky "coarse tailings," which would be put back into the ground as fill for retired mine shafts. The other half is powdery "fine tailings," which would be dumped into a waste pond covering 280 acres at least 90 feet deep. At a size of about 280 football fields, it would be the largest toxic waste dump in Wisconsin history.[6] The water table beneath these ponds is as close as 15 feet down. When metallic sulfide wastes have contact with water and air, the potential result is sulfuric acids and high levels of poisonous heavy metals like mercury, lead, zinc, arsenic, copper and cadmium.

After a decade of facing strong local opposition, Exxon withdrew from the project in 1986, citing depressed metal prices.[7] Exxon then returned in September 1993 to announce its intention to mine with a new partner—Canada-based Rio Algom—in their new "Crandon Mining Co." In its report on the Exxon/Rio Algom joint venture, *The Northern Miner* noted that "the only objections raised at the Crandon press conference…came from native Americans who expressed concern over archaeological aspects of the site. No objec-

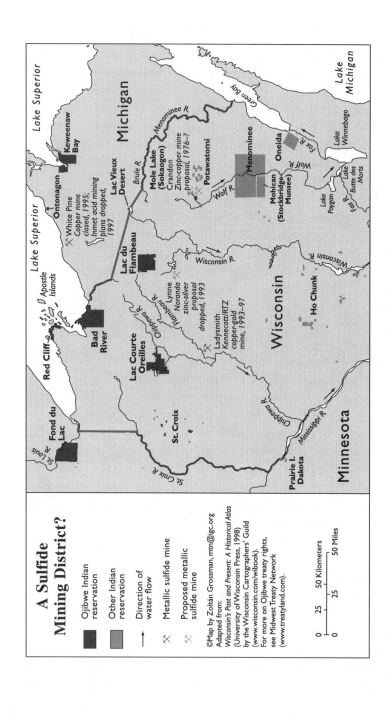

A Sulfide Mining District?

Ojibwe Indian reservation

Other Indian reservation

Direction of water flow

Metallic sulfide mine

Proposed metallic sulfide mine

©Map by Zoltán Grossman, mtn@igc.org
Adapted from:
Wisconsin's Past and Present: A Historical Atlas
(University of Wisconsin Press, 1998)
by the Wisconsin Cartographers' Guild
(www.wisconsin.com/wibook).
For more on Ojibwe treaty rights,
see Midwest Treaty Network
(www.treatyland.com).

0   25   50 Kilometers

0   25   50 Miles

Lake Superior

Keweenaw Bay

Ontonagon

White Pine Copper mine closed, 1995; Inmet acid mining plans dropped, 1997

Michigan

Lac Vieux Desert

Menominee R.

Brule R.

Mole Lake (Sokaogon)
Crandon
Zinc-copper mine proposal, 1976–?

Potawatomi

Menominee

Oneida

Mohican (Stockbridge-Munsee)

Wolf R.

Fox R.

Green Bay

Lake Winnebago

Lake Butte des Morts

Lake Poygan

Fox R.

Lake Michigan

Lac du Flambeau

Chippewa R.

Wisconsin R.

Flambeau R.

Lynne Noranda zinc-silver proposal, 1993

Ladysmith Kennecott/RTZ copper-gold mine, 1993–97

Lake Superior

Apostle Islands

Red Cliff

Bad River

Lac Courte Oreilles

St. Croix R.

Fond du Lac

St. Louis R.

St. Croix

Chippewa R.

Wisconsin

Wisconsin R.

Ho Chunk

Prairie I. Dakota

Mississippi R.

Minnesota

tions were heard from environmental groups."[8] The paper failed to mention that no environmental groups were present to voice their opposition. However, the paper's characterization of the objections from Native Americans as insignificant, compared to the possible objections from non-native environmental groups, is all too typical of the way native cultures have been ignored by the dominant society.

Mining vs. Native Subsistence

> The threat of annihilation has been hanging over this community since 1975. The mental stress and mental anguish are unbearable at times.[9]
>
> —Wayne LaBine, Sokaogon Chippewa tribal planner

The planned mine lies on territory sold by the Chippewa Nation to the United States in 1842, and directly on a 12-square mile tract of land promised to the Mole Lake Sokaogon Chippewa in 1855.[10] Treaties guaranteed Chippewa access to wild rice, fish and some wild game on ceded lands. The Mole Lake Reservation (formed in 1939) is a prime harvester of wild rice in Wisconsin. The rice, called *manomim,* or "gift from the creator," is an essential part of the Chippewa diet, an important cash crop and a sacred part of the band's religious rituals.[11] The Wisconsin Department of Natural Resources (DNR) emphasized the centrality of wild rice to Chippewa culture in their analysis of Exxon's proposed mine: "Rice Lake and the bounty of the lake's harvest lie at the heart of their identity as a people.... The rice and the lake are the major links between themselves, Mother Earth, their ancestors and future generations."[12]

Any contamination or drawdown of water would threaten the survival of both fish and wild rice. The Chippewa were not reassured when Exxon's biologist mistook their wild rice for a "bunch of lake weeds." Later, Exxon maintained that any pollutants from the mine would travel along the rim of Rice Lake and cause no harm to the delicate ecology of wild rice. The tribe asked the U.S. Geological Survey to perform a dye test to determine the path of potential pollutants. The results showed the dye dispersing over the entire lake. Exxon's own environmental impact report blandly mentioned that "the means of subsistence on the reservation" may be "rendered less than effective."[13]

Mole Lake tribal chairman Arlyn Ackley responded to Exxon's announcement to resume the mine permit process by recalling Exxon's previous attempt to develop the orebody and to the history of the industry with native peoples elsewhere:

> Exxon claimed it would be an "environmentally safe" mine in the 1970s. They claimed it wouldn't harm our sacred wild rice beds or water resources. We had to spend our own money on tests to prove their project would in fact contaminate our subsistence harvest areas and lower the water level of Rice Lake. Exxon's claims of environmentally safe mining were unfounded.
>
> I think these companies are willing to lie. Their history is one of pollution, destruction and death. Just last month, more than 70 Yanomami Indians were massacred by miners in the Amazon forest. As far as we are concerned, Exxon and Rio Algom are of the same mindset. Let it be known here and now that these companies are prepared to plunder and destroy our people and lands for their insatiable greed. They may be more polite in North America, but they are no less deadly to Native people. [14]

The major environmental threat to the tribe comes from the large piles of mine waste upstream from their wild rice lake. To control leakage into wells and streams, Exxon plans to place a liner under the waste pond. The U.S. Environmental Protection Agency (EPA) admits that tailings ponds are "regulated...loosely" and that leaks from even the best of dumps "will inevitably occur."[15] The U.S. Forest Service says that "there are currently no widely applicable technologies" to prevent acid mine drainage.[16] The mining industry cannot point to a single example of a metallic sulfide mine that has been successfully reclaimed (that is, returned to a natural state). This fact was confirmed by a 1995 Wisconsin DNR report.[17]

Besides the mine waste, the half-mile deep mine shafts would themselves drain groundwater supplies, in much the same way that a syringe draws blood from a patient. The waste water would be constantly pumped out of the shafts, "drawing down" water levels in a four-square mile area. If not adequately regulated, this "dewatering" could lower lakes by several feet, and dry up wells and springs.[18] An

Exxon engineer once pointed to the terrain map of the mine and said that, from the standpoint of the wetlands, the groundwater and the overall topography, "You couldn't find a more difficult place in the world to mine."[19]

The potential threat to the economy and culture of the Mole Lake Chippewa from Exxon's proposed mine must also be evaluated in the context of the cumulative environmental threats facing both Indian and non-Indian communities in the north woods. The Chippewa, along with other Native nations in northern Wisconsin, already suffer a disproportionate environmental risk of illness and other health problems from eating fish, deer and other wildlife contaminated with industrial pollutants like airborne polychlorinated biphenyls (PCBs), mercury and other toxins deposited on land and water. "Fish and game have accumulated these toxic chemicals," according to a 1992 U.S. EPA study, "to levels posing substantial health, ecological and cultural risks to a Native American population that relies heavily on local fish and game for subsistence. As the extent of fish and game contamination is more fully investigated by state and federal authorities, advisories suggesting limited or no consumption of fish and game are being established for a large portion of the Chippewa's traditional hunting and fishing areas."[20]

The Wolf Watershed Educational Project

> We like where we're living. They put us here years and years ago on federal land and now that we're here, they discover something, and they either want to take it from us or move us away from it. We don't want to do this. This is where I belong. This is my home. This is where my roots are, and this is where I'm gonna stay.[21]
>
> —Myra Tuckwab, Mole Lake Chippewa tribal member

If Exxon could have limited the conflict over the mine to a contest between itself and the Chippewa, the construction of the mine would be a foregone conclusion. Multinational mining companies have a long record of overwhelming native peoples whose resources they have sought to control.[22] In each case, the corporation has sought to reduce its political and financial risks by limiting the arena of conflict so that the victims are completely exposed to the reach of the corporation, but only one tentacle of the corporation's world-wide organization is exposed to the opposition.[23]

The nature of the proposed mine, however, posed a number of environmental and social threats that were of major concern to non-Native residents, environmental groups, sportfishing groups, and other Native nations. The nearby Menominee, Potawatomi and Stockbridge-Munsee Nations would also be severely affected by the mine pollution and the social upheaval brought by new outsiders. With Mole Lake, they formed the Nii Win Intertribal Council (Nii Win is Ojibwe for "four"). Unlike the last Exxon battle, Native Americans have considerably more revenues available from casino proceeds that can be used to fight Exxon's current proposal. Nii Win immediately began hiring lawyers and technical experts to challenge Exxon/Rio Algom's mine permit application. They also purchased a Nii Win house on a seven-acre parcel, across the road from the Crandon mine site, to monitor all activities at the site. The Oneida Nation, which is downstream from the mine near Green Bay, also joined the opposition. In the distant and recent past, these Native nations have survived relocation, termination and assimilation, against overwhelming odds. They now see the mine as one more threat to their cultures and their future generations.

All five Native nations are working in alliance with environmental and sportfishing groups within a campaign called the Wolf Watershed Educational Project, a campaign of the Midwest Treaty Network (MTN) in Madison, Wisconsin. The Wisconsin conflict over treaty spearfishing pitted Chippewas against some white fishermen from 1984 until the anti-Indian protests ended in 1992.[24] Mining companies had perhaps felt that sportfishing groups would never join hands with the tribes, yet some slowly realized that if metallic sulfide mines were allowed to contaminate rivers with sulfuric acid, there might not be edible fish left to argue about. Trout Unlimited's Wolf River chapter says that "the mine as proposed would be a threat to the Wolf River as a trout stream."[25]

Opening Up the Mine Permit Process

> Our reservation is directly adjacent to this mine project. The mine water will flow through it. How can the DNR possibly discuss so-

cioeconomic impacts without even notifying our tribe of this meeting? Our people stand to lose our very existence. Our wild rice beds will be devastated. Our cultural and spiritual traditions will be seriously damaged—or destroyed. Yet the DNR has the arrogance to assume we don't need to be invited to the table.[26]

—Arlyn Ackley, Sokaogon Chippewa Tribal Chairman

One of the characteristics of environmental racism, besides the disproportionate impact racial minorities experience from environmental hazards, is the exclusion of racial minorities from participation in the decision-making process. One of the objectives of mining opponents is to provide statewide press advisories of any activity by the Wisconsin DNR or the Crandon Mining Company (CMC) relating to the mine permitting process.

In January 1994, the DNR had planned a series of meetings over three days with CMC officials and consultants to determine the scope of the social and environmental studies that would be part of the company's mine permit application. Although the DNR did not notify any of the affected Indian and non-Indian communities, word leaked out, and the Watershed Alliance to End Environmental Racism (WATER), a Wisconsin grassroots environmental group, issued a statewide press advisory that was picked up over the wire services. On the morning of the first meeting, the headline in the state's largest morning newspaper, *The Milwaukee Sentinel*, was, "Indian leaders blast DNR over meetings on mining project."

The DNR's mine project coordinator, Bill Tans, said Chippewa leaders were not invited because the meetings were not set up for public comment. "These are strictly preliminary meetings, and everything can change," he said.[27] Tans explained that the tribes would have an opportunity to comment at the time of CMC's publication of a Notice of Intent and a scope of study for its mine permit application in April 1994. However, from the perspective of the tribes, this effectively excluded them from determining the agenda for the proposed studies related to the mine permit. It also contributes to a "psychology of inevitability" about the mine because all the planning would be done behind closed doors and presented to the public as an accomplished fact. As a result of the negative publicity generated by this story, the DNR agreed to set up a fax communication system to notify the tribes in advance of any planned meetings with CMC.

Mobilizing the Grassroots Opposition

> The women have been entrusted with the Water and the men with the Fire. These are two things that sustain life. If you take care of them, they will take care of you.[28]
>
> —Eddie Benton-Benai, Three Fires Midewin Society

Even before Exxon/Rio Algom filed its notice of intent to seek mining permits for the Crandon mine, the MTN announced a state-wide emergency rally at the state capitol in Madison to stop the proposed mine. In March 1994, over 400 people from all around the state rallied at the capitol building and listened as Frances Van Zile, an Anishinabekwe (Chippewa woman) spoke about the role of women as the "Keepers of the Water" in her culture:

> This isn't an Indian issue, nor is it a white issue. It's everybody's issue. Everybody has to take care of that water. The women are the ones who are the keepers of that water. I ask all women to stand up and support that and realize that if it wasn't for the water none of us would be here today, because when we first started out in life, we were born in that water in our mother's womb. And I'll bet you everybody here turned on that water today to do something with it. And that's what they're going to pollute. That's what they're going to destroy. I'm not going to have any more wild rice if that water drops down three feet from the mine dewatering. That is important to my way of life—to all Anishinabes' way of life. And they're taking that away—they're going to destroy our way of life.[29]

Following the rally at the capitol, demonstrators marched to the headquarters of the Wisconsin DNR and to the Wisconsin Manufacturers and Commerce Association. The latter is one of the chief lobbying organizations for the mining companies, as well as for the mining equipment manufacturing industry in Milwaukee. By their physical presence, the MTN intended to put corporate and governmental decision-makers on notice that the resistance to this mine project could reach into the centers of corporate and governmental power. Mole Lake Chippewa tribal members Fred Ackley and Frances Van Zile dramatically illustrated this determination to confront corporate decision-makers when they attended Exxon's annual shareholder meeting in Dallas, Texas, the following month.

The Exxon Shareholder Campaign

> We see our shareholder actions as a vehicle to give access to corporate board rooms for communities like Mole Lake.[30]
>
> —Toni Harris, Sinsinawa Dominican Sisters of Wisconsin

In addition to environmental and fishing groups, the WATER campaign also included various church groups that held stock in several mining companies and were willing to raise issues of social and corporate responsibility through shareholder resolutions. Shortly after Exxon announced its intention to seek mining permits at Crandon/Mole Lake, the Sinsinawa Dominican Sisters of Wisconsin, along with six other religious congregations, filed a shareholder resolution on behalf of the Sokaogon Chippewa and the other Native communities affected by Exxon's mining operations. The resolution specifically asked Exxon to provide a report to shareholders on the impact of the proposed mine on indigenous peoples and on any sacred sites within indigenous communities. The resolution also called upon Exxon to disclose "the nature of and reason[s] for any public opposition to our Company's mining operations wherever they may occur."[31]

As required by law, Exxon immediately informed the Securities and Exchange Commission, which has regulatory authority over shareholder resolutions, that it intended to omit the Sinsinawa resolution from its 1994 proxy statement. The company argued that the resolution was moot because "extensive studies covering the impact on the environment and indigenous people and all other material aspects of the project were prepared by both Exxon and the Wisconsin Department of Natural Resources" before Exxon suspended the project in 1986.[32]

Sister Toni Harris responded that the studies Exxon referred to did not address the specific questions raised in their resolution.

"Most significantly," said Harris, "the 446-page Environmental Impact Statement published in November 1986 was criticized as inadequate by the U.S. Department of the Interior and the Environmental Protection Agency."[33] In its letter to the Wisconsin DNR, in reponse to the environmental impact statement for the Crandon project, the Interior Department said it did not

> believe there is sufficient consideration of potential long-term impacts associated with the proposed mine development, or of contingency plans to assure that adequate environmental protection will be provided. We also feel that special attention should be paid to the effect of long-term discharge to the Wolf River, and to the water resources of the Mole Lake Indian Reservation.[34]

The SEC ruled that the Sinsinawa resolution was not "moot" and that Exxon could not exclude the resolution from stockholder consideration.

With the SEC victory in hand, the Chippewa were able to challenge Exxon on its home turf. Fred Ackley and Frances Van Zile spoke to the resolution and explained to the shareholders that the very existence of their culture was at stake in this proposed mining investment. The resolution received 6% of the vote, or 49 million shares. Most shareholder resolutions of this type receive less than 3% of the vote. While the resolution was defeated, the Chippewa won enough votes to reintroduce the resolution at the 1995 shareholders' meeting.

The Wolf River: Ecology and Economics

> Crandon Mining Co.'s proposed construction and operation of a hard-rock metallic sulfide mine at the headwaters of the Wolf River seriously threatens this magnificent river. Water quality and tremendous ecological diversity [are] imperiled, including bald eagle, wild rice, lake sturgeon and trout habitat. The Wolf River is the lifeline of the Menominee people, and central to our existence. We will let no harm come to the river.[35]

> —John Teller, Menominee Tribal Chairman.

"The environment comes first," says Jerry D. Goodrich, president of the Crandon Mining Company. "If we can't protect the Wolf, there'll be no Crandon mine."[36] Opponents of Exxon's proposed mine won't argue with Goodrich on this point. The Wolf River is at the center of the northeastern Wisconsin tourist economy and the meeting ground between Indians and sportfishers who have a history of bitter disagreement over Chippewa spearfishing.[37] Despite this conflict, Indians and sportfishermen share a "common ground" in their defense of the Wolf River, which both groups consider "sacred."[38]

The Wolf River is the state's largest whitewater trout stream, supporting brown, brook and rainbow trout fisheries. Over 50,000 tourists are attracted to the area every year to enjoy trout fishing, whitewater rafting, and canoeing.[39] The lower half of the river is designated a National Wild and Scenic River.

The Wolf River is also sacred ground to the Menominee Tribe which has occupied the Wolf River area for 8,000 years.[40] The name "Menominee" means "wild rice people." Their reservation, encompassing nearly 235,000 acres, features some of the finest managed forestland within the Great Lakes Basin. It is the Tribe's philosophy that actions that affect its natural resources must be judged according to their potential effect on the seventh future generation.

During Exxon's first attempt to develop the Crandon/Mole Lake deposit, the Wolf River became a rallying point for both environmental and tribal opposition. The Menominee Indian Nation strongly opposed the mine, partly because the Wolf River runs through their reservation. Exxon's mine proposal called for dumping over 2,000 gallons of mine waste water per minute into the trout-rich streams that drain into the Wolf River. A biological consultant hired by Trout Unlimited and other environmental groups, reviewed Exxon's proposal and concluded that "the discharge of waste water from the Crandon Project to Swamp Creek could result in the bioaccumulation of heavy metals in aquatic organisms and changes in the natural species composition of the area."[41]

By the time the DNR held public hearings on the draft environmental impact statement in June 1986, over 10,000 signatures had been collected on petitions asking the governor, the legislature and the DNR to oppose any dumping into the Wolf River. The Langlade County board had also passed a similar resolution. The mobilization of public sentiment about preserving the pristine quality of the Wolf River became a major turning point in the first Exxon battle because the widely perceived economic threat to the Wolf River tourism industry outweighed any potential economic benefits from the mine project.

Shortly after Exxon announced it would once again seek permits for the mine, the Wolf River Territory Association, a group of businesspeople promoting the area for tourism, passed a resolution against the mine. Herb Buettner, owner of the Wild Wolf Inn and president of the Wolf River chapter of Trout Unlimited, warned that "if the mine were to go in, it would wipe out the Wolf River trout stream and create a pile of tailings that in 50 years would be a Superfund [hazardous waste] site."[42]

Crandon Mining president Goodrich's concern for preserving the pristine quality of the Wolf River has not reassured those who are familiar with Exxon's strong opposition to DNR's proposed classification of the upper Wolf River as an "Outstanding Resource Water" (ORW) under the provisions of the federal Clean Water Act. If this status were granted, any water discharged into the Wolf would have to be as clean or cleaner than the water already in the river. The first indication that Exxon might revive its Crandon project came in May 1988, when James D. Patton, Exxon Minerals' manager of regulatory affairs, wrote to Wisconsin DNR Secretary Carroll Besadny warning that DNR's proposed classification of the Wolf River "could create a significant potential roadblock to any future resumption of the Crandon project."[43] Exxon's intense lobbying against the designation was counteracted by the combined forces of the Menominee Tribe and the Wolf River Watershed Alliance. The Wolf River received ORW status in November 1988.

Besides Exxon's opposition to ORW classification for the Wolf River, the company's record with the 1989 Exxon Valdez oil spill raised additional doubts about the company's ability to manage a high-risk mining venture in the ecologically sensitive Wolf River watershed. Adding to doubts about Exxon's environmental record is the fact that Crandon Mining's first public relations officer, J. Wiley

Bragg, handled public relations for Exxon in Alaska after the Exxon-Valdez spill.[44]

Prior to the first public hearing on Exxon's mine permit application, the WATER campaign ran a series of local newspaper ads that asked, "Will the Wolf River Be Exxon's Valdez? What If It Happened Here?" The ads emphasized that Wisconsin has abundant clean waters but that the history of metallic sulfide mining is one of poisoned rivers, lakes and groundwaters. The ads urged citizens to attend the DNR public hearing and state their concerns about the proposed mine. Over 300 people, including Native Americans, local property owners, fishers, small-business owners and environmentalists, packed into the Nashville Wisconsin Town Hall in April 1994 to express their concerns. Because of the large number of people who wanted to testify, the DNR stayed past midnight and still was not able to accommodate all those who wanted to speak. Of the 300 people who attended the hearing, only a handful were in favor of the project. Two thirds of the people who testified mentioned their concern about the Wolf River, local lakes, streams or groundwater.

Some mine opponents accused the DNR of manipulating the order in which testimony was heard and preventing several knowledgeable anti-mining citizens from speaking until late in the evening, when the media and the majority of the audience had left. Among those who had registered early in the evening but were not called until five hours after testimony had begun was Wisconsin Public Intervenor Laura Sutherland. The Public Intervenor is an office in the Wisconsin Department of Justice empowered to protect public rights in the natural resources of the state. Despite Exxon's objections, the Citizens Advisory Committee, which oversees the Public Intervenor, unanimously directed the Public Intervenor to review Exxon's mine proposal. One of Sutherland's principal concerns in the permitting process was the fact that "the DNR has never before permitted *any* discharge into ORW waters and this mine proposal, therefore, presents the possibility of a dangerous precedent."[45]

Although Sutherland's testimony was not covered in the press reports immediately after the meeting, the *Milwaukee Journal* featured her written testimony in a front page story the next week, followed by a strong editorial that warned that "the loss of recreation and tourism from a degraded environment could end up outweighing any economic gains from the mine."[46]

Prior to the DNR meeting, Crandon Mining president Jerry Goodrich sent out a letter to local residents warning that "certain groups opposed to mining and other industry development are planning to bus people in from Green Bay, Madison, Milwaukee and other distant locations to pack the hearing with opponents of the Crandon Project (or, at least, people who will say they are opponents of the project)."[47] It was the classic "outside agitator" ploy. It backfired when the WATER campaign took out ads in the local newspapers the following week that asked: "Can We Trust Exxon To Tell The Truth?" The ad pointed out that

> there were *no* busloads of opponents, there were never any planned. In fact, 68% of those who gave oral statements were from Forest County and the area immediately downriver of the project. The only people that came from "distant locations" were the employees of Exxon temporarily living near Crandon. Mr. Goodrich, where do you get your misinformation?[48]

In April, 1995, the national conservation group American Rivers named the Wolf River on its list of the nation's 20 most threatened rivers because of the possibility of pollution from Exxon/Rio Algom's proposed mine. The Menominee, along with the River Alliance of Wisconsin and the Mining Impact Coalition of Wisconsin, provided the documentation on the threat from mine pollution. The day after the Wolf's designation as a threatened river, Exxon announced it was abandoning its plans to dump treated waste water from the mine into the Wolf River. Instead, the company would build a 40-mile pipeline and divert the waste water into the Wisconsin River near Rhinelander, Wisconsin.

While the timing of Exxon's announcement may have been calculated to divert attention from the American Rivers announcement and the continuing controversy over mine waste discharges to the Wolf River, mine opponents were quick to point out that the new plan threatens pollution of both the Wolf and Wisconsin Rivers. David Blouin, a spokesperson for the Mining Impact Coalition of Wisconsin, said the threat to the Wolf would remain because tailings from the mine would still be stored at the headwaters of the Wolf. Also, since the Wisconsin River is not as clean as the Wolf, the company would not have to spend as much on treating the discharge. In addition, the plan could actually increase groundwater depletion in the area of the mine because of the amount of water necessary to pump the wastes to Rhinelander.[49] Whatever the motivation for the change of plans, it was a retreat from Exxon's previously stated position that they could meet the stringent requirements for discharge into a water body rated as an Outstanding Resource Water.

In all of these activities, Midwest Treaty Network (MTN), WATER and other mining opponents developed a multifaceted counterstrategy to Exxon's ecologically and culturally destructive mine plans. Through intertribal organization, alliance building with environmental and sportfishing groups, mass demonstrations, shareholder resolutions and mass media publicity, the Mole Lake Chippewa hope to increase the political and financial risks of the project for Exxon and Rio Algom. This was the reason why Mole Lake and the Nii Win Intertribal Council invited the Indigenous Environmental Network (IEN) to hold its fifth annual "Protecting Mother Earth Conference" on the Mole Lake Reservation in June 1994, in conjunction with a regional gathering coordinated by MTN.

International Networking

> There'll be decades of fallout regardless of who wins this battle. This is one of the great events. We want to put Mole Lake and Exxon on the map.[50]

—Walter Bresette, Red Cliff band of Lake Superior Chippewa.

Previous IEN conferences brought together community-based indigenous activists from throughout the Americas and the Pacific Islands to work together to protect indigenous lands from contamination and exploitation. IEN's previous efforts have helped grassroots activists defeat a 5,000-acre landfill on the Rosebud Lakota Reservation in South Dakota, and a proposed incinerator and an asbestos landfill on Diné (Navajo) land in Arizona.[51]

Approximately 1,000 people gathered on the Mole Lake Reservation during the five-day conference. "This is to put Exxon and

[Wisconsin] Governor Tommy Thompson on notice that we can bring people up here to stop the mine," said Bill Koenen, an IEN National Council member and a Mole Lake band member.[52] On the last day of the conference, over 300 Native and non-Native people participated in a "spirit walk" to the proposed mine site, where they conducted a spiritual ceremony while tresspassing on Exxon's property. Exxon called the Crandon police, but no arrests were made. The police were reluctant to interrupt the ceremony.

The Mole Lake gathering also featured a Wisconsin Review Commission to review the track records of Exxon and Rio Algom around the world. The commission included groups representing farmers, churches, workers, civil rights activists, women, small businesses, tribal governments and recreational groups. A similar commission was assembled in the 1970s by the Black Hills Alliance to investigate the track records of uranium mining companies that wanted to mine in the sacred Black Hills of the Lakota (Sioux).

The panel, chaired by Wisconsin Secretary of State Douglas LaFollette, heard testimony from Native people who came from Alaska, Colombia, Ontario and New Mexico. Testimony focused on people who have been directly affected by Exxon's mining and oil drilling activities and its chemical and oil leaks.

Nearly all of the testimony before the commission was delivered by Native peoples from North and South America, which reflects the fact that a disproportionate amount of resource extraction occurs on Native lands. Native Eyak fisher Dune Lankard explained how the Exxon Valdez spill damaged the resource-based cultures of local Native peoples on Prince William Sound:

> I grew up fishing since I was five years old on the ocean. I thought I had the most incredible way of life in the world, and I never believed once that anyone could ever kill the ocean. So when it happened, I was in shock. They leave you with the social impacts—the suicide, the alcohol, the drug abuse, the loss of jobs, the loss of a way of life, the loss of language, the loss of subsistence. How do you add all that up?
>
> How do you compensate somebody for taking everything away from you?[53]

After the oil spill, Eyak government leaders complained that Exxon simply refused to recognize their Native group. The company took the position that the Eyak were not adversely affected by the oil spill, and consequently, refused to provide food and services which were provided for Natives elsewhere.[54] Exxon was fined $5 billion in punitive damages for economic losses from the spill in 1995. The company has been fighting to have the damages award overturned ever since. Attorneys involved say the case could drag on for a few more years.[55]

Some of the most damning testimony came from Armando Valbuena Gouriyu, a Wayuu Indian from the Guajira peninsula, on the northern tip of Colombia, where Exxon operates the El Cerrejon open pit coal mine in a joint venture with the Colombian government. It is the largest coal mine in this hemisphere. Valbuena worked at the huge coal mine from 1983 until Exxon fired him for his union organizing activities in 1988. The construction of the mine had a devastating effect on the lives of approximately 90 Wayuu *apushis* (matrilineal kinship groupings) who saw their houses, corrals, cleared ground and cemeteries flattened for the construction of a road from El Cerrejon to the new port of Puerto Bolivar, with no respect for indigenous rights.[56] The excavation of the open pit has also caused the adjoining rivers and streams to dry up, along with people's drinking wells. The area affected is roughly 94,000 acres.[57] Colombian army troops and armored tanks were called in three times to break miners' strikes.[58]

In 1992, Survival International included Exxon on its list of the top ten companies who were doing serious damage to tribal peoples' land in the Americas.[59] The vice-president of the El Cerrejon mine, Jerry Goodrich, is the past president of Crandon Mining. While Goodrich was vice-president at El Cerrejon, more than 30 workers died during work at the mine.[60] Valbuena testified that Goodrich "promised us jobs and prosperity and instead worked to destroy our traditional ways and forced us from our land. This must not happen again…. To allow this mine is to disappear from the earth."[61]

The Wisconsin Review Commission released its report on the track records of Exxon and Rio Algom on March 24, 1995—the sixth anniversary of the Exxon Valdez oil spill. In releasing the report, Secretary of State LaFollette urged the state legislature to approve the mining "bad actor" legislation, which would require the state to consider a company's past performance before approving state mine permits. "Past violations," LaFollette said, "are taken into account for everything from driver's licenses to gaming licenses, but not permits for potentially harmful mining developments."[62] The commission presented its citizens' hearing panel as a model for public participation in the absence of governmental action, as well as for multinational citizens' tracking of multinational corporations.

The Federal Environmental Review Process

> Even if the mining company makes substantial financial commit-
> ments for restoration of the site, there will more than likely be
> damages not provided for with financial assurances. The neigh-
> bors, particularly the tribes, will receive a relatively meager pro-
> portion of the short-term economic benefit, but by virtue of the
> location of their lands, will inherit the brunt of the environmental
> problems and economic bust cycle. It seems unfair that a large
> and powerful, but temporarily involved, interested party can reap
> the benefits, but leave the majority of the costs to less powerful
> interests who cannot reasonably move from the area to escape
> long-term costs.[63]
>
> —Janet Smith, U.S. Department of the Interior,
> Fish and Wildlife Service, Green Bay, WI

The construction of the proposed Crandon mine would involve the filling of approximately 30 acres of wetlands. Under the provisions of the Clean Water Act, the U.S. Army Corps of Engineers (COE) must review such projects. In November 1994, the Fish and Wildlife Service of the U.S. Interior Department (DOI) expressed serious reservations about the project:

> The Department is particularly concerned about the proposed
> permit action because we believe that it could potentially result in
> a diminishment of Indian interests in exchange for benefits for
> the general public. The courts have held that federal agencies can-
> not subordinate Indian interests to other public purposes except
> when specifically authorized by Congress to do so.[64]

The DOI recommended that the affected tribes play a greater role in identifying environmental impacts and "impacts to Indian trust resources" as defined in the treaties with the federal government. Furthermore, the DOI recommended that the COE be the sole lead agency for the federal environmental impact statement (EIS) "so that the impacts to Indian trust resources can be appropriately assessed in a purely federal forum. The state does not have the authority to assess impacts to Indian trust lands, and thus should have no role in doing so."[65] The COE's decision to conduct its own EIS has provided mine opponents with two separate opportunities to argue their case.

The public hearings held by the COE on the Crandon project brought out overwhelming public opposition in the capital city of Madison, in Crandon itself and on the Mole Lake reservation. At the hearing on the reservation, tribal members expressed their determination to stop Exxon's proposed mine. Bill Koenen, a tribal member and environmental specialist, testified as his three sons stood beside him. "Our children will be right behind us to help us defend our sacred land and wild rice beds." And Robert Van Zile, a traditional pipe carrier, reflected the views of many who spoke when he said, "If I have to defend this land with my life, I will."[66]

While Exxon has claimed that its Crandon mine studies are "one of the most thorough environmental studies in state history,"[67] the COE has determined that the groundwater models used by Exxon to predict water drawdown around the mine are scientifically inadequate, and has proposed additional studies by an independent consultant with no ties to Exxon.[68]

Aside from the scientific adequacy of Exxon's studies, there was the issue of whether the studies fully disclosed all the impacts of the project. Until the fall of 1999, Exxon/Rio Algom had not disclosed where the electrical power necessary to run the mine and mill was coming from. As soon as that information was disclosed, the anti-mining movement added another important link to the chain of resistance.

Mines, Dams and Powerlines

> Our people have decided that they will no longer be beaten up in
> silence. We will tell our story and assert our rights—in churches,
> universities, human-rights forums, energy regulatory agencies
> and financial markets in Canada and elsewhere. That includes
> places where Manitoba Hydro sells electricity and bonds. If this
> causes U.S. electricity consumers to decline to buy power that is
> generated through the sacrifice of Cree lives and an entire envi-
> ronment, so be it. We know that the Americans have other energy
> options that are genuinely renewable, sustainable, equitable and
> consistent with morality.[69]

> —John Miswagon, Chief of Pimicikamak Cree Nation
> in Cross Lake, Manitoba, Canada

In November 1999, opponents of the proposed Crandon mine
joined forces with opponents to high-voltage transmission lines for
a rally just outside of Crandon. The rally, sponsored by the Wolf Watershed Educational Project, drew public attention to the proposed
construction of a 115-kilovolt (kv) spur line from nearby
Rhinelander to the mine site at Mole Lake. The larger, 345-kv transmission line, from Duluth, Minnesota, to Wausau, Wisconsin,
would use power from a controversial hydroelectric project at Cross
Lake, Manitoba, about 300 miles north of Winnipeg, opposed by the
Pimicikamak Cree Nation. Members of Save Our Unique Lands,
whose northern Wisconsin membership is about 10,000, spoke
about their concerns for the land that would be affected by the
250-mile high-voltage corridor that could cross the Lac Courte
Oreilles (LCO) Chippewa reservation near Hayward, as well as important wetlands, rivers and forests in central and northwestern
Wisconsin. From start to finish, the whole complex of mines, dams
and powerlines is based upon the exploitation of Native peoples'
lands and resources in Wisconsin and Manitoba. If the project were
allowed to proceed, Manitoba Hydro, a state corporation owned by
the province of Manitoba, would further destroy the environment
and economy of the Cree to provide cheap electrical power that
would allow a Canadian mining company (Rio Algom) to extract
zinc and copper that would contaminate the wild rice beds of the
Mole Lake Chippewa and the Wolf River watershed.

Manitoba Power Generating Dams

NUNAVUT

Hudson Bay

MANITOBA

Churchill

Churchill R.

York Factory

Laurie River I and II

South Bay Channel

Missi Falls Control

Leaf Rapids

Long Spruce

Nelson R.

Kettle

Limestone

South Indian Lake

Split Lake

Kelsey

Gillam

Ilford

Hays R.

Nelson House

Thompson

Cross Lake

Wabowden

Jenpeg

Ominawain Bypass

Kiskitto Control Dam

Norway House

ONTARIO

Eight Mile Channel

Cross Lake

Lake Winnipeg

Two Mile Channel

Grand Rapids

SASKATCHEWAN

Assiniboine R.

- Community
- Generating station
- River diversion, or Control dam

Winnipeg

UNITED STATES

Manitoba in Canada

ATLANTIC OCEAN

Manitoba

Canada

U.S.A.

In the 1970s, Manitoba Hydro diverted more than 85% of the flow of the Churchill River to the Nelson River. The Cree Indians of the boreal forests and lakes of northern Manitoba lost 3.3 million acres (50,000 square miles) of their traditional lands as a result of flooding or because the land became inaccessible. The Cree were never informed of Manitoba Hydro's plans, there were no public hearings and the utility did not ask for Cree consent, despite the fact that the flooded lands had been set aside as Reserve lands. The flooded lands also encompassed traditional Cree hunting, fishing and trapping, all inviolable rights guaranteed by treaty and never ceded. Luke Hertlein of Protecting Aboriginal Rights, Lands and the Environment has written that "the violation of the sacred treaty rights can be seen as a direct attack upon the Cree themselves, impacting their means to economically sustain themselves and continue their way of life."[70]

The higher water levels have submerged vegetation, which then decomposes and produces methane, a powerful greenhouse gas, in amounts rivaling that produced by fossil fuels.[71] The decomposition process also produces bacteria that transform naturally occurring mercury in the soil and rocks into toxic methylmercury. The mercury moves up the food chain to the fish and ultimately to the Cree, who depend on the fish for their diet. One out of six people in the impacted Nelson River area suffers from mercury contamination.[72]

According to the Chief of the Manitoba Cree: "The diversion resulted in widespread mercury contamination, erosion and injury to the way of life of the northern Cree. No environmental assessment has ever been done on this project."[73] Because there was no environmental assessment, the Cree do not know how many species have been lost or how many habitats have been destroyed. "We do know that we have lost burial sites, the entire fisheries of whitefish and sturgeon, our ability to travel safely on the waterways and much of our ability to sustain ourselves from the land."[74] Gideon McKay, an elder who lives in the community of Cross Lake along the Nelson River, describes graphically what happened to the land where his family's trapline used to support generations of McKays: "They poured filth over the clean dish that I once had while my kids were eating from there. They took our plate."[75] With the loss of traditional foods, the Crees have become dependent upon store-bought foods that have changed the diet, nutrition and health of the Cree.[76] Unemployment, alcoholism, drug abuse and suicide rates have sky-rocketed.

More than one third of the electricity generated from flooded Cree lands is exported to Minnesota.[77] In the fall of 1999, Manitoba Hydro announced plans to build another dam on the Nelson River and double its exports to the United States. For the Cross Lake Crees, more electricity means more environmental damage. The Cross Lake Crees then decided to enlist the support of environmental and human rights organizations in their fight against Manitoba Hydro. Their principal target is Minneapolis-based Xcel Energy (formerly Northern States Power Company), which buys much of Manitoba Hydro's electricity. Their campaign is focused "to turn Xcel away from Manitoba Hydro's cheap power and force the utility to agree to an acceptable compensation package for the tribe."[78]

The people from Cross Lake have rallied at the offices of Xcel; testified before the Minnesota Public Utilities Commission; sent speakers to schools and universities; and lobbied dozens of environmental, human rights and church groups and tribal organizations in the United States. Minnesota's North Star Chapter of the Sierra Club has gone on record opposing Manitoba Hydro's continued environmental destruction and exploitation of the Cree Nation and has called for Xcel to stop purchasing power from Manitoba Hydro. Minnesota Sierra Club members have met with the Clean Water Action Alliance of Minnesota, the North American Water Office and Minnesotans for an Energy Efficient Economy to put together a public education and advocacy campaign on this issue.[79]

Wisconsin Indian tribes and organizations have also expressed solidarity with the Crees. In September 1999, the Lac Courte Oreilles (LCO) passed a resolution opposing the construction of transmission lines anywhere on their reservation or within the ceded territory of the Lake Superior Chippewa. The 250-mile, 345kv powerline would cross a portion of the LCO reservation near Hayward, Wisconsin, as well as public lands where the Chippewa retain treaty rights. "LCO still suffers from our people's displacement when Northern States Power Company built a dam and reservoir 80

years ago on our traditional territory," said Gaiashkibos (pro-
nounced "gosh-ki-bosh"), chairman of the LCO band of Lake Superior Chippewa. "We refuse to be a party to more destruction of
indigenous peoples, their way of life and our environment."[80]

The Great Lakes Inter-Tribal Council (GLITC), a consortium
of tribes in Wisconsin, unanimously passed a resolution that calls for
increased investments by tribal, local, state and national governments in energy conservation and renewable resources. "We have
affirmed our historic commitment to protecting the lands, waters
and people of Wisconsin," said Tom Maulson, GLITC president.
"We are sending a clear message to our utilities that we oppose the
construction of powerlines that will bring more harm to the Lac
Courte Oreilles Band of Lake Superior Chippewa in Hayward, and
the Pimicikamak Cree Nation in Manitoba."[81] The Great Lakes Indian Fish and Wildlife Commission has also affirmed its opposition
to the powerline on Chippewa ceded territory.

Not only is Xcel's contract to import Manitoba Hydro's electricity destructive to the Crees, but it is unnecessary. At a recent conference on Environmental Justice and Energy Policy in the Upper
Midwest held in Minneapolis, Pat Spears, the President of the Intertribal Council on Utility Policy, emphasized the tremendous wind
resource that exists in the Great Plains:

> The Department of Energy estimates that 75% of the total energy
> needs in this country can be generated through development of
> wind energy. This is with technology that exists today, and it
> works. We can generate wind power on the Plains; we need sup-
> port to use the federal power grid system to move the power to
> the people who want green power in the states around us and in
> the Midwest. We say, Green Power is Red Power! [82]

In 1994, the *New York Times* described the anti-mining movement in Wisconsin as "one of the country's fiercest grassroots environmental face-offs."[83] With the strong grassroots opposition to the
proposed transmission line, the utilities have provided this movement with an opportunity to link the dam issues, transmission line
issues and mining issues into a single powerful movement.

A New Level of Resistance

> Resource extraction plans...proposed for Indigenous lands do not consider the significance of these economic systems, nor their value for the future. A direct consequence is that environmentally destructive programs ensue, many times foreclosing the opportunity to continue the lower scale, intergenerational economic practices that had been underway in the Native community.[84]
>
> —Winona LaDuke, Anishinabe (Chippewa) activist

Mining, by its very nature, constitutes an assault on the physical, social and cultural environment. When this assault occurs in ecologically sensitive areas inhabited by Native peoples who rely on traditional subsistence economies, the results can be disastrous. In the past, this corporate assault on Native cultures has frequently gone unnoticed and unreported. Chippewa resistance to Exxon's proposed mine emerged at a time when Native peoples all around the world were actively opposing large-scale destructive development projects on or adjacent to their lands. Their initial efforts to oppose Exxon were favorably viewed by some of their non-Indian neighbors, and an effective Native-environmental alliance was born. With the emergence of the Watershed Alliance to End Environmental Racism, the Midwest Treaty Network and the Wolf Watershed Educational Project, a new level of political organization and resistance has emerged to challenge the unquestioned assumptions of global industrialization and the inevitable disappearance of Native subsistence cultures. This new level of resistance has made it impossible for the mining industry to conduct business as usual. It has been forced to come up with new ways to separate Native people and rural communities from their resources, as we shall see in the next chapter.

1   Midwest Treaty Network, 1999.
2   Great Lakes Indian Fish & Wildlife Commission, 1996, p. 17.
3   Great Lakes Indian Fish & Wildlife Commission, 1991, pp. 1-2.
4   May and Shilling, 1977, p. 39.
5   Seely, 1982.
6   Sutherland, 1994, p. 2.
7   Gedicks, 1993, p. 76.
8   *Northern Miner*, 1993.
9   La Bine, 1995.
10   Danziger, 1978, p. 153.
11   Vennum, 1988; Gough, 1980.
12   Wisconsin Department of Natural Resources (DNR), 1986, p. 108. The importance of subsistence activity can be seen in the fact that 86% of the Chippewa families rely to some extent on hunting and fishing for food, and over 90% rely on gardening, ricing and picking wild plants. Ibid.
13   Exxon, 1983, p. 316.
14   *Masinaigan*, 1993.
15   Schmidt, 1982.
16   U.S. Forest Service, 1993, p. 3.
17   Wisconsin DNR, 1995.
18   Wisconsin DNR, 1986, p. 131.
19   Van Goethem, 1982.
20   U.S. Environmental Protection Agency, 1992, p. ix.
21   cited in Gedicks, 1993, p. 63.
22   Anthropology Resource Center, 1981; Burger, 1987; Howard, 1988.
23   Nader, 1982, p. 9.
24   Whaley and Bresette, 1993.
25   Trout Unlimited, 1994.
26   Causey, 1994.
27   Ibid.
28   cited in Erickson, 1994, p. 3.
29   Van Zile, 1994.
30   WATER, 1994.
31   Exxon, 1994, p. 16.
32   Ibid.
33   Harris, 1994.
34   Huff, 1986.
35   *Isthmus*, 1995.
36   Geniesse, 1994a.
37   Seppa, 1994.
38   Grossman, 2000, p. 4.
39   Van Goethem, 1986, p. 39.
40   Menominee Nation, 1995, p. 6.
41   Brooks, 1986, p. 10.
42   Seppa, 1994.
43   Patton, 1988, p. 4.
44   Seely, 1994.

45   Sutherland, 1994.
46   Behm, 1994; *Milwaukee Journal*, 1994.
47   Goodrich, 1994.
48   *Forest Republican*, 1994.
49   Seely, 1995a.
50   cited in Geniesse, 1994b.
51   Selcraig, 1994, p. 47.
52   Maller, 1994.
53   Lankard, 1995, p. 11.
54   U.S. Department of the Interior, 1993, p. 207.
55   Cooper, 1999, p. A8.
56   Minewatch, 1994, p. 1.
57   Vukelich, 1994.
58   Americas Watch and United Mine Workers of America, 1990, p. 23.
59   Survival International, 1992.
60   Moody, 1992, p. 367.
61   cited in Donato, 1994.
62   Seely, 1995b.
63   Smith, 1994, p. 3.
64   Ibid., p. 2.
65   Ibid., p. 3.
66   Van Zile, 1995.
67   *Forest Republican*, 1995.
68   U.S. Army Corps of Engineers, 1996, p. 1.
69   Miswagon, 2000a.
70   Hertlein, 1999, p. 125.
71   Kelly, et al., 1997, p. 1334; Rudd, et al., 1993
72   La Duke, 1991, p. 7.
73   Ross, 1991, p. 52.
74   Miswagon, 2000b.
75   Stewart, 1999.
76   Hertlein, 199, p. 126.
77   Miswagon, 1999.
78   Robertson, 2000, p. 25.
79   Ostberg, 1999.
80   *Spooner Advocate*, 2000.
81   Ibid.
82   Spears, 2000.
83   Schneider, 1994.
84   La Duke, 1992, p. 57.

CHAPTER 5

Silencing the Voice of the People

How Mining Companies Subvert Local Opposition

The political struggles over mining projects in Native American communities are about survival—the protection of human health, the culture of a people, and the preservation of the ecosystem. Equally important, as detailed here, they are struggles about democracy, as large corporations seek to exercise their power without effective public participation.

In 1993, the provincial government of British Columbia decided to safeguard a vast northern wilderness from the ravages of mining by designating a 2.5-million acre watershed of the Tatshenshini and Alsek rivers a provincial park. The area is approximately twice the size of the Grand Canyon. The decision effectively halted plans to build the hemisphere's largest open pit copper and gold mine, the $430 million Windy Craggy project. The original proposal called for shipping the ore 150 miles by truck or slurry pipeline to the deepwater port at Haines, Alaska. Among those opposing the project were the Chilkat tribe at Klukwan village near Haines. Tribal leaders feared that any ore spills would drain into the Chilkat River and threaten their main source of food—the salmon fishery.[1]

In 1997, President Clinton announced the cancellation of a huge $650 million gold mine near the border of Yellowstone National Park in Montana. Grassroots environmental groups said that acid mine drainage was inevitable because of the highly acidic ore. Moreover, the permanent storage of toxic mine waste at the proposed New World Mine would forever threaten fish, wildlife and water quality in the area, as well as human health. The cancellation was the culmination of a bitterly contested five-year battle to halt the project led by the Greater Yellowstone Coalition and the Beartooth Alliance.

While grassroots environmental organizing efforts were successful in halting both of these high-profile mining projects, the mining companies did not suffer major defeats. In both cases, the companies were ensured access to other government lands of comparable mineral worth. Nevertheless, the mining industry is not used to the kind of grassroots environmental organizing that stopped the New World and Windy Craggy projects. The permitting of new mines in sensitive areas where local residents place a high value upon a clean environment continues to be a major social problem for the mining industry in most advanced capitalist nations.[2]

The kind of resistance that occurred in Yellowstone and British Columbia is indicative both of the organizing skills of people whose livelihood and culture are threatened, and the failures of corporate strategies in seeking to buy off local communities in secret negotiations with elected officials.

While images of devastated Appalachian landscapes from coal strip-mining became part of the national environmental consciousness in the 1960s, the far more extensive damage from unregulated hard-rock mining of metals like gold, silver, copper and uranium has only quite recently come to be defined as a major environmental health problem. In a 1987 study, the EPA rated problems related to mining waste as second only to global warming and stratospheric ozone depletion in terms of ecological risk. The report concluded "with high certainty" that the release to the environment of mining waste "can result in profound, generally irreversible destruction of ecosystems."[3] In 1989, the U.S. Bureau of Mines reported that such mining has contaminated more than 12,000 miles of rivers and streams and 180,000 acres of lakes and reservoirs in the United States.[4] At least 60 of the 1,381 sites now on the U.S. Superfund hazardous waste cleanup list are former mineral operations.[5] The largest

Superfund site is a former copper and silver mining and smelting area, where pollutants have migrated 130 miles along Montana's Clark Fork River and contaminated a land area one fifth the size of Rhode Island.[6]

Even though the hard-rock mining industry generates about the same amount of hazardous waste as all other industries combined, Congress specifically exempted mining wastes from regulation as hazardous waste in the Resource Conservation and Recovery Act (RCRA) of 1976. Besides escaping regulation as hazardous wastes, for over a decade, the industry hid behind a reporting exemption to the Toxics Release Inventory (TRI) created in 1986 by the Emergency Planning and Community Right to Know Act (EPCRA), which provides citizens with vital information about toxic releases in their communities.

When this loophole was finally closed in 2000, the TRI report revealed what many critics had long suspected: that the hard-rock mining industry releases more toxins than any other industry in the United States.[7] In 1998, for example, Nevada mines released approximately 1.3 billion pounds of toxic pollutants such as mercury, arsenic, lead and cyanide. One Nevada mine reported releasing over 80,000 pounds of mercury, with over 9,000 pounds of mercury released directly into the air. According to EPA staff, this single mine's output is "equivalent to the mercury emissions of 40 average coal fired power plants and is one of the the single largest sources of mercury releases in the nation."[8]

Special exemptions enjoyed by the hard-rock mining industry have allowed it to avoid public scrutiny and the widespread public opposition that has characterized the siting of hazardous waste facilities in the wake of Love Canal and other toxic contamination disasters.[9] However, as the higher-grade mineral deposits are exhausted and new mining ventures exploit lower-grade ores in less accessible and more fragile environments, the conflicts between mineral extraction activities and environmental protection become more visible and more likely to generate grassroots opposition movements.[10] This is nowhere more evident than in the attempt over the last 25 years to transform large portions of northern Wisconsin into a new mining district.

A New Mining District in Northern Wisconsin?

Beginning with the discovery of the Flambeau copper-gold sulfide deposit in 1968, mining companies have been greedily eyeing northern Wisconsin. That relatively modest first 1.9-million ton Flambeau deposit was soon overshadowed by the 55-million ton zinc-copper sulfide deposit discovered by Exxon Minerals in the mid-1970s. By the early 1980s, as many as 15 multinational mining corporations were exploring the state for mineral deposits.

Despite several attempts by powerful mining corporations, only one mine, Kennecott/Rio Tinto's copper-gold mine at Ladysmith (1993-1997), has actually been constructed. Grassroots citizen, tribal, environmental and sportfishing groups have blocked mining projects in Ladysmith in 1976, Crandon in 1986 and Lynne in 1993. Faced with a series of embarrassing defeats, the mining industry, in cooperation with the state, initiated a variety of strategies to overcome grassroots environmental resistance to new mining projects. These strategies have included the following, among others: legislative initiatives to thwart local democratic control, legal challenges to local zoning authority, mass media campaigns and attacks on tribal sovereignty.

In his survey of the global anti-environmental movement, Andrew Rowell has argued that "the intensity of the corporate counterattack against a burgeoning environmental opposition has been so powerful that in countries like America, it has, at best, derailed, at most, destroyed democracy itself."[11] While this statement may sound like an exaggeration, for many Wisconsin rural communities that have had some degree of success in opposing new mining projects, this is an all too accurate characterization of the erosion of democracy.

Legislative Initiatives to Thwart Local Democratic Control

Before mining companies can receive permits to mine in Wisconsin, they must have the approval of local units of government—a major obstacle for both Kennecott Copper and Exxon Minerals. A decade after withdrawing from the Flambeau project, Kennecott reevaluated the project and discovered that the copper lode was an extraordinarily rich deposit. In 1987, Kennecott reactivated its mine application for a scaled-down version of the defeated project.

However, the company could not meet the tough environmental requirements contained in the county zoning ordinance and thus could not get a state permit. In one of Kennecott's "issue papers," the company identified "a small vocal opposition group" whose concerns about mining impacts could be "neutralized" if local leaders and company officials could negotiate a "local agreement" addressing some of these concerns.[12]

To avoid what the company called "onerous local approvals," a Kennecott official drafted the so-called "local agreement" law, which allows mining companies to negotiate a local agreement in lieu of zoning permission. Such negotiations are confined to elected officials. The bill was attached to a budget bill and passed without public hearings or debate in 1988. Shortly thereafter, Rusk County gave in to the mining company's threat to sue for "deprivation of economic use of its property" and signed a local agreement before the Wisconsin Department of Natural Resources (DNR) had even issued an environmental impact statement (EIS).[13]

Seven years after withdrawing from the Crandon project, Exxon and Canada-based Rio Algom formed the Crandon Mining Company (CMC) and resurrected plans to extract 55 million tons of zinc-copper sulfide ore at the headwaters of the Wolf River in northeastern Wisconsin. Shortly thereafter, CMC began closed-door negotiations with local units of government to secure advance permission for the mine through a local agreement. Citizens in the town of Nashville, Wisconsin, objected to the closed-door negotiations, but their protests were ignored.

Seeking to prevent their town board from giving advance permission for the proposed mine, 230 out of 301 Nashville voters petitioned for a special town meeting. Citizens wanted to vote on whether the town should enter into a local agreement with CMC before all the issues surrounding the mine had been discussed in a master hearing.

Among the major problems the citizens had with the local agreement was the attempt to exempt the mining company from all town zoning ordinances, regulations and laws, and to limit the powers of local government and the courts to directly or indirectly prohibit mining.[14] In effect, the local government gives up all authority to govern or to represent its citizens.[15] The agreement also gives final township approval for the disposal of all wastes associated with the project. Over its lifetime, the mine would generate an estimated 44 million tons of wastes.

In December 1996, over 350 town residents gathered to express their opinion on the draft local agreement. The town chairman declared that the meeting was illegal and shut it down before it started. Local police were called, and the crowd peacefully dispersed. "We were treated like Third World people," said George Rock, a mining opponent who owns a cottage in the township. "[The mining companies have] done it for years in other countries, and now they're doing it in northern Wisconsin."[16] The most telling comment about the controversy came from William Marquardt, one of three Nashville town board members who voted in favor of granting permission for the mine. He told a reporter that if there were a referendum on the local agreement, voters would likely reject it.[17]

Exxon used the full extent of its financial and political power to get the local agreements for its Crandon mine approved. It bought full-page ads in local newspapers, bombarded local residents with radio ads and bused in mine supporters to voice support for the local agreement at the Nashville township hearings. In December 1996, over the objections of a crowd of 250 citizens, the town board voted to approve the local agreement with CMC.

Five critics of the local agreement then filed petitions to run for town of Nashville positions in the April 1997 election. In February 1997, the Forest County chapter of the Wisconsin Resources Protection Council filed a lawsuit accusing the town board and CMC of holding more than a dozen illegal closed meetings to develop a local agreement. In announcing the lawsuit, one of the plaintiffs, also a candidate for town chairman, noted that it was being brought

> as a class action on behalf of all citizens whose right to speak out and be heard by their elected officials has been ignored. It is brought on behalf of all residents and tribal members who live and work in the Wolf River and Wisconsin River watersheds in harm's way of the potential havoc that this mine may cause, and

whose rights to clean air and water have been forgotten. These Local Agreements were hammered out in secret, behind closed doors. They are weak and ineffective. They do not protect the citizens of Nashville, Forest County and the state, or protect the rights of tribal members of the Native American nations who live in the two watersheds which will be directly affected by these Agreements.... We can't let our communities be sacrificed by corporate greed or let "feel-good" television commericals, paid for by Exxon, cause us to forget what is right.[18]

In the April 1997 local election, four out of the five town board members were voted out of office in "one of the most bitterly contested elections in state history."[19] The new town board, for the first time in recent history, included a member of the Mole Lake Chippewa Tribe.

In September 1998, the new town board rescinded the local agreement with the mining company. Without this agreement from the town, says Chuck Sleeter, the new town chairman, the state cannot grant a mining permit.[20] As soon as the town board voted to scrap the local agreement, CMC challenged the board in court, claiming that the town's cancellation of the agreement was illegal. In direct correspondence with Nashville citizens, the company implicitly threatened to bankrupt the town through expensive litigation.[21]

The township responded by setting up a legal defense fund and establishing a website called "Nashville Wisconsin Under Siege!" (www.nashvillewiundersiege.com). In June 1999, the town filed a countersuit in federal court in Milwaukee against CMC in which it charged that the local agreement "resulted from a conspiracy by the mining company and the town's former attorneys to defraud the town of its zoning authority over the proposed mining operations."[22] The town says its former attorneys agreed to recommend approval of the local agreement by the former board in exchange for the mining company's agreement to pay the attorneys more than $350,000 in past due legal fees and expenses incurred while representing the town.[23] Among the activities undertaken by the attorneys were the compilation of dossiers of local opponents of the mine and research into the sovereign powers of the Mole Lake Chippewa Tribe.

Meanwhile the citizen lawsuit against the old town board was settled out of court when the old town board members admitted they broke Wisconsin's open meetings law 55 times in their three years of closed-door discussions with the mining company. "Any time you have this many independent violations of the state open meetings law, you've got problems," said Sleeter. "This is a very dark day in the history of the town."[24] Despite the admission of wrong-doing by the former town board, the judge refused to overturn the local agreement. The judge's refusal was condemned by the state's environmental community. "If this flagrant corruption is upheld in the courts," wrote Jim Wise, president of Environmentally Concerned Citizens of Lakeland Areas (ECCOLA), "then what is left of democracy in Wisconsin? Regardless of the potential environmental pollution the mines may bring, the pollution of government in our state is far more dangerous."[25]

Legal Challenges to Local Zoning Authority

The power of large, multinational mining corporations to threaten lawsuits against small rural townships who dare to withhold permission for exploration and mining can be very intimidating. While Crandon Mining was meeting with the Nashville town board to develop a local agreement for a zinc-copper sulfide mine at the headwaters of the Wolf River, Australia's largest company, Broken Hill Proprietary Minerals International (BHP), was applying for a conditional use permit to conduct mineral exploration and drilling not far from Exxon's proposed Crandon mine. If both Exxon and BHP were to proceed with their mining plans, the township would be totally surrounded by metallic sulfide mines.

At the public hearing on BHP's application before the Nashville zoning committee, local residents testified that there were no examples of successful sulfide mine reclamation anywhere. They argued that the permit should be denied because the cumulative impacts of exploration and mining had not been identified, the use was not consistent with the development pattern in the town's land use plan and did not meet the health and welfare concerns of community residents as expressed in a public opinion survey.[26]

Shortly after the zoning committee voted to deny BHP's explor-
atory drilling request, the company filed a lawsuit against the township and the members of the zoning board, threatening each
member of the zoning committee with confiscation of their property and/or wages. The lawsuit accused the zoning board of voting
against BHP's application "for reasons that were unrelated to the
Ordinance standards." BHP also alleged that the committee's denial
was "arbitrary and capricious, and takes BHP's property without just
compensation in violation of the United States and Wisconsin Constitutions."[27] The latter argument, known as the "takings" argument,
has become a rallying point for the anti-environmental backlash em-
bodied in the so-called "Wise Use" and property rights movements.[28] The town's board of adjustment then overturned the zoning committee's decision and gave BHP permission to drill. The
company dropped the lawsuit.

In effecting the zoning committee's reversal, BHP was simply
applying the kind of political muscle that has worked so effectively
in the Third World. The company's Ok Tedi copper and gold mine
in Papua New Guinea (PNG) has been dumping 80,000 tons of
tailings into the Ok Tedi and Fly Rivers since 1984. The pollution
has wiped out the subsistence farming and fishing of 30,000 landowners downstream. To avoid compensating landowners adversely affected by the mine, BHP drafted legislation for the PNG
Parliament that subjected anyone who sued BHP to fines up to
$75,000. "Even more remarkably," reports the *Multinational Moni-
tor*, "the bill also applied the same fines to anyone who attempted
to challenge the constitutional validity of the proposed law in PNG
courts."[29]

Mass Media Campaigns

In 1994, Roper Research conducted a survey of how the public
perceived various industries. Mining came in last, even less liked
than tobacco.[30] While the mining industry attempts to portray the
mine permitting process as a purely technical and scientific process,
the industry cannot mine without public approval. A major component
of the backlash against environmentalism in the United States and
Canada consists of mass media campaigns to persuade the public to

permit mining.[31] In 1990, U.S. businesses spent an estimated $500 million on hiring the services of anti-environmental public relations professionals and on "greenwashing" their corporate image.[32] The former chairman and CEO of Freeport McMoRan encouraged his industry colleagues to establish organizations to coordinate and implement "image-enhancement programs for mining."[33]

The immediate impetus to Exxon's media campaign in Wisconsin was the "Save Our Clean Waters Speaking Tour," organized by the Wolf Watershed Educational Project and the Midwest Treaty Network, which built upon previous efforts of grassroots environmental groups, sportfishing groups and Native American nations. The original plan called for a speaking tour in communities along the Wolf River to alert people to the downstream pollution from Exxon's proposed Crandon mine. However, when Exxon announced its plan to divert mine wastewater into the Wisconsin River, the speaking tour expanded to include cities and towns along that river. This opened up a whole new constituency that had not previously been concerned with the project.

Beginning on Earth Day 1996, the 12-day tour drew over 1,000 people in 22 cities and towns along both the Wolf and Wisconsin Rivers. Each event featured three speakers—a tribal member, a sportfisher and an environmentalist—representing the three legs of the movement. "We were building ties between communities that didn't have ties," said Zoltan Grossman, a co-founder of the Wolf Watershed Educational Project.[34] After each community event, organizers left behind a core of grassroots supporters who carried on the work of coalition-building and community action. The tour was the most ambitious public education campaign about the environmental, economic and cultural effects of Exxon's proposed Crandon mine ever undertaken by the grassroots opposition.

Crandon Mining accused mine opponents of spreading misinformation about the project without specifically identifying a single example. Exxon's full-page ads emphasized that "the Wisconsin Department of Natural Resources (DNR) cannot approve a mine that will threaten public safety, harm the environment or be bad for the local economy."[35] Exxon's tactic of using the Wisconsin DNR to reassure the public was problematic because the pro-mining Governor, Tommy Thompson, had just eliminated the Public Intervenor's office, the state's environmental watchdog, and transformed the DNR into a political patronage agency. All of the state's environmental, conservation and sportfishing organizations were opposed to these moves. Both actions severely undermined public confidence in the state's ability and commitment to protect clean water and public health and safety from the risks of mine pollution. As in the case of hazardous waste facilities, public distrust of government regulatory agencies fueled the local opposition to the siting of these facilities.[36]

The speaking tour was also designed to build public support for legislative passage of a sulfide mining moratorium bill that would prohibit the opening of a new mine in a sulfide orebody until a similar mine had been operated for ten years elsewhere and closed for ten years without pollution from acid mine drainage. By focusing public discussion and debate on the problem of acid mine drainage, mine opponents were able to shift the discussion from the issue of mine *production*, which leaves the state, to the issue of mine *waste*, which remains in the local community and may have long-term and serious effects on both the environment and the health of local populations.

A study by the Institute for Environmental Studies at the University of Wisconsin warned that "the potential for damage may be so severe as to require perpetual monitoring and maintenance similar to that done by federal authorities with radioactive waste material."[37] The identification of acid mine drainage, with its characteristic orange-colored stream beds, as the most serious mining pollution problem became a "political icon" for the mining opposition in the same sense that the 55-gallon drum became a political icon for the toxic waste protest movement of the 1980s.[38]

Prior to the Wisconsin Senate's vote on the mining moratorium bill, slick CMC television commercials promoted the wonders of modern mining technology and associated it with the warm, fuzzy images of the idealized version of life in a small, northern Wisconsin town. The ads showed geese flying over a lake, a sparkling stream, school children and a place where young people didn't have to leave home to find work. It was a subtle attempt to split rural from urban people by suggesting that the anti-mining forces were primarily urban-based and out of touch with rural sentiments. However, the ads did not mention controversial issues about groundwater and surface water contamination from acid mine drainage and heavy metals, the drawdown of local water supplies in the vicinity of the mine and the effects of discharging upward of a million gallons of treated mine waste water into the Wisconsin River every day for 30 years. All of these issues were generating strong local opposition to mining proposals.

The second Crandon Mining Company television ad Exxon paid for featured United Steelworkers of America (USWA) union president Dennis Bosanac of Local 1114 in Milwaukee with the union seal in the background. This was an attempt to split the movement along class lines. Bosanac says:

> Some legislators in Madison want to stop mining. That's like asking over 10,000 working people to stop breathing. Don't they know that thousands and thousands of us work in jobs that depend on mining? Don't they know how important mining has been and will be to Wisconsin? We want to be part of it. Those high-paying jobs belong in Wisconsin, not someplace else.[39]

The Wolf Watershed Educational Project issued a press release explaining why the ad was misleading. First, the mining moratorium bill would not have banned mining in Wisconsin. Instead, the bill required that prior to obtaining a permit, the applicant must demonstrate that a similar mine had been operated successfully without pollution from acid mine drainage or heavy metal contamination. Second, if the Crandon mine were not opened, potential jobs would not travel out of state, because the ore could not be moved. Mining equipment companies would still receive contracts from outside Wisconsin. While Exxon promised 400 permanent high-paying jobs in the Crandon area, there was no assurance that these jobs would not go to already skilled miners from elsewhere who, after six months in Wisconsin, would become "local" residents. The 1997 shutdown of the White Pine copper mine in nearby Michigan had already created a pool of unemployed miners that would be attracted to any potential mine jobs at Crandon.

Third, the ad never mentioned that Exxon and Rio Algom, a Canadian mining company, are the co-owners of Crandon Mining Company. This was a significant omission, because the ad leads the viewer to believe that the United Steelworkers supported the companies behind CMC. Nothing could be further from the truth. The USWA has been in the forefront against Rio Algom on the issue of worker health and safety at the Elliot Lake uranium mines in Canada. As the main union involved in uranium mining at Elliot Lake, the USWA expressed deep concern over the health effects of radiation from the early days of mining. The Ontario Workmen's Compensation Board reported in 1969 that 16 out of 20 deaths of Elliot Lake miners were the result of lung cancer. A USWA survey showed that "Rio Algom had consistently underestimated hazards in virtually every part of the mining complex and mills, by deliberately under-reading radiation levels."[40] Wisconsin union members formed the Committee of Labor Against Sulfide Pollution to expose the company's health and safety track record.

Seeking to prevent passage of the moratorium bill in the Wisconsin assembly, Exxon set up and funded the Coalition for Fair Regulation (CFR) in the hope of mobilizing other industries, such as the paper mills, which had not yet been part of the mining moratorium battle. The mining industry has been advocating these kinds of broad-based coalitions with timbering, land development and paper production as a way to increase its political clout on key legislative battles. The CFR steering committee includes the largest mining and mining equipment manufacturers in the world. The attempt to turn workers against environmentalists failed. Several unions, including the steelworkers and the construction workers, many of whose members enjoy fishing in northern Wisconsin, passed resolutions in favor of the mining moratorium bill.

Despite an unprecedented media, lobbying and mass mailing campaign by Exxon, Kennecott and the Wisconsin Manufacturers and Commerce Association, the enormous public support for the moratorium bill resulted in legislative approval by an overwhelming margin (29-3). While the legislation does not permanently stop the mine permitting process, it creates environmental standards that the industry will be hard pressed to meet.

Attacks on Tribal Sovereignty

Indian control over air and water quality on reservations is long overdue. Tribal lands were ignored in the original versions of many federal environmental laws of the 1960s and 1970s, including the Clean Air Act and the Clean Water Act. To remedy this exclusion, amendments to these laws have been enacted to give tribes the same standing to enforce environmental standards as states.

At public hearings on the Sokaogon Chippewa's application for water regulatory authority, the mining industry tried to split the movement by race. The Wisconsin Mining Association warned that tribal water quality authority "could be the most controversial and contentious environmental development affecting the state in decades."[41] However, local citizens, lake associations and the Wolf River Watershed Alliance testified in support of the tribe's application.

The Mole Lake Chippewa reservation, famous for its wild rice, is just a mile downstream from Exxon's proposed Wolf River mine site. Tribal regulatory authority would affect all upstream industrial and municipal facilities, including Exxon's proposed mine. In 1995, the Mole Lake Chippewa became the first Wisconsin tribe granted independent authority by the U.S. Environmental Protection Agency (EPA) to regulate water quality on their reservation. Because Swamp Creek flows into the Chippewa's Rice Lake, the tribe has to give approval for any activity upstream that might degrade their wild rice beds.[42]

The Sokaogon Chippewa's water regulatory authority was not the only concern of powerful corporate interests. The Forest County Potawatomi Tribe was seeking federal approval of clean air standards that would affect the ability of large industry to pollute the region's air. The Potawatomi air quality regulations would only affect facilities that release at least 250 tons of pollutants per year. Exxon estimates that if the Crandon mine is built, it will emit about 247 tons of particulates into the air a year. Based on past experience, however, there is a good chance that Exxon's projections underestimate the amount of pollution that will be emitted.

Two pro-mining northern Wisconsin Republican legislators commented: "As legislators and concerned citizens, we stand united in opposing the imposition of obscure provisions in the federal Clean Air Act that deny the citizens of the state due process, violate state sovereignty and threaten the economic stability of many northern Wisconsin counties and communities in northern Michigan."[43] Both the governor and the secretary of the DNR urged the EPA to deny tribal regulatory authority over air and water quality standards.[44] Meanwhile, a coalition of legislators, business leaders and a banker called upon Congress to change the Clean Air Act to disallow tribal authority over clean air standards.[45] Powerful corporate interests were using scare tactics to suggest that Indian sovereignty over reservation resources is an economic threat to small-business owners and ordinary citizens, while they ignore the serious potential for long- term damage to the resource and economic base of northern Wisconsin from large-scale mining and waste disposal.

Within a week of EPA approval of Sokaogon Chippewa water quality authority, the Wisconsin attorney general sued the EPA in federal court, demanding that the federal government reverse its decision to let Indian tribes make their own water pollution laws. "All bodies of water in Wisconsin are public and belong to no one, not even an Indian tribe," said James Haney, a spokesman for the Wisconsin Justice Department. Therefore, according to Haney, it is the state's responsibility, not that of individuals or tribes, to set and enforce water pollution standards in Wisconsin.[46] In April 1999, the U.S. District Court in Milwaukee dismissed the Wisconsin lawsuit and upheld the tribe's right to establish water quality standards for its reservation near the proposed Crandon mine.[47] The state is appealing this decision.

Exxon's Defeat and the Future for Multiracial Coalitions

As grassroots resistance to environmentally destructive mining activities succeeds in delaying, modifying or stopping new mining projects, multinational mining corporations and state agencies have defined this resistance as a social problem in the same way that local opposition to the siting of hazardous waste facilities was defined as a problem in the 1980s.[48] Some of the same strategies that were used to overcome local opposition to the siting of hazardous waste facilities have been used to overcome local opposition to new mining projects.

Among the most important of these strategies have been state preemption of local siting authority and the use of financial compensation to offset community costs.[49] While preemption removes control over land use from the hands of local opponents, it does not preempt all forms of local opposition. If opponents of unwanted facilities cannot exercise their right to withhold needed zoning or other permit approvals, they will simply use more creative measures. Preemption laws may also encourage opponents of a facility to challenge the legality of these laws. In 1981, the state of Wisconsin adopted a negotiated siting process for hazardous waste facilities after the courts rejected the state's preemption effort.[50]

The strategy of offsetting community costs with benefits, such as additional public services or tax revenues, distracts attention from the potential environmental harm of a facility. The assumption that local opposition could be bought off has been offensive to many involved in the toxic waste protest movement.

Even if communities are willing to give up their health and safety concerns for financial compensation, there is still a fundamental issue of social injustice. If hazardous waste facilities were allocated to those communities most in need of any additional source of income, these facilities would end up in the poorest and most oppressed communities, exacerbating the already serious problem of "environmental racism."[51]

In the Wisconsin case of the local agreement negotiated between the town of Nashville and Crandon Mining, the Mole Lake Sokaogon Chippewa Tribe was not even consulted during the negotiations. Since the Mole Lake Tribe stands to be the community most adversely affected by the proposed mine and its toxic waste dump, and since reservation land is held in trust by the federal government, this could be one of the most serious obstacles to federal approval of the mine project. The courts have ruled that federal agencies cannot subordinate Indian interests to other public purposes except when specifically authorized by Congress to do so.[52]

The question remains: Have the corporate and state strategies for overcoming local resistance to new mining projects been any more effective than similar strategies that were developed to neutralize the toxic waste movement of the 1980s? In the case of local opposition to the Kennecott copper mine in Ladysmith, the strategy met with some degree of success. The mine was constructed after numerous delays, court challenges and civil disobedience actions at the mine site. However, this was a relatively small mine by industry standards, and the grade of ore was rich enough to allow the company to ship the unprocessed ore to Canada and thereby avoid the construction of a permanent waste disposal site in Ladysmith. While the local opposition was highly organized and motivated, the statewide opposition to the mine was limited.

The local resistance to Exxon's proposed Crandon mine is a different story. While the company has a local agreement for their proposed mine, they also have a full-blown citizen-tribal insurgency that has thrown out a pro-mining town board, replaced it with an anti-mining town board and filed legal challenges to the local agreement that could effectively halt the project. In contrast to the Ladysmith experience, Exxon and Rio Algom have not been able to restrict the resistance movement to the local area; it is statewide.

This was nowhere more evident than in the extensive grassroots lobbying campaign organized by supporters of the mining moratorium bill. It was hardly coincidental that after assembly approval of the bill, Exxon announced that it was selling out its 50% interest in the Crandon mine to Rio Algom. However, Exxon will receive about 2.5% of any profit from the mine under terms of the sale. Although the company emphasized that its decision was based on general business needs, industry observers complained that "the increasingly sophisticated political maneuvering by environmental special interest groups have made permitting a mine in Wisconsin an impossibility."[53]

While mine opponents cheered Exxon's withdrawal, it was not the end of the battle. However, the willingness of one of the world's largest corporations to walk away from a large mineral project potentially worth more than $4 billion tends to reinforce the conclusion that the environmental, sportfishing and Native nations coalition that came together in embryonic form during the Ladysmith mine battle has developed into an effective, mature and broad-based statewide movement.

The movement's strength is due in no small part to the delegitimation of state and industry authority as they try to force their mining agenda upon communities that are increasingly aware of the health risks of metallic sulfide mining. As indicated earlier, this increased awareness was largely a result of the strategic decision of mine opponents to focus public discussion and debate on the mine waste issue, and especially the industry's unsolved problem of acid mine drainage, which would affect the state's pristine rivers.

Unlike the hazardous waste movement of the 1980s, however, the resistance to mining is not a typical environmental movement. It is a rural-based, multiracial, grassroots rebellion that has forged significant links with an urban, labor and student constituency. The diversity of this coalition has continually confounded the mining industry and thwarted attempts to isolate the mining opposition from the political mainstream.

Does Exxon's defeat mean that the mining industry has exhausted its strategies for overcoming local resistance to new mining projects? Not at all. Rio Algom submitted three "example mines" to meet the criteria of the moratorium law (even though two of the mines had not been both open and closed for ten years). The third mine may not even qualify as a sulfide mine according to one independent evaluation.[54] However, by accepting the company's sleight-of-hand, the DNR effectively undermined the moratorium law.

Whether one looks at what has happened to township governments or the courts in mineral-rich areas, or to state regulatory agencies like the DNR, there is increasing evidence of mining industry dominance and/or outright collusion in promoting a corporate mining agenda. The multiracial anti-mining movement that has developed in Wisconsin does not assume that these institutions will

protect and defend the resources and cultures at stake in this resource colonization battle. This movement has continually developed its own political agenda rather than simply responding to the
agenda set by the state and the mining industry. It was precisely the
awareness of this capacity for grassroots political mobilization that
led Exxon to pull out of the Crandon project. And it is this same
awareness that has mining industry leaders worried about their
ability to contain a growing multiracial environmental resistance
movement in Wisconsin. The journal of the National Mining Association has complained that Wisconsin "barbarians in
cyberspace" were spreading anti-corporate tactics around the
world through the Internet.[55] And the *Mining Environmental Management Journal* portrayed the Wolf Watershed Educational Project as
an "example of what is becoming a very real threat to the global
mining inudustry."[56]

In October 2000, the London-based South African company
Billiton purchased Rio Algom. Company spokesperson Marc
Gonsalves soon reported that the company had received an "end-
less stream of e-mails" from Crandon mine opponents, adding that
"we don't like to be where we're not wanted."[57] Nonetheless,
Billiton has given no indication that it will abandon the project.
Billiton is the fourth in a series of mining companies that have tried
to develop the project since 1975.

In March 2001, Billiton merged with the notorious Australian
mining company, Broken Hill Proprietary to create the world's second-largest mining company known as BHP Billiton. At BHP's May
2001 annual meeting in Melbourne, Australia, activists from Friends
of the Earth, Melbourne greeted shareholders with signs urging
them to "Stop Billiton's Crandon Mine in Wisconsin, USA" and
"Protect Indigenous Rights in Wisconsin, USA: Drop the Crandon
Mine."[58]

A recent editorial in *North American Mining* warns industry leaders that if they continue to dictate to communities, they will face a
"time bomb of socioeconomic concerns that demand just as much
attention, patience, cost and effort from operators as environmental
protection does today." As examples of where the industry has ignored this reality, the editorial points to conflicts "still brewing be-

tween mining companies and local peoples in the state of Wisconsin in the United States, Irian Jaya in Indonesia, the provinces and territories of Canada and states and territories in Australia."[59] In all of these places, the industry faces similar political coalitions between environmentalists and Native peoples.

1   Darlington, 1992, p. 90.
2   Prager, 1997.
3   U.S. Environmental Protection Agency, 1987, p. 79.
4   Kleinman, 1989.
5   U.S. Environmental Protection Agency, 1997, p. 4.
6   Moore and Luoma, 1991, p. 8.
7   Mineral Policy Center, 2000b.
8   Madden, 2000, p. 12.
9   Szasz, 1994; Gerrard, 1994.
10 Gedicks, 1993, pp. 46-47.
11 Rowell, 1996, p. 69.
12 Kennecott, 1988.
13 Seely, 1991, p. 13A.
14 Although the Wisconsin law has not yet been judged unconstitutional, common law rules generally prohibit municipalities from bargaining away their policymaking powers. See Bacow and Milkey, 1987, p. 166.
15 Morris, 1997, p. 40.
16 Fantle, 1997.
17 Associated Press, 1996.
18 Sleeter, 1997.
19 Zaleski, 1997.
20 Imrie, 1998, p. 7C.
21 Cumming, 1998.
22 Seely, 1999.
23 Ibid.
24 Brook, 1999, p. 2B.
25 Wise, 2000.
26 Monte, 1996, p. 1.
27 *Broken Hill Proprietary v. Town of Nashville,* 1996, p. 7.
28 The concept of "takings" is rooted in the concern for private property found in the U.S. Constitution. The Fifth Amendment, in addition to guarding against self-incrimination, states, "nor shall private property be taken for public use without just compensation." Landowners, including mining and logging companies, have seized upon the language of the Fifth Amendment and argued that the enactment of environmental regulations over the last 20 years has restricted their right to use their own property and that such restrictions are tantamount to a "taking" of land. They argue that, just like landowners whose property is seized for roads, bridges, parks or other public purposes, they are entitled to just compensation as provided by the Fifth Amendment. See Schneider, 1992. In the late 1980s, the Pacific Legal Foundation, the Mountain States Legal Foundation and other "Wise Use" law firms began providing workshops and seminars on the value of takings in promoting the corporate agenda. See Bowling, 1994, p. 27.

29   Imhof, 1996, p. 16. The World Bank has called upon BHP to immediately close the troubled Ok Tedi mine due to the environmental damage being caused by the mine. Mineral Policy Center, 2000a.

30   Prager, 1997, p. 37.

31   Panos, 1997, p. 13.

32   Bleifuss, 1995.

33   Ward, 1992, pp. 33, 35.

34   Lavendel, 1998.

35   Crandon Mining Company, 1996, p. 8.

36   Bacow and Milkey, in Lake, 1987, p. 160; Szasz, 1994, p. 104.

37   McNamara, 1976, p. 51. The majority of Americans view the mining industry primarily as a source of valuable raw materials rather than as a major contributor to pollution. In a recent poll, 57% of the 1,000 people surveyed said that they view mining companies "primarily as producers of valuable resources." Only 21.9% said they viewed the industry primarily as a polluter. See *Engineering and Mining Journal,* 1997, p. 16EEE.

38   Szasz, 1994, pp. 63-64.

39   Crandon Mining Company, 1997.

40   Moody, 1991, p. 127.

41   Buchen, 1995, p. 1.

42   Behm, 1995, p. 1B.

43   Seratti and Ourada, 1995, p. 1.

44   Mayers and Seppa, 1994, p. 1B.

45   Walters, 1995, p. 3B.

46   Flaherty, 1996, p. 1B.

47   *State of Wisconsin v. U.S. EPA,* 1999.

48   Szasz, 1994, p. 105.

49   Mazmanian and Morell, 1992, p. 109.

50   Ibid., p. 189.

51   Szasz, 1994, p. 110. See also Bullard, 1993, p. 15.

52   Smith, 1994, p. 2.

53   *North American Mining Magazine,* 1998, p. 3.

54   Robinson, 1999.

55   Webster, 1998.

56   Khanna, 2000, p. 19.

57   Kallio, 2000.

58   Midwest Treaty Network, 2001.

59   *North American Mining Magazine,* 1997, p. 3.

CHAPTER 6

The Military, Trade and Strategies for Sustainability

Many of the Third World indigenous nations whose lands contain valuable resources have suffered dispossession and displacement from their traditional lands under the combined onslaught of corporations in alliance with the military might of the state. Some of these native peoples continue to suffer widespread discrimination, poverty and malnutrition as a result of this displacement; others, such as the Tetetes of Ecuador, have become extinct. Some of the larger groups, such as the Melanesians of West Papua, have taken up arms to defend themselves and their lands through the Free Papua Movement.

The vast majority of the armed conflicts in the world today are between nations and states.[1] Despite the misleading use of the term "nation-state" to refer to a single nation, the reality is that all states contain more than one nation. Nations can be defined as "geographically bounded territories of a common people."[2] These commonalities include language, culture, history and self-government. There are more than 5,000 nations that exist within the geographical boundaries of the more than 190 currently existing states.[3] The majority of these states have been created since World War II, whereas most nations have been around for hundreds or thousands of years.

The underlying cause of most of these wars boils down to state grabs for territory and resources: "Nations account for 10 to

15% of the world's population, but have traditional claims to 25 to 30% of the Earth's surface area and resources."[4] In a survey of minority political protest and rebellion between 1945 and 1989, one researcher reported that the expansion of state powers is most likely to provoke protest and resistance among indigenous peoples who are "most likely to lose autonomy, status and resources to hegemonic state elites."[5] Since World War II, at least 5 million people, mostly women, children and the elderly, have been killed as a result of such conflicts. More than 150 million others have been displaced, and some 15 million have fled to neighboring states as refugees.[6]

In addition to the resource wars between nations and states, there may be as many countries bordering on war as are actually engaged in it.[7] The widespread political violence that we have seen in the oil-rich communities of the Niger Delta would be an example of such a borderline situation. Moreover, the massive environmental degradation and resource depletion that provoke such conflicts are likely to become even more important in the future as climate change exacerbates the situation.[8]

According to geographer Bernard Nietschmann, most of these resource wars are hidden from view "because the fighting is against peoples and countries that are often not even on the map. In this war only one half of the geography is shown, and only one side of the fighting has a name."[9] Indonesia, for example, claims it is fighting separatist "Indonesian" citizens, not the Melanesian nation of West Papua, whose people do not consider themselves to be Indonesian. The territorial invasion of West Papua and its renaming as Irian Jaya is called "national integration." The military occupation and forced removal of native peoples in mineral-rich areas is called "economic development." And the armed Papuan resistance movement is dismissed as a handful of "trouble-makers" officially referred to as "wild terrorist gangs."[10]

Besides the human costs of resource wars, there is the spiraling debt of many Third World states that results from the purchase of weapons to put down native political protests and rebellions. Between 1974 and 1985, Third World debt increased by $580 billion; $250 billion of this represented arms imports from the developed world.[11] This is a massive diversion of scarce resources that could otherwise be available for social investments and economic development. In order to receive loans desperately needed to meet the payments on this debt, Third World governments need to comply with the terms set down by the IMF and the World Bank. These terms usually involve "structural adjustments" that require massive cut-backs in social spending and increased oil or mineral production for export. Both requirements are prescriptions for further military expenditures. As urban populations protest the imposition of spending cuts and the rising cost of basic necessities, the military is used to put down civil unrest, as we have seen in Ecuador. As Third World states invade more native lands to increase oil and mineral production to pay off the debt, they encounter resistance requiring further military repression. It is an endless cycle.

The Multinational-Military Connection

The entire system for maintaining this flow of resources from the Third World to the advanced capitalist countries requires an enormous annual consumption of resources for military purposes that has increased about 30-fold over the course of this century.[12] The United States currently accounts "for more than 30% of worldwide military expenditures and, given its predominant position as an arms producer, probably accounts for a significantly higher percentage of the total worldwide military consumption of raw materials."[13] A United Nations study shows that about 3.5% of the annual global consumption of a group of ten major metals—aluminum, chromium, copper, iron, lead, manganese, molybdenum, nickel, tin and zinc—is devoted to U.S. military purposes.[14] Nearly 40% of U.S. industrial plants and equipment are devoted to military manufacturing, while 30% of all U.S. industry output was purchased by the Pentagon in 1989.[15]

The preparations for waging resource wars by the worldwide armed forces consumes more aluminum, copper, nickel and platinum than all the developed nations. Almost 10% of all iron and steel used on the planet is consumed by the military.[16] Moreover, to transform these metals into tanks, bombers and fighter planes requires enormous quantities of energy. Mining and smelting alone take an estimated 5 to 10% of world energy use each year.[17] Among the pollutants released by smelting are sulfur oxides, which contribute to acid rain. Energy consumption in mining and smelting also contributes to such problems as global warming and the destruction of rivers for hydroelectric dams.[18] Thus, the problem for the mineral and energy industries is not that we're running out of resources, but that at current rates of consumption, the fragile ecosystems that provide us with renewable resources will collapse long before we run out of the minerals and energy.[19]

The impact of the military upon the environment is staggering. According to environmental analyst Ruth Leger Sivard: "The world's armed forces are the single largest polluter on Earth."[20] Over the past 50 years, the United States' nuclear weapons complex, encompassing 17 principal and 100 secondary weapons factories, disposed of some of the most toxic and radioactive substances into the air, soils and water. We are just now beginning to assess the extent of the damage to the environment and human health and the costs of cleanup. According to the U.S. Congress' Office of Technology Assessment, "There is evidence that air, groundwater, surface water, sediments and soil, as well as vegetation and wildlife, have been contaminated at most, if not all, of the Department of Energy [DOE] nuclear weapons sites."[21] The estimated cost of cleaning up these sites over the next 30 years is $200 billion, making it the largest public works project in U.S. History.[22] Moreover, a recent National Academy of Sciences' report concludes that the risks to human health and the environment will remain as a permanent legacy of the nuclear weapons complex:

> at most of DOE's waste sites complete elimination of unacceptable risks to humans and the environment will not be achieved, now or in the forseeable future. At many of DOE's sites, radiological and chemical contaminants posing potentially substantial risks are likely to remain on site and may migrate off site.[23]

At every step of the nuclear weapons cycle there has been significant damage to the lands and cultures of native peoples from the mining of uranium and rare metals for weapons production, to the use of native lands for the testing of nuclear weapons, to the siting of native lands for radioactive waste dumps, to the armed invasion of native territories with tanks and high-speed aircraft.[24] The same world view that has equated weapons development with "progress" has systematically invaded, colonized and dehumanized native cultures.

As the performance requirements for weapons become more demanding, so too does the use of rare minerals. The use of titanium in U.S. high speed combat aircraft is a good example. In the 1950s the F-8 and the F-105 had 8 to 10% of their airframe weights composed of titanium. The current generation of aircraft, such as the F-15 and F-16, have between one quarter and one third of their airframe weights composed of titanium.[25] It has been estimated that military consumption accounted for 10 to 20% of U.S. mineral consumption.[26]

To move its thousands of aircraft and ground vehicles and hundreds of ships, the U.S. military consumes millions of barrels of petroleum. A single B-52 Stratofortress consumed 3,612 fuel gallons per hour, while carriers like the USS Independence consumed 100,000 gallons of fuel in a single day, plus the same amount for the attached aircraft.[27] These figures do not take into account the petroleum products consumed in the production of weapons and military equipment. If "direct military" and "military-related" consumption of energy were added, the sum would account for 7 to 8% of total energy use in the United States.[28]

Despite the military's enormous impact on the environment, there has been very little public discussion of these issues at international meetings such as the UN Conference on Environment and Development held in Rio de Janeiro, Brazil in 1992. This is hardly accidental. In her study of the military and the envrionment, Dr. Rosalie Bertell noted that this issue was eliminated from the agenda, under pressure from the United States. "In the official documents of this UN conference, the US delegation had circled every mention of the 'military', disputing these sections until each reference was withdrawn."[29] In contrast, military and nuclear issues were at the forefront of the NGO parallel conference in Rio.

One way of measuring the impact of the military on the environment is to examine resource consumption in relationship to the biological and physical resources available to a country. This meth-

odology has been described as "ecological footprints" and was first
reported at the Rio plus 5 Conference in 1997, a meeting to assess
the progress made since 1992. According to Bertell, many of the
countries which are running up yearly ecological deficits, with their
resource consumption exceeding their national ecological capacity,
are precisely those countries with extensive weapons programs:

> Approximately 422 million hectares of ecological resources are
> used each year for weapons production in the United States, Rus-
> sia, China, United Kingdom, France, Germany and Japan. Based
> on the global average, this could provide sustainable life support
> for about 250 million people.[30]

The voracious wartime consumption of both metals and energy
is not only wasteful and destructive; it also highlights a critical aspect
of the multinational-military connection. Because the United States
is not self-sufficient in supplies of exotic minerals like titanium and
cobalt, the depletion of wartime stocks of these minerals propels the
next cycle of multinational mining extractive activities on the
world's resource frontiers, where these activities inevitably provoke
further protests and resistance from native peoples in these areas.
Assisting the multinational corporations in this invasive activity is
the U.S. military. Indeed, in the post-Cold War era, the U.S. Defense
Department and the Joint Chiefs of Staff have given a new emphasis
to the protection of U.S. overseas "access to certain strategic resources" including oil and minerals needed for military production.[31]

In many parts of the Third World, multinational mining and energy corporations work in partnership with the armed forces and the
police of the host country. We have seen this pattern with the oil industry in Nigeria, Ecuador and Colombia, and with the mining industry in Indonesia and the Philippines. An important, but
frequently overlooked, part of this dynamic is the booming trade in
armaments. Moreover, U.S. taxpayers are largely unaware that they
are paying for more than half of all U.S. weapons exports. In 1995,
for example, the federal government paid out $7.6 billion in subsi-
dies for arms exports, amounting to more than half the total value of
U.S. arms exports in that year.[32]

From 1989 to 1993, the U.S. State Department issued 39 licenses to U.S. firms to export small arms to Colombia, for a total value of $643,785.[33] While a detailed accounting of these sales is considered classified information by the State Department, the above figure is known to include sales of AR-15 rifles, produced by Colt Manufacturing Company, which "are commonly used by paramilitary forces even though they are forbidden to civilians."[34] Most of the Congressional debate about the recent $1.3 billion U.S. military aid package to Colombia focused on the relative merits of competing helicopters. At stake was $400 million in contracts for the Connecticut-based Sikorsky, maker of the more expensive and heavily-armed Blackhawk, versus the Texas-based Bell Technology, maker of the older, general-purpose Hueys.[35]

In some cases, corporations are directly involved in the arms trade. For example, in January 1996, Shell admitted that it had imported side arms for the Nigerian police who are assigned to Shell and guard the company's facilities. Among the weapons ordered were Beretta semi-automatic rifles, pump-action shotguns and material, such as tear gas, designed for crowd control.[36] When Shell's importation of arms was reported in the Sunday London *Observer*, the company received much public criticism, but nonetheless told Human Rights Watch that it couldn't promise to discontinue the practice "due to the deteriorating security situation in Nigeria."[37] In other cases, corporations are directly providing support services to the military. In January 1999, Chevron transported about 100 soldiers from the military base at Chevron's Escravos facility aboard its leased speedboats and a helicopter to Opia and Ikiyan, two Ijaw communities in Nigeria's Delta State. The soldiers opened fire indiscriminately. One of those wounded was the traditional leader of Ikenyan, who had come to negotiate with the invaders. Each village was burned by the soldiers. Human Rights Watch visited both communities and reported four deaths and 62 missing from the two villages.[38]

And in still other cases, multinational mining and oil corporations are hiring mercenaries to provide "security" services for their facilities, from Colombia, Guyana and Venezuela in South America; to Guinea, Liberia, Nigeria and Sierra Leone in West Africa; to Angola and Namibia in southern Africa; to former Zaire in central Africa; to Sudan and Uganda in East Africa; to Papua New Guinea and Indonesia in the Pacific; and to Kazakhstan in central Asia.[39] Many of these mercenaries are former intelligence officers and death squad veterans. They operate behind harmless sounding companies like "Executive Outcomes," "Diamond Works" and "Sandline International."

Mining consultant Roger Moody has noted that Western governments have little reason to be concerned about curbing these mercenaries, because they boost weapons sales in Europe and elsewhere. Executive Outcomes is estimated to bring in at least $290 million annually to the South African economy, much of it to arms suppliers.[40] The United States doesn't seem to regard the mercenaries as a problem, either. In June 1997, the Pentagon's Defense Intelligence Agency sponsored a high-level conference on mercenaries in Africa featuring representatives from Executive Outcomes and other advocates of armed force to support mining activities.[41]

As mining and oil companies have come under increasing criticism for human rights abuses committed by the armed forces assigned to protect their operations, political-risk consultants are advising their corporate clients to maintain some distance between themselves and the local military. "One big no-no, " warns the Control Risks Group, "is staffing the highest ranks of your company's security team with military figures or personalities closely associated with the state security forces."[42]

The Multilateral Agreement on Investment and the Military-Industrial Complex

Far more important than public relations for the security concerns of mining and oil corporations is the continued military spending by the advanced capitalist countries and the continued weapons consumption by Third World states. Both of these components of the military-industrial complex will receive special protection under the proposed Multilateral Agreement on Investment (MAI).[43] The MAI is the creation of the Organization for Economic Cooperation and Development (OECD), an intergovernmental organization made up of 29 of the world's richest industrialized countries, with headquarters in Paris. Nearly all of the world's 500 largest multinational corporations are based in OECD countries and, through their numerous corporate lobby groups, have been involved in shaping the MAI. Since 1995, members of the OECD have been negotiating what England's *Ecologist* magazine has described as "the latest plan of the economic globalization fraternity for dismantling barriers to investment all over the world in the march for a progressively more open global economy."[44]

The MAI, if adopted, would have the authority of an international treaty and would thus take precedence over the domestic laws of almost every country. Legislation incompatible with the provisions of the MAI would be thrown out by national courts, with one major exception: military spending and arms production. Rules and regulations that hinder foreign investment but that protect workers and jobs, public services, domestic businesses, the environment and culture would be dismantled under the MAI. Governmental actions or programs developed to promote national security are explicitly excluded from MAI governance. "Specifically," notes one analyst, "this includes government spending for the military, weapons development and production, and direct support for weapons corporations."[45]

The MAI would fuel the ongoing resource wars and further cement the relationship between multinational mining and oil corporations and the military.[46] In the first place, the MAI would give weapons corporations protection from government interference in the arms trade. If the U.S. Congress wanted to exercise its authority to restrict U.S. arms sales to countries that violate human rights, it could find itself required to compensate the weapons corporation for the value of the cancelled contract. Secondly, if Congress wanted to impose sanctions on companies doing business with countries like Indonesia, Colombia or Nigeria, it could be open to a series of legal challenges based on the MAI.

While the MAI would initially be adopted by the richest nations, eventually the rest of the world would be coerced into accepting the MAI through the World Trade Organization (WTO). Third World governments would then be subject to MAI provisions that require signatory nations to provide "fair and equitable treatment and full and constant protection and security" including "protection from strife" in times of war and unrest.[47] This is a prescription for military spending to protect those controversial mining and oil activities and repress political dissent. It would also guarantee that Third World states would suffer from escalating foreign debts to pay for the weapons and military training that could only be repaid by increasing exports of oil and minerals. In short, the MAI is a prescription for resource wars without end.

Despite the secretive negotiations surrounding the MAI treaty, Canadian activists illicitly obtained a draft version in early 1997 and immediately posted it on the Internet. Almost overnight, anti-MAI campaigns sprouted in one OECD country after another. The original May 1997 target date for ratification had to be postponed. Meanwhile, the international NGO community organized a successful International Week of Action against the MAI in February 1998, just before the OECD's high-level negotiation session.[48]

Canadian NGOs and citizen groups later challenged the right of their government to negotiate the MAI. The Vancouver-based Defence of Canadian Liberty Committee (DCLC) has taken the federal government to court, arguing that the MAI negotiations are in direct conflict with Canada's constitution and are therefore illegal. According to the DCLC, the MAI is fundamentally unconstitutional under Canadian law, because

> it gives entrenched rights to international banks and foreign corporations guaranteed by international law which Canadian citizens do not have. This is contrary to the principle of equality before the law which is part of the Canadian Constitution enshrined in the Charter of Rights and Freedoms.[49]

Canadian activists see their legal challenge as a model that can be used to challenge the MAI in other countries.

After the OECD negotiations broke down, the responsibility for ratification of the MAI was transferred to the WTO. As a result of the mass demonstrations in Seattle in 1999 and elsewhere more recently, the WTO negotiations on the MAI never got off the ground. Future meetings of the WTO and other international trade organizations will undoubtedly be the focus of a growing worldwide movement against globalized exploitation.

Resource Efficiency Strategies

While the consumption of minerals and energy for military purposes is even more concentrated in the main military powers than is resource consumption generally,[50] it would be a mistake to think that by eliminating this wasteful consumption the human and ecological costs of resource wars would disappear. Not only does the mining industry release more toxins than any other industry in the United States (see Chapter 5), it is also one of the world's biggest consumers of energy. As higher-grade ores are exhausted, the direct energy requirements of mining and milling rise rapidly as more ore must be mined and milled for each ton of metal recovered. In the 1920s, the United States was mining copper ores as rich as 20 to 30%; the average copper ore mined today is 1% copper, but ore as poor as 0.3% is also mined. It is estimated that while U.S. mineral production rose 50% in the last 50 years, energy consumption went up 600% in the last 25 years.[51]

Unfortunately, the human and ecological costs of this consumption are largely hidden from public view for most people in the advanced capitalist countries. Instead, the National Mining Association encourages U.S. consumers to believe that to maintain our standard of living, "it is now necessary to produce 40,000 pounds of new minerals each year for each American and to generate energy for each person equal to that produced by 30,000 pounds of coal."[52] This figure is highly misleading because it lumps together all mineral and energy consumption into a single figure that is then allocated over the entire U.S. population. There is no distinction made between military and civilian consumption or between the consumption levels of different social classes. Obviously, the mining and weapons industries have a far greater stake in maintaining this system than the vast majority of Americans. But there will never be a public understanding of these critical differences as long as everyone is led to believe that we are all equal consumers of minerals and energy. As we shall see, this rate of resource consumption is neither necessary nor sustainable.

The first step in addressing these problems is an immediate ban on new exploration in pristine, frontier ecosystems. The second step is a massive transfer of public funds from subsidizing fossil fuel ex-

traction "to be used instead entirely for investments in clean, renewable and decentralized forms of energy, with a particular focus on
meeting the energy needs of the poorest 2 billion people."[53] The
third step is for the energy corporations to take responsibility for
cleaning up the messes they have made around the globe. These
were the demands of over 200 organizations from 52 countries at
the Kyoto, Japan, meeting of the Climate Convention in 1997. The
urgency to take immediate steps to curb world energy consumption
stems from the understanding that "the burning of even a portion of
known economically recoverable fossil fuel reserves ensures climate
catastrophe."[54]

This is not an unreasonable demand. The present energy system
is based upon an extraordinary waste of resources:

> Each year the U.S. spends $56 billion on imported oil and another
> $25 billion for the military defense of our oil interests in the Mid-
> dle East. Federal subsidies to the oil industry drain another $20
> billion or so, while the environmental and health impacts of air
> pollution add another $150 billion. The total comes to more than
> $250 billion a year. [55]

Current reserves of oil and gas are sufficient to provide a bridge
to an economy based on renewable energy resources.[56] An immediate ban would also make available several hundred billion dollars annually in investment capital for the renewable energy industry. The
technology for renewable and efficient energy is now available and
could provide long-term savings of more than $300 billion a year in
energy costs while eliminating billions of tons of air pollution.[57] Investment in renewable energy also has the potential for providing a
significant source of jobs. In a 1997 report, the European Commission noted that, even taking job losses in fossil fuel energy sectors
into account, a half-million net additional jobs could be created in
the renewable energy sector and in supplies industries, and another
350,000 jobs through exports of renewables.[58]

One of the main driving forces in the continuing high consumption of metals, apart from the high military consumption, is the arti-
ficially low cost of the minerals because of the failure to account for
the environmental and human health costs of their extraction and

processing. Due to irresponsible mining practices and poor regulation, there are more than 557,000 hardrock abandoned mines in at least 32 states. This encompasses at least 50 billion tons of untreated, unreclaimed mine wastes on public and private lands in the United States.[58] Much of the potentially recoverable minerals are also left in the abandoned mine when mining companies "high grade" the deposits in an attempt to extract the highest grades of ore in the shortest possible time at the lowest possible cost.

Another major reason for the continuing high consumption of metals is that the economic policies of most advanced capitalist countries actually discourage the efficient use of materials:

> Industrial societies continue to waste materials at phenomenal rates because our regulations, taxes, subsidies and other policies make it pay to do so. Virtually all industrial countries provide explicit or hidden subsidies for raw materials production. In the United States, these subsidies take the form of large tax exemptions for mineral producers, bargain prices for resources on public lands and wink-and-look-the-other-way environmental regulations. Policies like these have stacked the deck against efficiency. [59]

A prime example of government subsidy of the mining industry is the 1872 Mining Law, which governs mining on federal lands in the western United States. Under the provisions of the this law, miners have the right to purchase mineral-bearing government lands for $5 per acre or less, with no royalties on production and no obligation to clean up the mess they leave behind. Through massive lobbying efforts, the industry has convinced Congress to resist calls by the environmental community to force the industry to pay the costs of environmental cleanup. The cost of cleaning up these sites is projected to cost between 32 and 72 billion dollars.[60] Of the total number of abandoned mine sites, at least 16,000 have "considerable surface and groundwater contamination problems that seriously degrade water resources."[61] The ecological damage from mining is even more extensive in the Third World, as we have seen in the case of West Papua, the Philippines and Guyana.

The policies of the United States, and most other advanced capitalist countries, have been to encourage the production of virgin minerals, which causes the greatest environmental damage and poses the most serious threat to the survival of the world's native peoples. "A far less destructive policy," says the Washington, DC-based Worldwatch Institute, "would be to maximize conservation of mineral stocks already circulating in the global economy, thereby reducing both the demand for new materials and the environmental damage done to produce them."[63] The logical place to begin to implement this policy is in the advanced capitalist countries that are the world's largest consumers of minerals. This is quite feasible in light of the fact that

> the trend in both per capita use and intensity of use [volume relative to gross national product] of minerals in industrialized countries is down; mature economies with infrastructures in place become increasingly tied to high technology and service industries that require less intense use of raw materials, thanks to miniaturization, economies of scale and substitution.[64]

Moreover, this decline in the per capita needs for virgin minerals reflects a major shift in the structure of the economy rather than simply a temporary drop in demand.[65]

The simplest way to encourage more efficient use of minerals would be to tax, rather than subsidize, the production of virgin minerals so that mining companies are forced to cover the full environmental costs of their activities.[66] This would mean eliminating the industry's depletion allowance and the accelerated depreciation for large capital expenses that was made possible during the Reagan administration. It would also mean getting rid of corporate welfare for mining companies, which take minerals from public lands without paying any royalties. The Mineral Policy Center, a Washington, DC-based environmental advocacy group, has proposed the imposition of a 12.5% royalty (the same rate charged to producers of oil and gas on public land) upon mining companies. This, along with an annual $100 rental fee for mining claims on public lands, could provide about $400 million annually.[67] This would provide the government with a way to pay for the costs of cleaning up the nation's abandoned mine sites.

Another obvious way of increasing the efficiency of mineral use is recycling. According to the U.S. Bureau of Mines, U.S. consumers discard 10.6 million tons of iron and steel, 800,000 tons of zinc and 250,000 tons of copper each year.[68] In addition, Americans have discarded well over 200 million cars in the last 40 years; currently we junk 12 million cars annually, each containing a ton of steel and nearly 40 pounds of copper.[69] One of the goals of the Alliance for a Sustainable Materials Economy (ASME), a national coalition of more than 90 natural resources reform groups and recycling and community development advocates formed in 1993, is to view materials from a life cycle perspective. That means "mining the waste stream for glass, metal and paper the way corporations now mine the earth for ores and with much less expenditure of energy and much less damage to the environment."[70]

Production of aluminum from scrap uses only 5% of the energy required to extract the metal from bauxite ore; copper recovery from scrap uses 5 to 33% of the energy costs of using virgin copper ores, depending upon the type of scrap input and the end-use desired.[71] Recycling a ton of steel takes half the energy of original manufacture and avoids 25 tons of water use, nearly three tons of mining waste, 200 pounds of air pollutants and 100 pounds of water pollutants.[72] This is not to minimize the pollutants from metal smelting and refining. But it avoids the additional environmental costs of mining. And the more complete the recovery of metals, such as associated zinc and tin, the less the pollution as these metals are released.[73]

Another major source of mineral waste is poor product design. There is little point in promoting metals recycling if the products you put them in, from washing machines and toasters to cars and trucks, are not designed for long lives but for planned obsolescence. As early as 1979, a study by the U.S. Office of Technology Assessment concluded that reuse, repair and remanufacturing of metal-containing products were the most promising methods of conserving metals.[74] Finally, technological advances have made it possible to substitute less environmentally damaging new materials, such as optical fibers made of glass, for copper wires used in communications. The increasing use of plastic panels in cars is reducing the demand for zinc in coated steel sheet.[75] While most plastics today are petroleum-based, there is a growing use of plastics derived from wood, or silvichemicals, as they are sometimes called. Moreover, the production of plastics from wood could be completed with sources not suitable for pulping or conversion into solid wood products.[76] Similar substitutions are possible with ceramics and composites, in which several substances are combined into a coherent structure.[77] Composites are presently used in aircraft, textile equipment and sporting goods. Their lighter weight and good mechanical properties suggest they will find increasing use in autos as their costs become competitive with steel.[78]

This strategy of the efficient use of materials will not come about overnight or without a major commitment of capital, skills, government-funded research and development, and public commitment. It will also require a fundamental cultural shift from a "throw-away" culture to a reusable one. This redesigned economy will create a multitude of economic opportunities in the area of re-use, repair and remanufacture of materials. It will also require a fundamental shift in how and where materials are produced. Contrary to the National Mining Association, it is not necessary to produce 40,000 pounds of new minerals each year for each American. As we phase out the vast majority of mining operations we can replace them with smelters fed by recycled metals. This, in turn, will shift the major production sites from the frontier areas of the planet to cities, "where used resources, factories and labor are concentrated." Urban areas "will become a more important source of materials than rural mines or forests."[79]

Finally, an effective resource efficiency strategy requires a drastic reduction in the consumption of materials for military production and development of new weapons systems. What about national security? "At present, " says Rosalie Bertell,

> the greatest threat to our security is not invasion by "the enemy"; it is the destruction of the natural resources upon which we all rely for life and health. Without efficient use and responsible management of these resources, the fabric of our civilisation will disintegrate and we will be reduced to fighting each other over basics such as clean air and water.[80]

This is a far-reaching vision that provides an alternative to the unquestioned culture of consumption in the United States and other industrial societies.

Globalization and the Environmental Justice Movement

In 1992, the number of U.S. and Canadian mining corporations exploring or operating in Latin America doubled from the year before.[81] Latin America quickly became the leading region for new mining investment, followed by Africa and Asia. What accounts for this dramatic increase in mining investment? Mining executives complained about stiffer environmental regulations and the long delays in the mine permitting process because of objections from environmentalists in the United States and Canada. Ironically, the development of a North American environmental justice movement, which provided for greater environmental protection and greater citizen involvement in the permitting process, contributed to an intensified assault against native peoples in the Thirld World whose lands contained valuable resources. Assisting the multinational mining corporations in this assault were the structural adjustment policies of the World Bank and the IMF, which pressured many Third World countries to change their mining laws to make them more attractive to foreign investment. The results of this global expansionary process were quite predictable: an escalation of human rights and environmental rights violations.

Increased mining and oil activity in the Third World provoked numerous grassroots native resistance movements. In many cases where these movements faced state-sponsored terror and repression, they have tried to avoid a direct confrontation with the state by shifting the conflict to the international arena. They formed alliances with international environmental and human rights groups, exchanged information, shared resources, used the international media and exerted political leverage over multinational corporations, development-oriented states and multilateral development agencies. These tactics were critical to the success of the rubber tappers and dam opponents in Brazil, the Zapatistas in Mexico and the indigenous uprising in Ecuador. In all of these cases, native peoples opened up the traditionally exclusive decision-making process to allow greater native participation in policies affecting their lands and resources.

Many of the leading environmental organizations realized that environmental victories in the northern industrial countries could easily be negated by an expansion of polluting industries in the Third World. Environmental problems such as deforestation, acid rain and climate change were global problems requiring global solutions. This emerging global perspective was reflected in the fact that it was precisely those environmental groups that concentrated on international issues that grew most successfully throughout the 1980s.[82]

As a result of the assassination of Chico Mendes in Brazil and the execution of Ken Saro-Wiwa and eight other Ogoni leaders in Nigeria, there is a much greater international awareness of the inseparable connection between environmental injustice and human rights abuse. In a letter smuggled out of his Nigerian prison cell, Saro-Wiwa wrote, "The environment is man's first right."[83] In 1994, the UN's Draft Declaration of Principles on Human Rights announced the universal human right to a "secure, healthy, ecologically sound environment."[84] And in upholding the right of the Ecuadorian Indians to sue Texaco for environmental damages, Judge Broderick cited the 1992 Rio Declaration, which declared the right to a clean and healthy environment as a fundamental and inalienable human right. In their analysis of international advocacy networks, Keck and Sikkink emphasize that the "environmental campaigns that have had the greatest transnational effect have stressed the connection between protecting environments and protecting the often vulnerable people who live in them."[85]

What has been the effect of the growth and development of these international networks on the global oil and mining industries? The Canadian mining industry publication, *The Northern Miner,* complained that any company developing a mineral project anywhere in the world must be prepared for NGOs who "come knocking to ensure that social, environmental and other non-technical objectives are being given their rightful due by the project's proponent." In so doing, they "are usurping the role of government and other elected bodies that are supposed to set the standards for resource development and then enforce them."[86] However, in many

Thirld World countries, the government has been unwilling or unable to enforce environmental protection standards against multinational mining and oil corporations. In the absence of governmental regulation, grassroots and popular movements have emerged to defend native cultures, protect human health and preserve fragile ecosystems. In many cases, including Indonesia under Suharto and Nigeria under General Sani Abacha, the governments were in collusion with multinational oil and mining corporations. While *The Northern Miner* may complain that "there are simply too many" NGOs and that "corporations are being overwhelmed with bureaucratic demands that are strangling their projects,"[87] these same corporations have no hesitation in calling upon the military to suppress democratic opposition movements, or lobbying for a phony "drug war" that will provide military protection for U.S.oil investments in the Andean Amazon region.

What has changed in the last decade is that the globalization of these industries has multiplied the points of connection between grassroots resistance movements and the larger international community. This is why the *Oil and Gas Journal* warned its industry readers that the continuing standoff between Oxy and the U'wa in Colombia could "put the white-hot spotlight of the world on a single well" with negative repercussions for the entire industry. The international coalitions between environmental, human rights and indigenous groups that we have examined cannot always prevent developmental genocide but, as one industry consultant report emphasized, "heightened international scrutiny means that perceived transgressors truly have 'no hiding place'."[88]

The native peoples of the world are indeed the modern world's equivalent of the miner's canary. When these birds died from breathing the poisonous gases in underground mines, it was a warning that the miners would be next if they didn't leave the area immediately. Those native peoples who inhabit the world's sensitive ecosystems have been providing us with a powerful warning that "there is no development that can be constructed with the blood and death of our Peoples and the destruction of Mother Earth."[89] It is time for the rest of the world to heed this warning.

1 Clay, in Johnston, 1994, p. 24; Nietschmann, 1987, p. 7; Renner, 1996, p. 21.
2 Nietschmann, 1987, p. 1.
3 Hitchcock and Twedt, 1995, p. 486.
4 Clay, in Johnston, 1994, p. 21.
5 Gurr, 1993, p. 187.
6 Clay, in Johnston, 1994, p. 24.
7 Renner, 1996, p. 21.
8 Ibid. p. 26.
9 Nietschmann, 1987, p. 1.
10 Ibid; Budiardjo and Liong, 1988, p. vii.
11 *Christian Science Monitor*, 1987; cited in Nietschmann, 1987, p. 3.
12 Huisken, 1975, p. 230.
13 Ibid., p. 231.
14 Westing, 1980, p. 115.
15 Thomas, 1995, p. 8.
16 Ibid., p. 16.
17 Young and Sachs, 1994, p. 13
18 Ibid.
19 Ibid.
20 Ostling and Miller, 1992.
21 Center for Defense Information, 1994, p. 1; see also Coyle, et al., 1988.
22 Pasternak and Cary, 1992, p. 34.
23 National Research Council, 2000, p.x.
24 Churchill and La Duke, 1986; Johnston, 1994, pp. 131-141.
25 Huisken, 1975, p. 231.
26 Fine, 1980, p. 50.
27 Thomas, 1995, p. 111.
28 Hveem, 1978, p. 16.
29 Bertell, 2000, p.152.
30 Ibid. p. 154.
31 Center for Defense Information, 1992, p. 1; U.S. Navy, 1978, p. 3.
32 Washburn, 1997, p.27.
33 Human Rights Watch, 1996, p. 90.
34 Ibid.
35 Tate, 2000, p. 18.
36 Human Rights Watch, 1999a, pp. 174-175.
37 Ibid., p. 175.
38 Project Underground, 2000f; Human Rights Watch, 1999b, p. 14.
39 Project Underground, 1997c.
40 Moody, 1998, p. 17.
41 Ibid.
42 Barrett, 1997, p. 47.
43 Staples, 1999, p. 36.
44 Hoedeman, et al., 1998, p. 154.
45 Staples, 1999, p. 36.
46 This account of the MAI draws heavily upon Staples.
47 Ibid., p. 37.

48 Hoedeman, et al., 1998, p. 156.
49 Chossudovsky, 1999, p. 449.
50 Hveem, 1978, p. 20.
51 Lovering, 1969, p. 122.
52 National Mining Association, n.d., p. 7.
53 Rainforest Action Network and Project Underground, 1998, p. 46.
54 Ibid., p. 44.
55 Berger, 1997, p. 32.
56 Ibid., p. 6.
57 Berger, 1997, p. 32.
58 Renner, 2000, p. 174.
59 Lyon, et al., 1993, p. 4.
60 Young, 1994, p. 34.
61 Da Rosa and Lyon, 1997, p. 13.
62 Ibid.
63 Young, 1992, p. 41.
64 Hodges, 1995, p. 1307.
65 Ibid.
66 Young and Sachs, 1994, p. 23.
67 Lyon, et al., 1993, p. 9.
68 Ibid., p. 42
69 Morris, 1995, p. 15.
70 Bernstein, et al., 1994, p. 5.
71 Morris, 1995, p. 15.
72 Bernstein, et al., 1994, p. 5.
73 Morris, 1995, p. 15.
74 Young, 1992, p. 42.
75 *Northern Miner*, 1994.
76 Goldstein, 1976, p. 179.
77 Hodges, 1995, p. 1307.
78 Hillig, 1976, p. 135.
79 Young, 1994, p. 34.
80 Bertell, 2000, p. 5.
81 Charlier, 1993.
82 Yearley, 1996, p. 87.
83 cited in Sachs, 1995, p.53.
84 Sachs, 1995, p. 45.
85 Keck and Sikkink, 1998, p.27.
86 *Northern Miner,* 2000, p. 4.
87 Ibid.
88 Bray, 1997, p.2.
89 Mining and Indigenous Peoples Declaration, 1996, p. 23.

Bibliography

Abrash, Abigail, 2001. "The Amungme, Kamoro & Freeport: How Indigenous Papuans Have Resisted the World's Largest Gold and Copper Mine." *Cultural Survival Quarterly* 25:1:38-43 (Spring).

ACERCA, 2000. Press Release. Action for Community and Ecology in the Regions of Central America. Burlington, VT (May 11).

Adeola, Francis O., 2000. "Cross-National Environmental Injustice and Human Rights Issues: A Review of Evidence in the Developing World." *American Behavioral Scientist* 43:4:686- 706 (January).

Agence France Press, 1999. Jakarta (June 4).

— 1998. Jakarta (October 23).

Aigbogun, Frank, 1998. "Pipeline Explosion Kills 250." Associated Press. *Wisconsin State Journal* (October 19).

Ake, Claude, 1996. Interview cited in Andrew Rowell, *Green Backlash: Global Subversion of the Environmental Movement.* London and New York: Routledge.

Albuquerque Declaration, 1999. *Native Americas: Hemispheric Journal of Indigenous Issues* 16:3-4:98 (Fall/Winter).

Alden, Edward and David Buchan, 2000. "Oil Groups Back Initiative to Guard Human Rights." *Financial Times* (London) (December 21).

Allen, Terry, 2000. "With Friends Like These: Kissinger Does Indonesia." *In These Times* 24:10:11-12 (April 17).

Americas Watch and United Mine Workers of America,1990. Petition Before the U.S. Trade Representative on Labor Rights in Colombia. 35 pages (May).

Anthropology Resource Center,1981. "Transnational Corporations and Indigenous Peoples." ARC Position Paper. *ARC Newsletter* 5:3:2-7 (September).

Arthaud, Victoria C.,1994. "Environmental Destruction in the Amazon: Can U.S. Courts Provide a Forum for the Claims of Indigenous People?" *The Georgetown International Environmental Law Review* 7:1:195-233.

Associated Press,1996. "Lawmaker Opposes Mining Pact." *Wisconsin State Journal* (December 7).

— 1995. "Guyana in Uproar over Cyanide." Guyana Legal Defence Fund (August 24).

— 1992. "Ecuador Indians Regain Title to Amazon Forest." *Milwaukee Sentinel* (June 20).

Austin American-Statesman, 1995. "Freeport Threatens Action Against Critics" (December 14).

Australian Council for Overseas Aid, 1995. *Trouble at Freeport: Eyewitness Accounts of West Papuan Resistance to the Freeport McMoRan Mine in Irian Jaya, Indonesia and Indonesian Military Repression, June 1994-February 1995* (April).

Barrett, Justine, 1997. "Managing Energy Company Security Risks in Latin America." *Oil and Gas Journal* 95:23:44-47 (June 9).

Barsh, Russel, 1999. "The World's Indigenous Peoples." Investment Philosophy Social Screens Social Funds White Paper. Department of Native American Studies, University of Lethbridge, Canada.

Beanal, Tom, 1996. *Beanal v. Freeport McMoRan*. U.S. District Court, Eastern District for Louisiana, Case No. 96-1474 (April 29).

Behm, Don, 1995. "2 Tribes Hope to Control Reservation's Water Quality." *Milwaukee Journal* (February 5).

— 1994. "Proposed Giant Mine Raises Fears: State Official Questions Impact on Water Supply of Zinc, Copper Project." *Milwaukee Journal* (April 28).

Berger, John, 2000. *Beating the Heat: Why and How We Must Combat Global Warming*. Berkeley, CA: Berkeley Hills Books.

— 1997. "A Future Without Fossil Fuel." *Earth Island Journal* 13:32-33 (Winter).

Bernstein, Scott, Laura Power, and John Young, 1994. "Recycling Revisited." *Clementine*: 4-6 (Winter).

Berry, Jason, 1996. "CEO Defends Mining Firm in Full-Page Ads." *National Catholic Reporter* (December 22).

Bertell, Rosalie, 2000. *Planet Earth: The Latest Weapon of War: A Critical Study into the Military and the Environment*. London: The Women's Press.

Birnbaum, Michael, 1995. *Nigeria: Fundamental Rights Denied: Report on the Trial of Ken Saro-Wiwa and Others*. Bar Human Rights Committee of England and Wales and the Law Society of England and Wales (June).

Bleifuss, Joel, 1995. "Covering the Earth with Green PR." *PR Watch* 2:1:1-7 (First Quarter).

Bodley, John H.,1990. *Victims of Progress*. Mountain View, CA: Mayfield, 3rd ed.

— 1977. "Alternatives to Ethnocide: Human Zoos, Living Museums, and Real People," in Elias Sevilla-Casas (ed.) *Western Expansion and Indigenous Peoples: The Heritage of Las Casas*. Paris: Mouton.

Bonura, C.,1995. "Knoth Delays Forum to Discuss Money." *Maroon*. New Orleans: Loyola University (October 6).

Bosshard, Peter and Roger Moody, 1997. "Brave New World Bank?" *Higher Values* 11:7-11. (February).

Bowling, John, 1994. "Wise Use Wet Dream Interrupted!" *Earth First! Journal* 55:2:27 (December 21).

Bray, John, 1997. *No Hiding Place: Business and the Politics of Pressure*. London: Control Risks Group.

Broken Hill Proprietary (BHP) v. Town of Nashville, 1996. Complaint filed in State of Wisconsin Circuit Court, Forest County (June 12).

Brook, Tom Vanden, 1999. "Crandon Mine Meetings Broke Law, Judge Rules." *Milwaukee Journal Sentinel* (December 15).

Brookes, Terry, 1996. "Freeport and RTZ: Complicity in Crime in West Papua." *Higher Values* 8:3-5 (April).

Brooks, Dr. Arthur S., 1986. "Comments on the DEIS's Description of Water Impacts of the Crandon Project" (June).

Bryce, Robert, 1997. "Freeport Shareholders are Secured." *Austin Chronicle*. May 9-15.

— 1996. "Spinning Gold." *Mother Jones* 21:5:66-69 (October).

— 1995. "U.S. International Agency Cancels Insurance Because Mine Operations Have Severely Degraded the Rainforest." *Texas Observer* (November 17).

Bryce, Robert and Susan A. Brackett, 1996. "Controversy at the Grasberg Mine in Indonesia." *Clementine*: 10-13 (Spring-Summer).

Brysk, Alison, 2000. *From Tribal Village to Global Village: Indian Rights and International Relations in Latin America*. CA: Stanford University Press.

Buchen, James, 1995. "Delegation of Federal Clean Water Act." *Badger State Miner* (October November).

Budiardjo, Carmel and Liem Soei Liong, 1988. *West Papua: The Obliteration of a People*. Great Britain: The Indonesian Human Rights Campaign (TAPOL).

Bullard, Robert D., 1993. *Confronting Environmental Racism: Voices from the Grassroots*. Boston: South End Press.

Burger, Julian, 1987. *Report from the Frontier: The State of the World's Indigenous Peoples*. London: Zed Books.

Burton, Bob, 2000. "Freeport Sued Over Audit." *Mining Monitor* 5:3 (September).

Catholic Church of Jayapura, Irian Jaya, 1995. *Violations of Human Rights in the Timika Area of Irian Jaya, Indonesia* (August).

Causey, James E.,1994. "Indian Leaders Blast DNR Over Meetings on Mining Project." *Milwaukee Sentinel* (January 10).

Center for Defense Information, 1994. "Nuclear Threat at Home: The Cold War's Lethal Leftovers." *The Defense Monitor* 23:2:1-8.

— 1992. "Armed Force and Imported Resources." *The Defense Monitor* 21:2:1-8.

Center for Economic and Social Rights (CESR), 1994. *Rights Violations in the Ecuadorian Amazon: The Human Consequences of Oil Development*. New York: CESR.

Charlier, Marj, 1993. "Going South: U.S. Mining Firms, Unwelcome at Home, Flock to Latin America." *Wall Street Journal* (June 18).

Chatterjee, Pratap, 1997. "Environment: Lawsuit over Guyana Mine Calls for Company to Cleanup." Inter Press Service (March 28).

— 1996. "The Mining Menace of Freeport-McMoRan." *Multinational Monitor* 17:4:11-14 (April).

— 1995. "Indonesian Mining Project Posed 'Unreasonable Hazard.'" Inter Press Service (November 3).

Chauvel, Richard, 2000. "Indonesia's Dead End." *The Age* (December 27).

Chethik, Sunita, 1996. "Oil Protestors Attacked." *Earth Island Journal* 11:2:20 (Spring).

Chomsky, Noam, 2000. "The Colombia Plan: April 2000." *Z Magazine* 13:6:26-34 (June).

— 1992. *Deterring Democracy.* New York: Hill and Wang.

— 1990. "A Gleam of Light in Asia." *Z Magazine* 3:9:15-23 (September).

— 1970. *At War With Asia: Essays on Indochina.* New York: Vintage.

Chossudovsky, Michel, 1999. "Fighting MAIgalomania: Canadian Citizens Sue Their Government." *The Ecologist* 29:8:449-451 (December).

Christian Science Monitor, 2000. "Investing in Human Rights" (December 28).

— 1987. "The Cost of Arming the World" (August 24).

Churchill, Ward and Winona La Duke, 1986. "Native America: The Political Economy of Radioactive Colonialism." *The Insurgent Sociologist* 13:3:51-84 (Spring).

Clark, John, 1997. "Freeport and the Conscience of the University." *Maroon.* New Orleans: Loyola University (April 11).

Clay, Jason, 1990a. *Indigenous Peoples and Tropical Forests: Models of Land Use and Management from Latin America.* Cambridge, MA: Cultural Survival, Report 27.

— 1990b. "Indigenous Peoples: The Miner's Canary for the Twentieth Century," in Suzanne Head and Robert Heinzman (eds.) *Lessons of the Rainforest.* San Francisco: Sierra Club.

Cockburn, Alexander, 2000. "Gore's Debts to Richardson and Coelho." *Counter Punch* 7:6:2-3 (March 16-31).

Cohen, Mitchel, 1996. "Murder in Nigeria." *Z Magazine* 9:2:38-41 (February).

Collins, Jennifer, 2000. "A Sense of Possibility: Ecuador's Indigenous Movement Takes Center Stage." *NACLA Report on the Americas* 33:5:4-46 (March-April).

Contract of Work, 1991. Contract between Freeport Indonesia and the Indonesian Government.

Cooper, Christopher, 1999. "Sound and Fury: The Spillionaires' Tales Illuminate the Legacy of the Exxon Valdez." *Wall Street Journal* (March 12).

Cooper, Marc, 1992. "Rain Forest Crude." *Mother Jones* 17:2:39-47, 75-76 (March-April).

Coyle, Dana, Lisa Finaldi, Elana Greenfield, Minard Hamilton, Ed Hedemann, William McDonnell, Marvin Resnikoff, Jennifer Scarlott and Jennifer Tichenor, 1988. *Deadly Defense: Military Radioactive Landfills.* Radioactive Waste Campaign. Brooklyn, N.Y: Faculty Press.

Crandon Mining Company, 1997. Television ad (Fall).

— 1996. Full page ad. Rhinelander, WI *Daily News* (May 5).

Cumming, Donald, 1998. Letter to Nashville Property Owners from Nicolet Minerals Company (November 9).

Da Cunha, Manuel Carneiro, 1989. "Native Realpolitik." *NACLA Report on the Americas.* 22:1:19- 22 (May).

Da Rosa, Carlos and James S. Lyon, 1997. *Golden Dreams, Poisoned Streams: How Reckless Mining Pollutes America's Waters and How We Can Stop It.* Washington, DC: Mineral Policy Center.

De Palma, Anthony, 1996. "Mexican Oil-Well Blockade Threatens Election Reforms." *New York Times* (February 11).

Dames and Moore, 1996. PFTI (Freeport) Environmental Audit Report.

Danziger, Edmund Jefferson, 1978. *The Chippewas of Lake Superior.* Norman: University of Oklahoma Press.

Darlington, David, 1992. "Copper Versus Grandeur." *Audubon* 94:4:86-91 (July-August).

Davis, Shelton H., 1977. *Victims of the Miracle: Development and the Indians of Brazil.* New York: Cambridge University Press.

Donato, Marla, 1994. "To Allow This Mine is to Disappear from the Earth: Intercontinental Victims of Exxon-Rio Algom Mining Rally behind Mole Lake Anishinabe." *The Circle: News from a Native Perspective* 15:7 Minneapolis (July).

Dow Jones Newswires, 2000. "U.S. Embassy Supports Indonesia's Position on Papua" (June 5).

Dudley, N., 1997. "The Year the World Caught Fire." Washington, D.C.: Worldwide Fund for Nature International. Discussion Paper (December).

Dudley, Steven and Mario Murillo, 1998. "Oil in a Time of War." *NACLA Report on the Americas* 31:5:42-46 (March/April).

Duodo, C., 1996. "Shell Admits Importing Guns for Nigerian Police." *The Observer* London (January 28).

Durning, Alan Thein, 1992. "Guardians of the Land: Indigenous Peoples and the Health of the Earth." Washington, D.C.: *Worldwatch* Paper 112 (December).

Earth Island Journal, 2000. "Al Gore and Big Oil Genocide" 15:2 (Summer).

— 1996-97. "British Petroleum Hires Colombia's Army" 12:1 (Winter).

Egan, Timothy, 2001. "The Death of a River Looms Over Choice for Interior Post." *New York Times* (January 7).

Engineering and Mining Journal, 2000. "Indonesian Mines Outstrip the Competition" 201:3:ww8 (March).

— 1999. "Freeport McMoRan Copper & Gold's Grasberg mine" 200:7:16ww (July).

— 1997. 198:11 (November).

Environmental Rights Action, 2000. Press Release (July 5).

Epstein, Paul R., 2000. "Is Global Warming Harmful to Health?" *Scientific American* 238:2:50-57.

— 1999. "Profound Consequences: Climate Disruption, Contagious Disease and Public Health." *Native Americas: Hemispheric Journal of Indigenous Issues* 16:3-4:64-67 (Fall Winter).

Erickson, Sue, 1994. "Of Women and the Water." *Masinaigan.* Odanah, Wisconsin: Great Lakes Indian Fish and Wildlife Commission (Spring).

Esparza, Luis and Monica Wilson, 1999. *Oil for Nothing: Multinational Corporations, Environmental Destruction, Death and Impunity in the Niger Delta.* Washington, DC: Essential Action.

Exxon, 1994. Proxy Statement.

— 1983. "Forecast of Future Conditions: Socioeconomic Assessment, Crandon Project." Prepared for Exxon Minerals by Research Planning Consultants, Inc. (October).

Fantle, Will, 1997. "Mining Plans Poison Town." *The Progressive* 61:6:15 (June).

Far Eastern Economic Review, 1991. (July 4).

Fein, Helen, 1984. "Scenarios of Genocide: Models of Genocide and Critical Responses," in Israel W. Charny (ed.) *Toward the Understanding and Prevention of Genocide.* Boulder: Westview Press.

Fine, Daniel, 1980. "Mineral Resource Dependency Crisis: Soviet Union and United States." in James Arnold Miller, Daniel I Fine and R. Daniel McMichael (eds.) *The Resource War in 3-D: Dependency, Diplomacy, Defense.* Pittsburgh, PA: World Affairs Council.

Flaherty, Mike, 1996. "State Sues Over Indian Water Law." *Wisconsin State Journal* (January 30).

Flavin, Christopher, 1996. "Facing Up to the Risks of Climate Change," in Lester R. Brown (ed.) *State of the World 1996: A Worldwatch Institute Report on Progress Toward a Sustainable Society.* New York: W.W. Norton.

Forest Republican, 1995. Crandon Mining Company Full Page Newspaper Ad, Crandon,WI (October 11).

— 1994. Watershed Alliance to End Environmental Racism (WATER), Quarter Page Newspaper Ad, Crandon, WI (May 5).

Fox, Julia D., 1997. "Leasing the Ivory Tower at a Social Justice University." *Organization & Environment* 10:3:259-277 (September).

Freeport McMoRan, 1998. *Freeport-McMoRan Inc. and Freeport-McMoRan Copper and Gold, Inc.v. Yosefa Alomang and others,* the Supreme Court of the State of Louisiana, Case No. 98-C-1352 (July 2).

Gardner, Gary and Payal Sampat, 1999. "Forging a Sustainable Materials Economy," in Linda Starke (ed.) *State of the World 1999: A Worldwatch Institute Report on Progress Toward a Sustainable Society.* New York: W.W. Norton.

Garten, Jeffrey 1999. "CEO's Prepare for More Protests." *Wall Street Journal* (December 6).

Gedicks, Al, 1993. *The New Resource Wars: Native and Environmental Struggles Against Multinational Corporations.* Boston: South End Press.

— 1985. "Multinational Corporations and Internal Colonialism in the Advanced Capitalist Countries: The New Resource Wars," in Maurice Zeitlin (ed.) *Political Power and Social Theory: A Research Annual-5.* Greenwich: JAI Press.

Geniesse, Peter A., 1994a. "Wolf Key to Mining Fortunes." *Post-Crescent.* Appleton, WI (April 24).

— 1994b. "Fighting Exxon." *Post-Crescent.* Appleton, WI (June 19).

Gerrard, Michael B., 1994. *Whose Backyard, Whose Risk: Fear and Fairness in Toxic and Nuclear Waste Siting.* Cambridge, MA: MIT Press.

Gill, James, 1995. "Unendowing of a University Chair." *New Orleans Times-Picayune* (November 12).

Gladstone, Rick, 2000. "Private Sector: He May Win the Pennant, but Easy on the Champagne." *New York Times.* Business Section (December 17).

Goldstein, Irving S., 1976. "Potential for Converting Wood into Plastics," in Philip H. Abelson and Allen L. Hammond (eds.) *Materials: Renewable and Nonrenewable Resources.* Washington, D.C.: American Association for the Advancement of Science. Publication 76- 4.

Gonzalez, Mario, 1996. "Government Suspends Texaco's Environmental Repair Plan." Inter Press Service (September 19).

Goodman, Amy and Jeremy Scahill, 1998. "Drilling and Killing: Chevron and Nigeria's Oil Dictatorship." *The Nation* 267:16:6-7 (November 16).

Goodrich, Jerry, 1994. Letter to Forest County Residents (April 15).

Gore, Al, 1993. *Earth in the Balance: Ecology and the Human Spirit.* New York: Penguin/Plume.

Gough, Robert P.W., 1980. "A Cultural-Historical Assessment of the Wild Rice Resources of the Sokaogon Chippewa," in *An Analysis of the Socio-Economic and Environmental Impacts of Mining and Mineral Resource Development on the Sokaogon Chippewa Community.* Madison, WI: COACT Research.

Great Lakes Indian Fish & Wildlife Commission (GLIFWC), 1996. *Sulfide Mining: The Process and the Price: A Tribal and Ecological Perspective.* Odanah, WI: GLIFWC (September).

— 1991. "A Guide to Understanding Chippewa Treaty Rights." Odanah,WI: GLIFWC (September).

Green, Jennifer, 2001. Personal interview. New York: Center for Constitutional Rights (January 9).

Grossman, Zoltan, 2000. "Unlikely Alliances: Treaty Conflicts and Environmental Cooperation between Native American and Rural White Communities." Unpublished paper. Department of Geography, University of Wisconsin-Madison.

Gurr, Ted Robert, 1993. "Why Minorities Rebel: A Global Analysis of Communal Mobilization and Conflict Since 1945." *International Political Science Review* 14:2:161-201.

Guyana Geology and Mines Commission, 1996. *Final Report on Technical Causation: Omai Tailings Dam Failure* (July 31).

Harris, Toni, 1994. Letter to Amy Bowerman, Office of Chief Council, Securities and Exchange Commission (January 4).

Hawtrey, R.G., 1952. *Economic Aspects of Sovereignty.* New York: Longmans, Green and Co.

Hecht, Susanna B., 1989a. "Murder at the Margins of the World." *NACLA Report on the Americas* 23:1:36-38 (May).

— 1989b. "The Sacred Cow." *NACLA Report on the Americas* 23:1:23-26 (May).

Hechter, Michael, 1975. *Internal Colonialism: The Celtic Fringe in British National Development, 1536-1966.* Berkeley: University of California Press.

Hertlein, Luke M.A., 1999. "Lake Winnipeg Regulation Churchill-Nelson River Diversion Project and the Crees of Northern Manitoba." *Indigenous Affairs:* 3-4:120-135 (June-December). International Work Group for Indigenous Affairs. Copenhagen, Denmark.

Hillig, William B., 1976. "New Materials and Composites," in Philip H. Abelson and Allen L. Hammond (eds.) *Materials: Renewable and Nonrenewable Resources.* Washington, D.C: American Association for the Advancement of Science. Publication 76-4.

Hitchcock, Robert K. and Tara M. Twedt, 1995. "Physical and Cultural Genocide of Various Indigenous Peoples," in Samuel Totten, William S. Parsons and Israel W. Charny (eds.) *Genocide in the Twentieth Century: Critical Essays and Eyewitness Accounts.* New York: Garland Publishing.

Hodges, Carroll Ann, 1995. "Mineral Resources, Environmental Issues, and Land Use." *Science* 268:5215:1305-1312 (June).

Hoedeman, Olivier, Belen Balanya, Ann Doherty, Adam Ma'anit and Erik Wesselius, 1998. "MAIgalomania: The New Corporate Agenda." *The Ecologist* 28:3:154-161 (May/June).

Houck, Oliver, 1996. "Major Money Influence in Freeport-Indonesia Affair." *New Orleans Times-Picayune* (February 29).

Howard, Michael C., 1988. *The Impact of the International Mining Industry on Native Peoples.* Sydney, Australia: Transnational Corporations Research Project.

Huff, Sheila Minor, 1986. Letter from Regional Environmental Officer, U.S. Dept. of the Interior, to Howard Druckenmiller, Director, Bureau of Environmental Analysis and Review, Wisconsin DNR (July 31).

Huisken, Ronald H., 1975. "The Consumption of Raw Materials for Military Purposes." *Ambio* 4:5-6:229-233.

Human Rights Watch, 1999a. *The Price of Oil: Corporate Responsibility and Human Rights Violations in Nigeria's Oil Producing Communities.* New York: Human Rights Watch.

— 1999b. "Nigeria: Crackdown in the Niger Delta." 11:2A. New York: Human Rights Watch. 25 pages.

— 1998. *War Without Quarter: Colombia and International Humanitarian Law.* New York: Human Rights Watch.

— 1996. *Colombia's Killer Networks: The Military-Paramilitary Partnership and the United States.* New York: Human Rights Watch.

Hveem, Helge, 1979. "Militarization of Nature: Conflict and Control Over Strategic Resources and Some Implications for Peace Policies." *Journal of Peace Research* 16:1:1-26.

— 1978. "Arms Control Through Resource Control: The Link Between Military Consumption of Raw Materials and Energy and the Disarmament Question." *Bulletin of Peace Proposals* 9:1:14-23.

Hyndman, David, 1988. "Melanesian Resistance to Ecocide and Ethnocide: Transnational Mining Projects and the Fourth World on the Island of New Guinea," in John H. Bodley (ed.) *Tribal Peoples and Development Issues: A Global Overview.* Mountain View, CA: Mayfield.

Inter Press Service, 1994. "Ecuador/U.S. Indians Oppose Plans to Move Texaco Trial to Ecuador." (March 10).

International Federation of Chemical, Energy, Mine, and General Workers' Unions (ICEM), 1998. *Rio Tinto: Tainted Titan: The Stakeholders Report 1997*. Brussels, Belgium.

Idemyor, Vincent (Dr.), 1999. "The Role of Multinational Oil Companies in Nigerian Federalism." *Indigenous Affairs* 2:56-61 (April/May/June) International Work Group for Indigenous Affairs. Copenhagen, Denmark.

Imhof, Aviva, 1996. "The Big, Ugly Australian Goes to Ok Tedi." *Multinational Monitor* 17:3:15-18 (March).

Imrie, Robert, 1998. "Mining Company Protests Town's Renege on Deal." *Wisconsin State Journal* (September 24).

In These Times, 1990. "Safe for Democracy" 14:28 (June 20-July 3).

Indonesia Human Rights Campaign (TAPOL), 1997. "Timika Placed Under Virtual Army Occupation." (December 27).

— 1996. "Open Revolt Against Freeport/RTZ." Bulletin No.134. London (April).

Indonesia Human Rights Network, 2001. "U.S. Congress Shows Support for Human Rights in Indonesia." Washington DC. Press release (May 17).

Indonesian Observer, 1999 (June 16).

— 1998. (September 4).

Intergovernmental Panel on Climate Change (IPCC), 1995. *Climate Change 1995: A Report of the Intergovernmental Panel on Climate Change*. New York: United Nations.

Isacson, Adam, 2000. "Getting in Deeper: The United States' Growing Involvement in Colombia's Conflict." *International Policy Report*. Washington, DC: Center for International Policy.

*Isthmus,*1995. Madison, WI (May 26).

Jakarta Post, 2000a. "Demand for Freeport Contract Review Blasted." (February 4).

— 2000b. "Environmentalists Demand Freeport's Temporary Closure." (May 16).

— 1999. (June 16).

— 1997. "River Ajkwa Polluted." (March 27).

Jardine, Matthew, 1995. *East Timor: Genocide in Paradise*. Tucson, AZ: Odonian Press.

Jochnick, Chris, 1995. "Amazon Oil Offensive." *Multinational Monitor* 16:1-2:12-15 (January/February).

Jodah, Desiree Kissoon, 1995. "Courting Disaster in Guyana." *Multinational Monitor* 16:11:9-12 (November).

Johnson, Tim, 1999. "World Out of Balance: In a Prescient Time Native Prophecy Meets Scientific Prediction." *Native Americas: Hemispheric Journal of Indigenous Issues,* 16:3-4:8-25.

Johnston, Barbara Rose, 1997. *Life and Death Matters: Human Rights and the Environment at the End of the Millennium*. Walnut Creek, CA: Alta Mira Press.

— 1994. *Who Pays the Price?: The Sociocultural Context of Environmental Crisis*. Washington, D.C: Island Press.

Kallio, Nikki, 2000. "New Mine Owners Face Opposition." *Wausau Daily Herald* WI (October 8).

Keck, Margaret and Kathryn Sikkink, 1998. *Activists Beyond Borders: Advocacy Networks in International Politics*. Ithaca: Cornell University Press.

Kelly, C.A., et al., 1997. "Increases in Fluxes of Greenhouse Gases and Methyl Mercury Following Flooding of an Experimental Resevoir." *Environmental Science & Technology* 31:5

Kennecott, 1988. "Issue Paper # 1: Local Agreement/Local Approvals." (April 25).

Kennedy, Danny, 1999. Personal interview (June 22).

— 1997a. "Freeport Follies" *Down to Earth Newsletter.* London (August).

— 1997b. "U.S. Mine Gouges for Gold." *Earth Island Journal* 12:2 (Spring).

Kennedy, Danny with Pratap Chatterjee and Roger Moody, 1998. *Risky Business: The Grasberg Gold Mine: An Independent Annual Report on P.T. Freeport Indonesia.* Berkeley, CA: Project Underground.

Khanna, Tracey, 2000. *Mining Environmental Management* 8:3:19 (May).

Kilvert, Andrew, 2000. "Machete Militias Clash as Self-Rule Tensions Heat Up." *Sydney Morning Herald* (June 8).

Kimerling, Judith, 1996. "Oil, Lawlessness and Indigenous Struggles in Ecuador's Oriente," in Helen Collinson (ed.) *Green Guerrillas: Environmental Conflicts and Initiatives in Latin America and the Caribbean.* London: Latin America Bureau.

— 1994. "The Environmental Audit of Texaco's Amazon Oil Fields: Environmental Justice or Business as Usual?" *Harvard Human Rights Journal* 17:7-8:199-224 (Spring).

— 1991. *Amazon Crude.* Natural Resources Defense Council.

Kleinman, Robert, L.P., 1989. "Acid Mine Drainage." *Engineering and Mining Journal* 190:7: 16i-16n (July).

Knight, Danielle, 2000. "U.S. Aid Cut to Indonesian Environmental Groups that Criticized U.S. Mining Corporations." Inter Press Service. Washington, DC (May 16).

— 1998. "Indonesians Sue U.S. Mining Giant." Inter Press Service (March 15).

Knoester, Matthew, 2000. "On the Fence: Human Rights or Big Oil for Al Gore?" *In These Times* 24:8 (March 20).

Knol, Ann Schottman, 1999. "Menominee Leader Blames U.S. for Deaths." *Milwaukee Journal Sentinel* (March 7).

Kompas, 2000. "Satgas Papua Should Be Disbanded" (June 7).

Krauss, Clifford, 2000. "An Aimless War in Colombia Creates a Nation of Victims." *New York Times* (September 10).

Kretzman, Steve, 1997. "Nigeria: Hired Guns." *In These Times* 21:6 (February 3).

— 1995. "Nigeria's 'Drilling Fields': Shell Oil's Role in Repression." *Multinational Monitor* 16:1-2:8-11,25 (January February).

La Bine, Wayne, 1995. Testimony Before the U.S. Army Corps of Engineers, Public Hearing, Mole Lake Sokaogon Chippewa Reservation (March 29).

La Duke, Winona, 1992. "Indigenous Environmental Perspectives: A North American Primer." *Akwe:kon's Journal of Indigenous Issues* 9:2:52-70 (Summer).

— 1991. "Drowning the North for Minnesota Electricity." *The Circle: News from a Native Perspective* (December).

Lake, Robert W., 1987. *Resolving Locational Conflict.* New Brunswick, NJ: Center for Urban Policy Research.

Lankard, Dune, 1995. Testimony to the Wisconsin Review Commission, Mole Lake, WI (June 18) in *Report on the Track Records of Exxon and Rio Algom*. Madison, WI: Midwest Treaty Network (March 24).

Lavendel, Brian, 1998. "A Model of Citizen Action: Diverse Coalition Forced Passage of Mining Moratorium." *Isthmus*, Madison, WI (April 17).

Leeman, Sue, 1997. "As Forests Burn, We Destroy 'Insurance' for the Future: WWF." Associated Press. *Wisconsin State Journal* (December 17).

Lembaga Masyarakat Amungme (LEMASA), 1996. Resolution (July 5).

Lewan, Todd, 1997. "Amazon Rain Forest on the Brink of Fiery Disaster." Associated Press. *Wisconsin State Journal* (December 4).

Lipka, Mitch, 1994. "Rally at Texaco Ends in 9 Arrests." *Reporter-Dispatch* Westchester County (April 5).

Los Angeles Times, 1997. (April 25).

Lopez, Atencio, 1996. "Panama: the Indigenous People and the Mining Threat." *Indigenous Affairs* 2:20-22 (April/May/June). International Work Group for Indigenous Affairs. Copenhagen, Denmark.

Lovering, T.S., 1969. *Resources and Man*. San Francisco: Freeman.

Lyon, James S., Thomas J. Hilliard and Thomas N. Bethell, 1993. *Burden of Gilt: The Legacy of Environmental Damage from Abandoned Mines and What America Should Do About It*. Washington, DC: Mineral Policy Center.

Madani, Puspa and Jay Solomon, 2000. "Indonesia Orders Freeport to Reduce Mining Output." *Wall Street Journal* (May 24).

Madden, Francine, 2000. "Mining Tops Toxic Polluter List." *Mineral Policy Center News* (Spring).

Maller, Peter, 1994. "Mole Lake Expect Allies in Mine Fight." *Milwaukee Sentinel* (June 16).

Marr, Carolyn, 1993. *Digging Deep: The Hidden Costs of Mining in Indonesia*. London: Down to Earth and Minewatch.

Marquis, Christopher, 2000. "Ambitious Antidrug Plan for Colombia is Faltering." *New York Times* (October 15).

Masinaigan (Talking Paper), 1993. "Chippewa Leaders Voice Concerns about Proposed Wisconsin Mine" (Fall).

Marshall, Andrew, 2000. "Indonesia Says Freeport Agrees to Cut Output." *Reuters* (May 24).

Maull, Samuel, 1993. "Ecuadorian Tribes Sue Texaco, Inc." *News from Indian Country* 7:22 (Late November).

May, Edward R. and Robert W. Shilling, 1977. "Case Study of Environmental Impact – Flambeau Project." *Mining Congress Journal* 39-44 (January).

Mayers, Jeff and Nathan Seppa, 1994. "Thompson Vexed by Tribe's Move." *Wisconsin State Journal* (December 13).

Mazmanian, Daniel and David Morell, 1992. *Beyond Superfailure: America's Toxics Policy for the 1990s*. Boulder, CO: Westview Press.

McBeth, John, 1997. "Global Activists Have a New Target: Freeport." *Far Eastern Economic Review* (December 4).

McCaffrey, Barry R., 2000. Statement by General McCaffrey, Director, Office of National Drug Control Policy to Senate International Narcotics Control Caucus and Finance Committee, Subcommittee on International Trade – US Counterdrug Assistance for Colombia and the Andean Region (February 22).

McCawley, Tom, 2000. "Indonesia Copper Mine Spillage." *Financial Times* (May 6).

McKinney, Cynthia, 2000. "McKinney Expresses Outrage at Absence of U'wa." Press Release. (August 15).

McKinney, Cynthia et al. 2000. Letter to Dr. Madeline Albright (October 30).

McMenamin, Brigid, 1996. "Environmental Imperialism." *Forbes*. 157:124-136 (May 20).

Menominee Nation, 1995. *Can the Wolf River Survive the Impacts of Hardrock Metallic Sulfide Mining?* Menominee Tribal Environmental Services. Keshena, WI.

Midwest Treaty Network, 2001. "Protestors Oppose Crandon Mine at BHP Shareholders Meeting in Melbourne, Australia." Press release (May 19).

— 1999. "Multicultural Alliance Stymies Wisconsin Mining." *Earth First! Journal* 19:4 (March-April).

Milwaukee Journal, 1994. "Mining Mustn't Spoil the North." Editorial (May 8).

Mineral Policy Center, 2000a. "World Bank Calls for Ok Tedi Mine Closure." Press release (March 7).

— 2000b. "Mining Exposed as Top Toxic Polluter in U.S." Press release (May 11).

Minewatch, 1996. "Omai Gold Mine Disaster, 19-22 August 1995." *Higher Values*. 7:6-7 (January).

— 1994. "Summary of Material about the El Cerrejon Coal Mine and the Wayuu in the El Guajira Peninsula, Colombia." Materials Collected by Survival International and Summarized by Minewatch, London.

— 1993. "Development by Invasion: Mining and Human Rights in Melanesia." Briefing Sheet No. 23. (April).

— 1990. "Freeport Indonesia." Briefing Sheet No. 11.

Mining and Indigenous Peoples Declaration, 1996. *Indigenous Affairs* 2:23 (April/May/June). International Work Group for Indigenous Affairs. Copenhagen, Denmark:

Mining Journal, 1999. London (February 6).

Miswagon, John, 2000a. "We Won't Be Beaten Up in Silence." *Toronto Globe & Mail* (March 6).

— 2000b. "Only Beavers Should Build Dams." Remarks at Environmental Justice and Energy Policy in the Upper Midwest Conference. Minneapolis, MN (April 15).

Miswagon, Kenny, 1999. Pimicikamak Cree Nation Statement to Minnesota Public Utilities Commission (November 19).

Mokhiber, Russell, 1993. "The 1993 Corporate Hall of Shame." *Multinational Monitor* 14:12 (December).

Monbiot, George, 2000. "Another Massacre Is On the Way." *The Guardian* (November 30).

Monte, Mike, 1996. "BHP Minerals International Meets with Nashville Zoning." *Pioneer Express* (April 22).

Moody, Roger, 1999. Personal correspondence (June 26).

— 1998. "Diamond Dogs of War." *The New Internationalist* 299:15-17.

— 1997a. "Terror and Resistance, as Philippines goes 'Code Red' " *Higher Values.* 11:26-27 (February).

— 1997b. "MIGA Excuses." *Higher Values* 11:12 (February).

— 1996. "Mining the World: The Global Reach of Rio Tinto Zinc." *The Ecologist* 26:46-52 (March/April).

— 1994. "The Ugly Canadian: Robert Friedland and the Poisoning of the Americas." *Multinational Monitor* 15:21-23 (November).

— 1993. "South Counts the Cost of North's Bonanza." *Panoscope* 35:11-13 (April).

— 1992. *The Gulliver File: Mines, People and Land: A Global Battleground.* London: Minewatch.

— 1991. *Plunder!* Partizans/Campaign Against Foreign Control of Aotearoa. London, England.

Moore, Johnnie N. and Samuel N. Luoma, 1991. "Large Scale Environmental Impacts: Mining's Hazardous Waste." *Clementine* 8-15 (Spring).

Morgan, John D. Jr., 1973. "Future Use of Minerals: The Question of Demand," in Eugene N. Cameron (ed.) *The Mineral Position of the United States, 1975-2000.* Madison: University of Wisconsin Press.

Morris, Jane Anne, 1997. "Coming Soon: A Futures Market in Constitutional Rights?" *Earth Island Journal* 12:4:40 (Spring).

— 1995. "Homo Metallicus." *Midwest Headwaters* 8:2:1,9-11,14-16 (Spring).

Multinational Monitor, 1996. "BHP's Dirty Deeds." 17:9:5 (September).

Murdoch, Lindsay and Andrew Kilvert, 2000. "Golkar Youth Funding Separatists." *Sydney Morning Herald* (June 3).

Murillo, Mario A. 1999. "Under Fire from All Directions: Colombia's Indian Communities." *Native Americas: Akwe:kon's Journal of Indigenous Issues* 16:2:44-47.

Murphy, Paul S., 1998. Senior Vice President-External Affairs, Freeport McMoRan Copper & Gold. Personal correspondence.

Myers, Norman, 1988. "Threatened Biotas: 'Hotspots' in Tropical Forests." *The Environmentalist* 8:3.

Naanen, Ben, 1995. "Oil-Producing Minorities and the Restructuring of Nigerian Federalism: The Case of the Ogoni People." *Journal of Commonwealth and Comparative Politics* 33:1:46-78 (March).

Nader, Ralph, 1982. "Approaching Strategy for Confronting the Corporate Threat." *Akwesasne Notes* 14:6 (Winter).

Nash, June, 1995. "The Power of the Powerless in the New World Order: A View from Chiapas." *Indigenous Affairs* 1:22-30 (January/February/March). International Work Group for Indigenous Affairs. Copenhagen, Denmark.

National Mining Association, no date. "What Mining Means to Americans." Washington, DC

National Research Council, 2000. *Long-Term Institutional Management of U.S. Department of Energy Legacy Waste Sites.* Washington, DC: National Academy Press.

*Native Americas, Akwe:kon's Journal of Indigenous Issues.*1996. "World Bank Quietly Insures Major Polluters." 13:1:4-5 (Spring).

Nepstad, D.C., A.G. Moreira and A.A. Alencar, 1999. *Flames in the Rain Forest: Origins, Impacts and Alternatives to Amazonian Fire.* Pilot Program to Conserve the Brazilian Rain Forest. Ministry of the Environment, Secretariat for the Coordination of the Amazon.

Nettleton, Geoff, 1997. "Gold Mining and the Threat to Indigenous People's Rights in the Philippines." *Indigenous Affairs* 3-4:36-41 (July-December). International Work Group for Indigenous Affairs. Copenhagen, Denmark.

— 1996a. "Philippines: The New Mining Code." *Higher Values* 7:3-5 (January).

— 1996b. "Constitution Undermined by Mining Code." *Higher Values* 9:18-19 (July).

New York Times, 2000a. "Who is Al Gore? " Ad (March 6).

— 2000b. "Oil Company Abuses." Editorial (December 29).

Nietschmann, Bernard, 1987. "Militarization and Indigenous Peoples: The Third World War." *Cultural Survival Quarterly* 11:3:1-16.

— 1986. "Economic Development by Invasion of Indigenous Nations." *Cultural Survival Quarterly* 10:2:2-12.

North American Mining Magazine, 1998. "Troubled Times; Brighter Future." 2:4 (August- September).

— 1997a. "Smart Mining Companies Emphasize Local Partnerships." 1:9 (November).

— 1997b. "Guerrillas Attack Coal Company." 1:5:23 (June).

Northern Miner, 2000. "NGOs and the Global Village: Ruling the World." 86:24:4 (August 7- 13).

— 1997. Ad for JKS Boyles Drilling Co. 83:6:18 (April 7).

— 1995a. "Mineral Projects Held Hostage." 80:46:4 (January 16).

— 1995b. "Summitville Mine Employee Indicted by Federal Grand Jury." 81:19 (July 10).

— 1994. "Car Design and Metals." 80:41 (December 12).

— 1993. "Rio, Exxon Team Up in Wisconsin." 79:29:1 (September 20).

Nwiado, Deebii, 1996. "Militarizing Commerce in Africa." *Indigenous Affairs* 2:40-43 (April/May/June). International Work Group for Indigenous Affairs. Copenhagen, Denmark.

Oil and Gas Journal, 2000. "Environment-Finance: Activists Target Investors of US Company Drilling in Colombia." (December 27).

— 1999. "Potential Oil Industry Flashpoint Centers on Oxy's Colombian Rainforest Wildcat." 97:18-21 (November 29).

Ondawame, John Otto, 2000. "Self-Determination in West Papua (Irian Jaya)." *Indigenous Affairs* 1:32-35 (January/February/March). International Work Group for Indigenous Affairs. Copenhagen, Denmark.

Organizacion Nacional Indigena de Colombia (ONIC), 1996. *Desecrated Land: Large Projects and Their Impact on Indigenous Territories and the Environment in Colombia.* National Indigenous Organization of Colombia and Survival. London.

Onishi, Norimitsu, 2000. "Nigeria: Oil Blast Kills 30." *New York Times* (December 1).

— 1998. "Nigeria Combustible as South's Oil Enriches North." *New York Times* (November 22).

Organization of American States (OAS), 1997. *Report on the Situation of Human Rights in Ecuador.* Washington, DC: OAS. Document 10 (April 24).

Ortman, David E., 2000. "Comment on Collapse of Freeport's Wanagon Dump Site." *Joyo Indonesian News* (May 16).

Osborne, Robin, 1985. *Indonesia's Secret War: The Guerrilla Struggle in Irian Jaya.* Sydney: Allen and Unwin.

Ostberg, Anne, 1999. "Northern States Power's Electricity Destroying Canadian Cree Land." North Star, MN Sierra Club webpage. www.northstar.sierraclub.org

Ostling, Kristen and Joanna Miller, 1992. "Taking Stock: The Impact of Militarism on the Environment." Science for Peace. Cited in William Thomas, *Scorched Earth: The Military's Assault on the Environment.* Philadelphia, PA.: New Society Publishers, 1995.

Pacari, Nina, 1996. "Ecuador: Taking on the Neoliberal Agenda." *NACLA Report on the Americas* 29:5:23-32 (March April).

Panos, 1997. "Green or Mean? Environment and Industry Five Years on from the Earth Summit." Panos Media Briefing No. 24. London, England.

— 1996. "The Lure of Gold: How Golden is the Future?" Panos Media Briefing No. 19.

Papuan Peoples Center, 1992. "Freeport's Attack on the Futures of the Papua Peoples." *IWGIA Newsletter* 2:13-17 (April/May/June). International Work Group for Indigenous Affairs. Copenhagen, Denmark.

Parlow, Anita, 1991. "Worlds in Collision." *The Amicus Journal* 13:33-37 (Spring).

Partizans, 1995. *Parting Company* (Spring).

— 1990. "Special Report on the 1990 RTZ Annual General Meeting." *Parting Company* (Autumn).

Pasternak, Douglas and Peter Cary, 1992. "The $200 Billion Scandal at America's Bomb Factories." *U.S. News and World Report* 113:23:34-47 (December 14).

Patton, James D., 1988. Letter to Carroll D. Besadny, Secretary, Wisconsin Department of Natural Resources (May 20).

Pembaruan, Suara, 2000. "Tom Beanal: Papua's Desire to Separate from Indonesia Is Now Unstoppable." (June 5).

Petras, James, 2000. "Rebellion in Ecuador." *Z Magazine* 13:4:7-8 (April).

Petromindo, 2001. "Wanagon Lake Capable to Contain Freeport's Overburden: ITB." Jakarta (January 3).

Posey, Darrell, 1989. "From Warclub to Words." *NACLA Report on the Americas,* 23:1:13-18 (May).

Prager, Sharon, 1997. "Changing North America's Mind Set About Mining." *Engineering and Mining Journal* 198:2:36-44 (February).

Press, Eyal, 1999. "Texaco on Trial." *The Nation* 268:20:11-16 (May 31).

— 1997. "The Suharto Lobby." *The Progressive* 61:5:19-21 (May).

— 1996. "Jim Bob's Indonesian Misadventure." *The Progressive* 60:6:32-35 (June).

— 1995. "Freeport-McMoRan at Home and Abroad." *The Nation* 261:4:125-130 (July 31- August 7).

Project Underground, 2000a. "Vital Statistics: A Sampling of the World Bank Group Investment in Mining, Oil and Gas." *Drillbits and Tailings* 5:6 (April 17).

— 2000b. "Convergence Demands that World Bank Get Out of Mining, Oil and Gas." *Drillbits and Tailings* 5:6 (April 17).

— 2000c. *Independent Annual Report on Newmont.*

— 2000d. "U'wa Surrounded by Colombian Military." *Drillbits and Tailings* 5:1 (January 28).

— 2000e. "Freeport Faces Investigation Due to Disaster and Mismanagement." *Drillbits and Tailings* 5:8 (May 31).

— 2000f. "Visit the World of Chevron." Informational Poster.

— 2000g. "U'wa Attacked, Indigenous Confederation Demands Occidental Petroleum Leave Ecuador." *Drillbits and Tailings* 5:11 (June 30).

— 1999a. "More Blood is Spilled for Oil in the Niger Delta." *Drillbits and Tailings* 4:20 (December 11).

— 1999b. "Ecuadorian Indigenous Tribes March Against Oil Development Project." *Drillbits and Tailings* 4:13 (September 8).

— 1999c. "Human Rights Activists Protest Freeport Gold Mine in Indonesia." *Drillbits and Tailings* 4:9 (June 1).

— 1998. *Blood of Our Mother: The U'wa People, Occidental Petroleum and the Colombian Oil Industry.*

— 1997a. "Occidental: Supporting Suicide." Briefing paper. .

— 1997b. "Freeport Faces Challenges from All Sides." *Drillbits and Tailings* 2:8 (April 21).

— 1997c. "Militarization and Minerals Tour: Introduction." Briefing paper.

— 1996. *Drillbits and Tailings.* September 18.

— no date. Mission Statement

P.T. Freeport Indonesia, no date. "Tailings Management." *Fast Facts.*

Quarto, Alfredo, 2000. "In a Land of Oil and Agony." *Earth Island Journal* 15:2:7 (Summer).

Raeburn, Paul, Sheridan Prasso, Suzanne Timmons, and Michael Shari, 2000. "Whose Globe? In the Third World, Multinationals Face a New Era of Accountability." *Business Week* (November 6).

Rainforest Action Network (RAN), 2000a. "Grassroots Pressure Forces Fidelity Investments to Dump 60% of their Oxy Stock!" San Francisco, CA: U'wa Emergency Updates.

— 2000b. "Call for V.P. to take action for U'wa People." (October 6).

— 1991. "Ecuador: ARCO, UNOCAL Drilling in Amazon." *World Rainforest Report* 7:1:4.

Rainforest Action Network and Project Underground, 1998. *Drilling to the Ends of the Earth.* Berkeley, CA.

Reinsborough, Patrick, 2000. "U'wa Win a Critical Injunction." *Earth First! Journal* 20:5:14 (May-June).

Renner, Michael, 2000. "Creating Jobs, Preserving the Environment," in *State of the World, 2000*. Washington, DC: Worldwatch Institute.

— 1996. *Fighting for Survival: Environmental Decline, Social Conflict, and the New Age of Insecurity*. New York: W.W. Norton & Co.

Risse, Thomas, Stephen C. Ropp and Kathryn Sikkink (eds.), 1999. *The Power of Human Rights: International Norms and Domestic Change*. New York: Cambridge University Press.

Rio Tinto, 1999. Reports and Accounts. London.

Ripley, Earle A., Robert E. Redman and Adele A. Crowder, 1996. *Environmental Effects of Mining*. Delray Beach, FL: St. Lucie Press.

Robertson, Bud, 2000. "Power Play." *Utne Reader* 97:24-25 (January February).

Robinson, Deborah, 1996. *Ogoni: the struggle continues*. Geneva, Switzerland: World Council of Churches, 2nd edition.

Robinson, Paul, 1999. "Evaluation of the Nicolet Minerals Application For the Use of the Sacaton Mine Under the Wisconsin Sulfide Ore Body Permit Moratorium of 1997." Albuquerque, New Mexico: Southwest Research and Information Center (November).

Rohter, Larry, 2000. "As U.S. Military Settles In, Some in Ecuador Have Doubts." *New York Times* (December 31).

Ross, Alan, 1991. "The Manitoba Hydro-Electric Projects." *Northeast Indian Quarterly* 8:4:52-54 (Winter).

Ross, John, 1996. "Is Zapastista Rebellion Rooted in Oil?" *Earth Island Journal* 11:2:20 (Spring).

Ross, Renee, 1996. "Philippines: Mining Accident Prompts Criminal Charges." *Clementine* 12-13 (Winter 1996-97).

Rowell, Andrew, 1996. *Green Backlash: Global Subversion of the Environmental Movement*. London and New York: Routledge.

Rowell, Andy and Dr. Peter F. Moore, 2000. "Global Review of Forest Fires." Washington, DC: World Wide Fund for Nature (WWF) and the International Union for Conservation of Nature (IUCN).

Rudd, John W. M. et al.,1993. "Are Hydroelectric Resevoirs Significant Sources of Greenhouse Gases?" *Ambio: A Journal of the Human Environment* 22:4 (June).

Runyan, Curtis, 1998. "Indonesia's Discontent" *World Watch* 11:3:12-23 (May-June).

Sachs, Aaron, 1995. "Eco Justice: Linking Human Rights and the Environment." Washington, DC: *Worldwatch* Paper 127 (December).

Saro-Wiwa, Ken, 1992. *Genocide in Nigeria: The Ogoni Tragedy*. Port Harcourt: Saros International Publishers.

Sawyer, Suzana, 1996. "Indigenous Initiatives and Petroleum Politics in the Ecuadorian Amazon." *Cultural Survival* 20:1:26-30 (Spring).

Schemo, Diana Jean, 1998a. "Ecuadoreans Want Texaco to Clear Toxic Residue." *New York Times* (February 1).

— 1998b. "Fires Posing Greater Risk as Amazon Grows Drier." *New York Times* (September 13).

Schmidt, Jack, 1982. "Problems with Tailings Ponds: Incomplete Regulation, Inconsistent Review, Threats to Water." *Down to Earth* (July-August) Helena, MT.

Schneider, Keith, 1994. "A Wisconsin Tribe Tries to Turn Back a Giant." *New York Times* (December 26).

— 1992. "Owners Fight U.S. for Use of Land." *Wisconsin State Journal* (January 20).

Schwartzman, Stephan, 1999. "Reigniting the Rainforest: Fires, Development and Deforestation." *Native Americas: Hemispheric Journal of Indigenous Issues*, 16:3-4:60-63 (Fall-Winter).

Schwartzman, Stephan, Ana Valeria Araujo and Paulo Pankararu, 1996. "The Legal Battle over Indigenous Land Rights." *NACLA Report on the Americas* 29:5:36-43 (March April).

Scripps Howard News Service, 2000. "Lawmakers Fear Military Involvement in Colombian Anti- Drug Campaign." *Milwaukee Journal Sentinel* (February 16).

Seely, Ron, 1999. "Firm, Town Trade Barbs." *Wisconsin State Journal* (June 18).

— 1995a. "Plan Changes for Mine Wastes." *Wisconsin State Journal* (April 19).

— 1995b. "Exxon Mine Plans Opposed." *Wisconsin State Journal* (March 24).

— 1994. "Exxon's PR Man: J. Wiley Bragg." *Wisconsin State Journal* (April 25).

— 1991. "Northern Officials Give State Poor Grades." *Wisconsin State Journal* (March 24).

— 1982. "Mining Has Strong Potential in Wisconsin." *Wisconsin State Journal* (January 31).

Selcraig, Bruce, 1994. "Native Americans Join to Stop the Newest of the Indian Wars." *Sierra Magazine* 79:3 (May-June).

Selverston, Melina H., 1999. "Negotiating Kyoto," *Native Americas: Hemispheric Journal of Indigenous Issues*. 16:3-4:72-75 (Fall-Winter).

Seppa, Nathan, 1994. "Old Foes Now Allies: Indians, Sports Fishermen Join to Oppose Mine." *Wisconsin State Journal* (February 11).

Seratti, Lorraine and Tom Ourada, 1995. "Air Redesignation Concerns Legislators." *Forest Republican* (May 4).

Shari, Michael, 1995. "Gold Rush in New Guinea." *Business Week*: 66-68 (November 20).

Silverstein, Ken, 2000. "Gore's Oil Money." *The Nation* 270:20:11-13,15 (May 22).

— 1998. "Nigeria Deception." *Multinational Monitor* 19:1-2:36.

Silverstein, Ken and Alexander Cockburn, 1995. "Major U.S. Bank Urges Zapatista Wipe Out." *Counter Punch* 2:3 (February 1).

Simon, Suzanne, 2000. "Texaco's Ecological Terrorism of the Ecuadorian Amazon." *Z Magazine* 13:10:52-57 (October).

Simons, Marlise, 1988. "Brazil Accuses Scholar of Aiding Indian Protest." *New York Times* (August 14).

Sleeter, Charles, 1997. Press release (February 10).

Smith, J., 1989. "Problems Flow into Amazon." *Los Angeles Times* (December 14).

Smith, Janet, 1994. Comments to the U.S. Army Corps of Engineers on a Section 404 Permit Application for the Proposed Crandon Mine (November 18).

Solidarity Action Group for Indigenous People, 1996. "Philippines: Massacre in the Highlands." *Indigenous Affairs* 1:48-49 (January/February/March) International Work Group for Indigenous Affairs. Copenhagen, Denmark.

Solomon, Jay, 2000. "Four Feared Dead in Indonesia's Freeport Mishap." *Asian Wall Street Journal* (May 7).

South East Asia Mining Letter, 1995. London (November 30).

Spears, Pat, 2000. "How Energy Development Affects Indigenous Peoples." Presentation to the Environmental Justice and Energy Policy in the Upper Midwest Conference at the University of St. Thomas, Minneapolis, MN (April 15).

Spooner Advocate, 2000. "Tribal Consortium Opposes Power Line." Spooner, WI (March 20).

Staples, Steven, 1999. "Militarism and MAI." *Earth Island Journal* 14:1:36-37 (Summer-Fall).

State of Wisconsin v. U.S. EPA and Sokaogon Chippewa Community, 1999. U.S. District Court for the Eastern District of Wisconsin; Case No. 96-C-90 (April 30).

Steller, Tim, 1992. "Ecuador's Rain Forest Natives Struggle for Lands." *The Circle:News from a Native Perspective* 13:5 (April) Minneapolis.

Stewart, Ann, 1999. "Pull the Plug on Manitoba Hydro." *Masinaigan.* Odanah, WI: Great Lakes Indian Fish & Wildlife Commission (Winter).

Sutherland, Laura, 1994. "Comments on Exxon/Rio Algom's Notice of Intent." Wisconsin Department of Justice. Madison (April 23).

Survival International, 1999a. "Philippines-Subanen Kicked and Beaten by Canadian Mining Company." *Urgent Action Bulletin* (October).

— 1999b. "Bulletin Update on Subanen." (December).

— 1998a. "Rio Tinto Backs Off." *Bulletin* (August).

— 1998b. "Rio Tinto Critic Gagged." Media Briefing (May).

— 1996. "Freeport's Mine Incites Wrath of Tribal Peoples in West Papua." *Urgent Action Bulletin* (April).

— 1995a. "Mining Law Threatens Tribal Lands in Philippine Gold Rush." *Bulletin* (August).

— 1995b. "West Papua: Indonesian Military Torture and Murder at Mining Site." *Urgent Action Bulletin* (October).

— 1992. "Top Ten List." (September).

— 1987. "Ecuador: Indians Kill Bishop as Oil Companies Invade." *Bulletin* (August).

Switkes, Glenn, 1994. "The People vs. Texaco." *NACLA Report on the Americas* 28:2:6-10 (September October).

Szasz, Andrew, 1994. *Ecopopulism: Toxic Waste and the Movement for Environmental Justice.* Minneapolis: University of Minnesota Press.

Tarabay, Jamie, 2000. "Indonesia May Probe U.S. Mining Co." *Associated Press* (May 25).

Tate, Winifred, 2000. "Repeating Past Mistakes: Aiding Counterinsurgency in Colombia," *NACLA Report on the Americas* 34:2:16-19 (September October).

Texas Observer, 1996. "Primitive People." (June 14).

Thomas, William, 1995. *Scorched Earth: The Military's Assault on the Environment.* Philadelphia, PA: New Society Publishers.

Treakle, Kay, 1998. "Ecuador: Structural Adjustment and Indigenous and Environmentalist Resistance," in Jonathan A. Fox and L. David Brown (eds.) *The Struggle for Accountability: The World Bank, NGOs and Grassroots Movements.* Cambridge, MA: The MIT Press.

Trout Unlimited, 1994. "Mining Policy Statement" Wolf River Chapter (January).

Udin, Jeffrey, 1996. "The Profits of Genocide" *Z Magazine* 9:5:19-25 (May).

U.S. Army Corps of Engineers, 1996. Evaluation of Groundwater Modeling at the Crandon Mining Site. St.Paul District (February 21).

U.S. Department of the Interior, 1993. "Social Indicators of Alaskan Coastal Villages." Part 1, Technical Report No. 155. Minerals Management Service, Anchorage, Alaska.

U.S. Department of State, 1995. *Report on Indonesia.* Washington, DC.

U.S. Environmental Protection Agency (EPA), 1997. "Risks Posed by Bevill Wastes." Washington, DC: EPA (F-98-2P4F-S0032).

— 1992. *Tribes at Risk: The Wisconsin Tribes Comparative Risk Project.* Washington, DC: EPA (October).

— 1987. "Unfinished Business: A Comparative Assessment of Environmental Problems." Washington, DC: EPA.

U.S. Forest Service, 1993. *Acid Drainage from Mines on the National Forests: A Management Challenge.* Washington DC: Department of Agriculture.

U.S. Navy, 1978. *U.S. Life Lines: Imports of Essential Materials and the Impact of Waterborne Commerce on the Nation.* Office of the Chief of Naval Operations, Dept. of Navy. Washington, DC: U.S. Government Printing Office O-253-338.

U'wa, 2000. "Oxy Invades U'wa Territory." Press Release (January 20).

Valdmanis, Richard, 2000. "Colombian Tribe Steps Up Battle Against Occidental." Reuters (December 13).

Van Cott, Donna Lee, 1995. *Indigenous Peoples and Democracy in Latin America.* New York: St Martin's Press.

Van Goethem, Larry, 1986. "Exxon and the Wild Wolf River." *Wisconsin Sportsman* 15:38-42 (March).

— 1982. "Exxon Mine Will Feature Elaborate Waste Water Plan." *Milwaukee Journal* (March 28).

Van Zile, Frances, 1994. Statement to Madison Rally (March).

Van Zile, Robert, 1995. Public Testimony to the U.S. Army Corps of Engineers on Exxon's Crandon Project, Sokaogon Chippewa Reservation, Wisconsin (March 29).

Veilleux, Peter G., 1992. "Ecuador: 500 Kilometers of Resistance." (International Work Group for Indigenous Affairs) *Newsletter* 3:36-38 (July/August/September). Copenhagen, Denmark.

Vennum, Thomas Jr., 1988. *Wild Rice and the Ojibway People.* St. Paul: Minnesota Historical Society Press.

Vukelich, George, 1994. "Minding the Mine." Interview with Armando Valubuena Gouriyu. *Isthmus,* Madison, WI (July 8).

Waldman, Peter, 1999. "A Rain Forest Tribe Brings Its Eco-Battle to Corporate America." *Wall Street Journal* (June 7).

— 1998. "How Suharto's Circle and a Mining Firm Did So Well Together." *Wall Street Journal:* 1, A10 (September 29).

Walters, Steven, 1995. "Tribe's Request Could Jeopardize Current, Future Jobs, Groups Say." *Milwaukee Journal Sentinel* (April 27).

Ward, Milton, 1992. "Mining and the Environment." *Minerals Industry International: Bulletin of the Institution of Mining and Metallurgy* 1006:33-41 (May).

Washburn, Jennifer, 1997. "Twisting Arms: The U.S. Weapons Industry Gets its Way." *The Progressive* 61:5:26-27 (May).

WATER (Watershed Alliance to End Environmental Racism), 1994. "Religious Investors Group Wins SEC Action Against Exxon Crandon Project." Press Release (February 7).

Webster, Bob, 1998. "Barbarians at the Gates of Cyberspace." *Mining Voice* 4:1:38-43 (January/February).

Weissman, Robert, 1990. "Exxon Crushes Colombian Strike." *Multinational Monitor* 11:5:8 (May).

Westing, Arthur, 1980. "At War with Nature: Military Activities and the Environment." in Kathleen Courrier (ed.) *Life after '80: Environmental Choices We Can Live With.* Andover, MA: Brick House Publishing.

Whaley, Rick and Walter Bresette, 1993. *Walleye Warriors: An Effective Strategy Against Racism and for the Earth.* Philadelphia, PA: New Society Publishers.

Whirled Bank Group, 2000. "Mining and the World Bank." www.whirledbank.org/environment/mining.html.

Whittaker, A. (ed.), 1990. *West Papua: Plunder in Paradise.* Indigenous Peoples and Development Series. Vol. 6. London: Anti-Slavery Society.

Whittemore, Hank, 1992. "A Man Who Would Save the World." *Parade Magazine,* 4-7 (April 12).

Whitten, Norman E. Jr., 1978. "Amazonian Ecuador: An Ethnic Interface in Ecological, Social and Ideological Perspectives." International Work Group for Indigenous Affairs Document 34. Copenhagen, Denmark.

— 1976. "Ecuadorian Ethnocide and Indigenous Ethnogenesis: Amazonian Resurgence Amidst Andean Colonialism." International Work Group for Indigenous Affairs Document No. 23. Copenhagen, Denmark.

Wilson, Walter, 1996. "El Cerrejon: Power for the World." *The Lamp* 78:1:11-18 (Spring).

Wise, Jim, 2000. "Sad Times for Democracy in Wisconsin." Madison *Capital Times* (March 17).

Wisconsin Department of Natural Resources (DNR), 1995. "An Overview of Mining Waste Management Issues in Wisconsin." Bureau of Solid and Hazardous Waste Management, Madison, WI (July).

— 1986. *Final Environmental Impact Statement, Exxon Coal and Minerals Co., Zinc-Copper Mine, Crandon, Wisconsin.* Madison, WI (November).

Wiwa, Owens, 1996. "A Call to End the Shelling of Nigeria: An Interview with Dr. Owens Wiwa." *Multinational Monitor* 17:7-8:28.

Wolf, Paul, 1999. "United States and Colombia." *Z Magazine* 12:3:6-8 (March).

Wollock, Jeff, 1999. "Eclipse Over Colombia: Events and Consequences of the Murder of Ingrid Washinawatok and Her Companions." *Native Americas:Akwe:kon's Journal of Indigenous Issues* 16:2:10-31 (Summer).

Wood, Charles H. and Marianne Schmink, 1993. "The Military and the Environment in the Brazilian Amazon," *Journal of Political and Military Sociology,* 21:81-105 (Summer).

World Development Movement, 1996. "Protests and Profits: Mining in West Papua." London.

Wright, Shannon and Steve Kretzman, 1999. "Murder, Genocide and Petrol in Colombia." *Earth First! Journal* 19:5 (May-June).

Yearley, Steven, 1996. *Sociology, Environmentalism, Globalization.* London: Sage Publications.

Young, John, 1994. "The New Materialism: A Matter of Policy." *World Watch* 7:5:30-37 (September-October).

— 1992. "Mining the Earth." *Worldwatch* Paper 109. Washington, DC: Worldwatch Institute.

Young, John E. and Aaron Sachs, 1994. "The Next Efficiency Revolution: Creating a Sustainable Materials Economy." *Worldwatch* Paper 21. Washington, DC: Worldwatch Institute.

Young, Oran R., 1993. "Regime dyanamics: the rise and fall of international regimes," in Stephen D. Krasner (ed.) *International Regimes.* Ithaca: Cornell University Press.

Youngers, Coletta, 1998. "U.S. Entanglements in Colombia Continue." *NACLA Report on the Americas* 31:5:34-35 (March April).

Zackrison, James L. and Eileen Bradley, 1997. "Colombian Sovereignty Under Siege." *Strategic Forum* 112. National Defense University: Institute for National Strategic Studies.

Zagorin, Adam, 1999. "Freeport's Lode of Trouble." *Time* 153:22 (June 7).

Zaleski, Rob, 1997. "Mine Foes Coo Over Coup." *Capital Times.* Madison, WI (May 10).

Index

225

About Al Gedicks

Al Gedicks is the author of *New Resource Wars: Native and Environmental Struggles Against Multinational Corporations,* a classic book in environmental and Native studies. Gedicks is professor of sociology at the University of Wisconsin, La Crosse, and a longtime activist in environmental and Native solidarity movements in the upper Midwest. He is executive director of the Wisconsin Resources Protection Council and director of the Center for Alternative Mining Development Policy.

About South End Press

South End Press is a nonprofit, collectively run book publisher with over 200 titles in print. Since our founding in 1977, we have tried to publish books that encourage critical thinking and constructive action on the key political issues shaping life in the United States and in the world. For more information, please visit our website, www.southendpress.org, or call 1-800-533-8478.

Related Titles

New Resource Wars: Native and Environmental Struggles Against Multinational Corporations
by Al Gedicks $18.00

All Our Relations: Native Struggles for Land and Life
by Winona LaDuke $16.00

Confronting Environmental Racism: Voices from the Grassroots
Edited by Robert Bullard $16.00

Earth for Sale: Reclaiming Ecology in the Age of Corporate Greenwash
by Brian Tokar $18.00

Made in Indonesia: Indonesian Workers since Suharto
by Dan La Botz $18.00

Propaganda and the Public Mind: Conversations with Noam Chomsky
by Noam Chomsky and David Barsamian $16.00

(Orders may be sent to: South End Press, c/o CBSD, 1045 Westgate Dr., St. Paul, MN 55114-1065. Please include $3.50 shipping and handling for the first book and an add'l 50 cents for each thereafter. Or all 1-800-533-8478 for credit card orders and more information.)